Greetings from
the
FINGER
LAKES

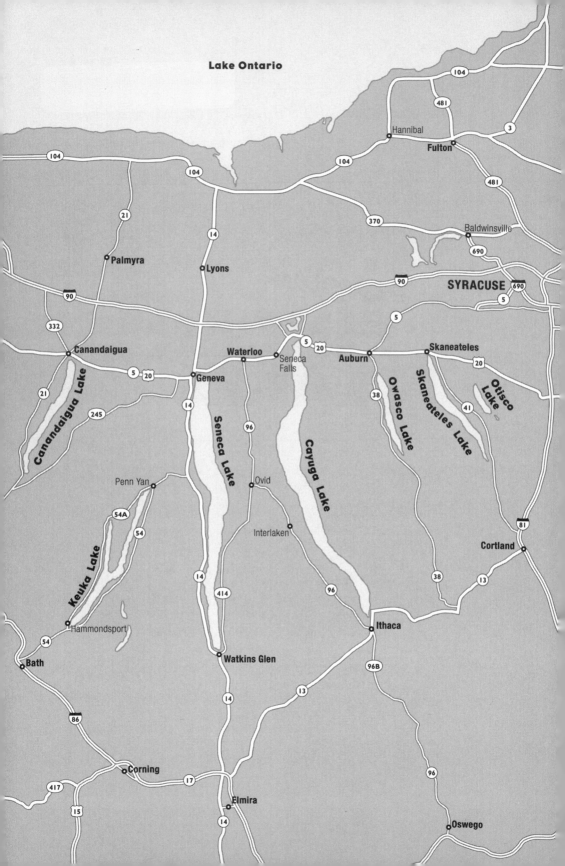

Greetings from the FINGER LAKES

A **Food** and **Wine Lover's** Companion

TEN SPEED PRESS
Berkeley / Toronto

To Marlowe and Layla

Ten Speed Press
Box 7123
Berkeley, California 94707

www.tenspeed.com

Distributed in Australia by Simon and Schuster Australia, in Canada by Ten Speed Press
Canada, in New Zealand by Southern Publishers Group, in South Africa by Real Books, and in
the United Kingdom and Europe by Airlift Book Company.

Cover and text design by Jeff Puda
Cover and interior photography by Juliet Turback

Turback, Michael.
   Greetings from the Finger Lakes : a food and wine lover's companion / Michael Turback.
      p. cm.
   Includes index.
   ISBN-10: 1-58008-607-1 (pbk.)
   ISBN-13: 978-1-58008-607-3 (pbk.)
   1. Grocery trade—New York (State)—Finger Lakes—Guidebooks. 2. Restaurants—
New York (State)—Finger Lakes—Guidebooks. 3. Wine and wine making—New York
(State)—Finger Lakes—Guidebooks. 4. Cookery—New York (State)—Finger Lakes. I. Title.
   TX907.3.N72F558 2005
   381'.456413'0257478—dc22
                                        2005000035

Printed in the United States of America

First printing, 2005

1 2 3 4 5 6 7 8 9 10 — 09 08 07 06 05

Contents

Acknowledgments

The main players who helped with this book are detailed on the pages that follow, and I wish to acknowledge a deep debt of gratitude to each of them.

I owe special thanks to Dennis Hayes of Ten Speed Press, who first saw the potential of this book and championed it, and to Julie Bennett, my editor, for her guidance and care. Thanks also for more-than-able assistance from Jessika Drmacich and Philip Aubrey Bobbs.

To Jeffrey Turback, my brother and business partner, thank you for allowing me the time to devote to this project.

For her professionalism, artistic eye, and steady hand, I want to thank my wife, photographer Juliet Turback.

Finally, I want to acknowledge the most important people in the life of this book—the readers. Thank you!

Introduction

The geography of the Finger Lakes makes it an easy area to romanticize. The glacially sculpted bodies of water in the heartland of New York State have long stirred the imagination of locals and travelers alike.

The five largest of the fabled lakes join together to form a shape like the human hand that gives the region its name. Native Americans, the first settlers of the area, believed that as God was creating the earth, He rested His hand on this place, leaving His imprint for all to see.

So, too, the earliest European immigrants understood that the curious and wonderful agricultural abundance of this land was a precious gift. With the help of the moderating effect of the deep lakes, they were able to harvest bumper crops of produce not otherwise expected to prosper this far north.

Hammondsport, at the southern end of Keuka Lake, was the site of both the birth and rebirth of the wine industry in the region. In 1860, an enterprising Frenchman by the name of Charles Champlin founded Pleasant Valley Wine Company to produce bottle-fermented sparkling wines from Catawba grapes, all but certain that only the indigenous Labrusca varieties were hearty enough to survive upstate winters. Then, almost exactly 100 years after winemakers first persisted with the grapey native wines, a proud Ukranian-born professor of plant science cultivated New York State's first classic Vinifera grapes in his Hammondsport vineyard. Konstantin Frank proved that European-style wines could be made here, notwithstanding the problematic climate. After Dr. Frank, an old way of thinking was gone forever.

The success of new wines from the Finger Lakes led inevitably to the reestablishment of small family farms and the production of regional foods, which then led to the inspiration of professional chefs and the advancement of local cooking—without the constraint of a singular culinary tradition. Closely intertwined with this enlightenment was the recognition of something the French call *terroir*. The word refers to the geology and microclimate of a particular place, but it means much more than that. It speaks to what we grow in this place, how the soil and the lakes are unmistakably expressed in the harvest, and how the disparate components of locale account for the uniqueness of our food and wine. The natural affinity between vineyard and farm is responsible for this region's emergence as the most important enological and culinary destination in the Eastern United States.

Greetings from the Finger Lakes is meant to be not only an introduction to the region's culture and identity, but the guide to an adventure you may never have imagined. If you plan to visit, please remember that not every small producer is open to the public without appointment. With the courtesy of a call in advance, you will be warmly welcomed at a convenient time for tours and tastings.

Although it was impossible to include every place, every grape, and every enterprise, for this book I have crafted a "blend" of the highest achievements in winemaking, artisan farming, and culinary invention. I hope you will savor its textures and complexities.

There is no other place on earth quite like this. My book is intended to whet your appetite for food and wine on the threshold of greatness. I invite you to share our generous table.

CANAN-DAIGUA
LAKE

(ˌka-nən-ˈdā-gwə)

THE WESTERNMOST OF NEW YORK'S major Finger Lakes lies cradled between pastoral hills, partly covered in forest, partly in tidy rows of grapevines. Pristine Canandaigua Lake is fifteen and a half miles long and one and a half miles wide, surrounded by thirty-two miles of shoreline where, during the romantic steamboat era, fourteen major boats provided service to sixty commercial docks.

At the northern end stands the busy little city of Canandaigua, a bedroom community for nearby Rochester and a popular summer retreat for wealthy city folk. Canandaigua boasts a Performing Arts Center, summer home of the Rochester Philharmonic Orchestra, and Sonnenberg Gardens, a Victorian-era setting for the Finger Lakes Wine Center.

There's more to wine country than just wine, and, as a winter diversion, Bristol Mountain, just south and west of Canandaigua, provides the highest ski slopes between the Adirondacks and the Rockies.

Imbedded at the southern end of the lake is a place whose serenity and beauty were once proclaimed comparable to the Italian city of Naples. Tourism is the primary venture in the Finger Lakes village of Naples, where tree-lined streets display architectural styles ranging from nineteenth-century vernacular houses to magnificent Victorian mansions. Fire hydrants in Naples are painted purple during an annual Grape Festival that has made eating grape pies part of the local culture.

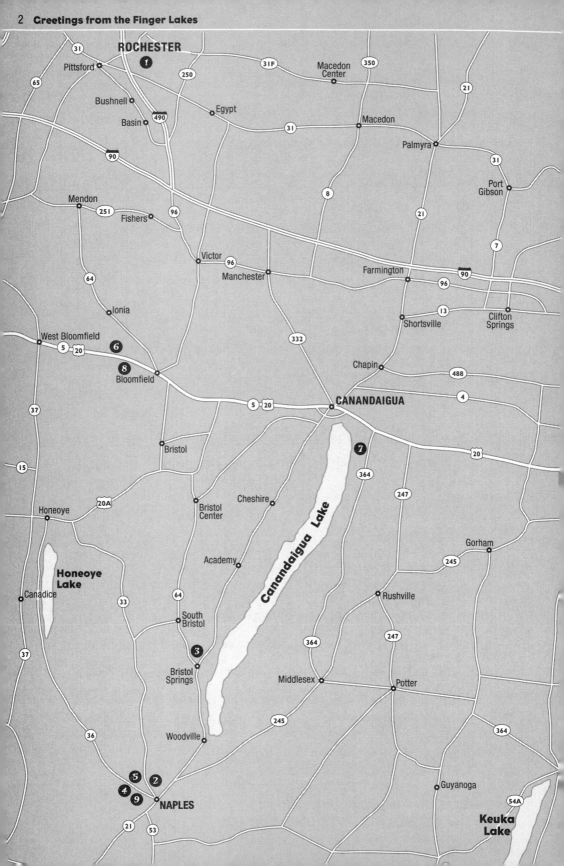

Wineries

1 Casa Larga Vineyards *(FAIRPORT)*

2 Widmer's Wine Cellars *(NAPLES)*

3 Arbor Hill Grapery *(BRISTOL SPRINGS)*

 Farms/Food Producers

4 Springwater Sprouts *(HONEOYE FALLS)*

5 Clute's Pure Maple Products *(NAPLES)*

6 Mountain Rise Organics *(NAPLES)*

 Restaurants

7 Thendara Inn *(CANANDAIGUA)*

8 Holloway House *(BLOOMFIELD)*

9 The Creek Café *(NAPLES)*

WINERIES

6461 Route 64
Bristol Springs, NY 14512
(585) 374-2406
(800) 554-7553

Hours: Monday–Saturday,
10:00 a.m.–5:00 p.m.;
Sunday, 11:00 a.m.–5:00 p.m.
(June through December);
Saturday, 10:00 a.m.–
5:00 p.m.; Sunday,
11:00 a.m.–5:00 p.m.
(January through May)

www.thegrapery.com

Arbor Hill Grapery

While the Gewürztraminer grape is prized for its spicy, aromatic wine, it has bewildered growers in the Finger Lakes. It buds early in the spring, so the vines are vulnerable to frost, and, to make matters worse, it puts up a weak defense to common diseases. Even healthy vines develop only small clusters, so vineyard productivity is relatively poor in most of our region.

An appealing solution seems to be the cross between Gewürztraminer and Joannes Seyve, developed at Cornell University's grape breeding program. Although the hybrid, called "Traminette," produces wine with pronounced varietal characters likened to its acclaimed parent, the vines are more prolific, at least partially resistant to several fungal diseases, and designed to outwit our notorious winters.

Arbor Hill Grapery has mounted the biggest challenge to skeptics who insist that temperatures near Canandaigua Lake are too cold to grow fine wine grapes. Owner and winemaker, John Brahm, became fascinated with the potential of Traminette during field trials conducted at the Geneva

Experiment Station in 1985. As a senior vice president at Widmer's Wine Cellars for many years, John was the viticultural innovator who pioneered the commercial production of Cayuga, a successful hybrid variety developed at Geneva, and he was eager to blaze another trail with Traminette. His own vineyard, situated above Canandaigua Lake at an elevation of 1,150 feet, was an unlikely site for the difficult-to-grow Gewürztraminer. Instead, he decided the proper goal would be to produce a wine from its hybrid offspring. Arbor Hill released the first-ever varietal Traminette in 1996.

After several years of practiced experience, Arbor Hill demonstrates the grape's versatility in three different versions. Spicy notes seem to show up best in the Dry Traminette, a wine that emulates the Traminer Aromatico of Italy. Exotic floral and straw aromatics are more obvious in the Semi-Dry, a well-structured wine with notes of honey and apricot in a lengthy finish. A dessert-style wine, called "Ambrosia," the blend of Traminette and an experimental Muscat Ottenel-Couderc hybrid, is spiked with a small amount of grape brandy. Its rich, textural palate and intensity are reminiscent of an ice wine.

While Traminette lacks some of the strong, fresh-ground spice flavors characteristic of fully ripe Gewürztraminer, it doesn't develop the distinct bitter finish. And, without strong lychee flavors, Traminette is more food-friendly than its ancestor. "It out-Gewürz's Gewürztraminer," says

John, an articulate defender of the fledgling grape. "With some aging it begins to take on the character of a superb French Sauterne."

One of the great pleasures of a visit to Arbor Hill is the opportunity to taste different interpretations of the same varietal and to understand the influence a single winemaker can have in his region. It was John Brahm's entrepreneurial vision that launched Traminette wines into the market, and his pioneering effort gives other wineries something to aspire to.

A footnote about Arbor Hill: Shelves of the winery gift shop are filled with wine sauces, jams, jellies, and preserves, flavored vinegars, barbecue sauces, and salad dressings—all made on the property one batch at a time.

Casa Larga Vineyards

Gaeta, an Italian coastal town that is caressed by the deep blue waters of the Mediterranean, was the boyhood home of Andrew Colaruotolo. Following in the footsteps of his father, he became a stone mason and, like his father, learned to grow grapes and olives on the family farm. In 1950, Andrew journeyed to America and settled in Rochester, New York.

2287 Turk Hill Road
Fairport, NY 14450
(585) 223-4210

Hours: Monday–Saturday,
10:00 a.m.–6:00 p.m.;
Sunday, noon–6:00 p.m.

www.casalarga.com

He was an ambitious young man who put his masonry skills to work and was soon building single-family homes in the growing suburbs of the city. In 1970, Andrew purchased property on Turk Hill that would not only provide a home for his family, but would support a small vineyard where he could make his own wines. He understood traditions of winemaking in Italy, but was intent on putting his own stamp on the craft. He christened the property "Casa Larga," inspired by the family vineyard in Italy, and, combining his passions for building and winemaking, he erected a Tuscan-style villa to house the facility.

Andrew, or "Mr. C," as he was known to his crew, was a man who believed in old-fashioned ideals of close family and hard work. He was an innovative builder and a visionary vintner. By the time he passed away in 2004, his son John had been well-groomed to assume control of the family enterprises. John studied construction engineering at the University of Wisconsin, then worked side by side with his dad, inheriting Andrew's dual passions for building homes and making wines.

Today, Casa Larga produces twenty-four European-style still and sparkling wines from forty-four acres of vines. Even with an elevation so high that it permits a view of the Rochester skyline, this favored location between Canandaigua Lake and Lake Ontario provides moderate temperatures and a lengthened growing season. Vibrant grapevines, arrayed in perfectly manicured rows beneath the winery campanile, produce superb wines.

The winery's workhorse is DeChaunac, a vineyard curiosity the Colaruotolos mastered early on. By cluster-thinning its prolific vines and picking the fruit at the right time, not necessarily fully ripe, they are able to harness its deep color and complex berry flavors; in the cellar they tame its acidic edge and wild characters.

Petite Noir, made entirely of DeChaunac, has a nose of ripe fruit, nuts, and plums and a full, round palate with hints of blackberry, licorice, and delicate oak. It's an unpretentious table wine, in the tradition of *vino da tavola*. Tapestry, a soft and fruity pale blend of DeChaunac (40%) and

Cabernet Sauvignon (60%), shows palate-lovely cherry, some wood, and a generous finish. But perhaps it is the Estate Red ("Tramonto"), a full-bodied, masculine wine with obvious Italian roots, that best defines Casa Larga. Dark garnet in color with plummy fruit in the nose, it displays a wonderful density of fruit on the palate; dark macerated fruit provides much of the character, with hints of blackberry and roasted tomatoes; smoky, toasty nuances suggest some oak influence. All three of these wines seem to be fashioned with Old World profiles. They remind me of traditional "abboccato," mouth-filling, easy, everyday wines that go enticingly well with a great range of foods. John calls them "conceptual Italian wines" and insists they are not the sort to be laid away or fussed over. Casa Larga has been named among America's great dessert wine producers by the Beverage Testing Institute for its consistently excellent vintages of Fiori Delle Stelle, an ice wine produced from part of a dozen acres of Vidal grapes on the estate.

Dependably cold winters combined with the constant airflow from the lakes, which prevents mold and mildew, mean this wine can be made here every year. The tough-skinned grapes are left on the vine long after harvest season, and then, usually between Christmas and the first week in January, they are picked and pressed while still frozen. Any water content in the grape is frozen solid, and only pure grape alcohol, high in sugars and acidity, is released. Concentrated nectar of the juice is then fermented into a rich and golden-colored dessert wine with warm, sensuous tangerine, peach, mango, maple, and apricot flavors. Fiore Delle Stelle is the jewel in Casa Larga's crown.

Mr. C's legacy lives on both in the architecture of the more than one thousand custom homes he built in greater Rochester and, of course, in the compelling collection of family wines that not only speak volumes about heritage, but add range and breadth of styles to the Finger Lakes.

PENNE WITH ASPARAGUS
AND PROSCIUTTO

Serves 4 to 6

Mama Colaruotolo traces this dish back to her ancestral home in Italy. While it originally called for Italian white wine, she substitutes her family's Finger Lakes Chardonnay to create a New World masterpiece. The Finger Lakes wine adds distinctive fruitiness to the dish, even better the next day, allowing the flavors to integrate even more.

Sea salt

1 pound penne pasta

1 pound asparagus

½ cup extra virgin olive oil

1 large yellow onion, chopped

½ cup Casa Larga Vineyard Hill Chardonnay

¼ pound prosciutto, diced

Freshly ground black pepper

Bring a large pot of water to a boil. Grind some sea salt into the water and add the pasta. Cook until al dente and drain.

Bring another large pot of water to a boil and grind some sea salt into it. Blanch the asparagus in the boiling salted water for less than 1 minute and then shock in ice water. Drain, remove, and discard the bottoms of the asparagus and slice the spears into 1-inch lengths.

In a large skillet, heat the olive oil over medium-high heat and add the onion. Sauté until softened, about 3 minutes. Add the wine and simmer for about 2 minutes, stirring occasionally.

Add the prosciutto and asparagus to the pan with the onion and cook for about 8 minutes, stirring occasionally. Season with freshly ground sea salt and freshly ground black pepper, toss with the pasta, and serve.

Widmer's Wine Cellars

One Lake Niagara Lane
Naples, NY 14512
(800) 836-5253

Hours: Call for schedule

www.widmerwine.com

John Jacob Widmer was a remarkable man who played an important part in the formative years of the Finger Lakes wine industry. He came to Naples from Switzerland in 1882, and, finding the fertile slopes above Canandaigua Lake suited to grape growing, he decided to make wine his life work. He bought his first plot of hillside woodland with borrowed money, cleared it, planted vines in the spring of 1883, and started production of wine five years later. Until his death in 1930, Widmer remained active in the cultivation and processing of the grapes from his vineyards.

During Prohibition, Widmer's survived by producing unfermented grape juice. Upon Repeal in 1933, the company was able to quickly revive its winemaking and reestablish its brand among wine consumers. The winery changed hands several times in the late twentieth century and is now a unit of Constellation Brands, the world's largest wine conglomerate. Manischewitz kosher wines and Taylor Lake Country wines are produced at the facility, besides Widmer's nostalgic sherries, ports, and its best-known wine, Lake Niagara, which senior winemaker Glenn Curtis politely refers to as one of his "mature brands."

The most exciting development at Widmer's is the fledgling Brickstone Cellars project, which, although it represents a mere 3,000 cases out of a total output of 3 million, produces a roster of varietals that compete at the highest level of winemaking in the region.

Brickstone takes its name from a separate small facility, located in a century-old underground stone cellar with a brick ceiling. Using small, stainless-steel tanks with individually controlled fermentation temperatures and the best coopered oak barrels, Glenn personally oversees the hand crafting of Chardonnay, Dry Riesling, Semi-Dry Riesling, Cabernet Franc, Pinot Noir, Meritage, and Late Harvest Vidal Blanc. Besides technical nurturing in the cellar, the grapes for these wines are harvested from a revitalized Gold Seal vineyard block in the "banana belt" of Seneca Lake, where cluster-thinning and leaf-pulling help to achieve a true measure of *terroir*.

Thirty-year-old Chardonnay vines produce small yields of intense flavor and concentration. "Sur lie" (aging on the yeast) and partial malolactic fermentation add richness and subtle oak influences to apple and tropical fruit characters. Warm fermentation on the skins, punching down several times a day, and minimal filtering give Cabernet Franc a deep, rich color, abundant tannins, and flavor profiles of raspberry, violet, and cedar.

Perhaps most impressive of all is Dry Riesling, with grapes picked from the Valois Vineyard, late enough for more ripeness and flavor development, then allowed to remain in contact with the skins for twenty-four hours before a very gentle pressing. Cold fermentation, stopped at just under 1% residual sugar, results in a lithe, elegant "Audrey Hepburn" of a Riesling, with just-ripe peach aromatics and delicate notes of honeydew and citrus.

These groundbreaking wines go a long way in reinvigorating a reputation to match the engaging history of this Finger Lakes institution. I expect the Widmer Brickstone label to become a popular standard, essential on any serious wine list in the region.

FARMS/FOOD PRODUCERS

405 Clute Road
Naples, NY 14512
(585) 374-6371

Hours: (Windmill Market)
Saturday, 8:00 a.m.–
4:30 p.m. (April through
December)

Clute's Pure Maple Products

When winter grudgingly gives way to spring, Lane Clute prepares to gather sap from the fragrant sugar maple trees on his land to make into maple syrup, just as his father and grandfather did before him. The family's 500-acre farm includes two vigorous stands of maples, whose lifetimes span centuries.

The annual ritual of "sugaring" at the Clute family farm usually begins in early March. When daytime temperatures reach above freezing and nighttime temperatures dip below, trees in the sugarbush begin to emerge from their dormant period and their sap begins to flow. Lane carefully drills a small hole, waist-high, into each trunk and inserts a tap at the opening.

In earlier times sap was collected in buckets, which hung from the taps. When the sap was "running," workers would trudge on snowshoe into the sugarbush twice a day to collect the clear, slightly sweet liquid in buckets. It was hard work toting five-gallon pails of sap through deep snow. Since the 1980s, Lane has used a less labor-intensive delivery system. Small plastic tubes are attached to the taps, and the sap is vacuum-pumped from the trees through the small tubes to larger collection tubes. These main tube lines carry the sap directly to the sugar shack on Clute Road.

Clouds of sweet steam billowing from the sugar shack are a sure sign that sap is beginning to boil in the flat, shallow steel pan called an evaporator. As it thickens, the syrup is drained off and filtered. Depending on sugar level, it takes thirty to fifty gallons of sap to make one gallon of syrup.

Early in the season, sap has a higher sugar content and requires less boiling. This sap produces a fine, light colored and delicately flavored syrup called Grade A Light Amber. As the season progresses, the sugar content of the sap decreases, and the syrup gets a little darker and begins to have a heavier, more robust maple flavor. The greatest demand is for Grade A Medium syrup, ideal for drenching a plate of hot pancakes. Lesser grades are used commercially as a flavoring for cakes and cured meats.

High-quality maple syrup has flavors of honey, sugar, roasted nuts, and praline, with a unique "fire" that coats your insides and warms your belly. Lane believes there is a secret in his soil that gives his syrup a distinctive balance of sweetness and acid, with hardly any bitter notes. "Like wine," he says, "you never find two syrups exactly the same."

In recent years, Lane has culled trees from the sugarbush to allow more room for the wide, deep crowns of his best trees. A larger crown means higher sugar and greater sap production. He takes out any trees that show signs of disease, protects root systems by keeping vehicles out of the woods, and follows proper taping procedures to ensure the health and vitality of the trees.

Besides producing nearly a thousand gallons of syrup every year, Lane does even more to ennoble the art of sugaring. He turns out a wide variety of maple confections under "Clute's Pure Maple Products" and "Good Old Boys" brands, including maple cream, granulated maple sugar, maple mustard, maple barbecue and dipping sauces, maple roasted peanuts and pecans, maple walnut and pecan toppings, maple pepper, and other maple seasonings.

Maple syrup is the best proof that the cuisine of the Finger Lakes is not without its luxuries. Think about warm syrup on sweet potatoes or butternut squash, and so many other dishes that taste better sauced, glazed, or infused with the liquid gold.

6

7556 County Road 33
Naples, NY 14512
(585) 374-9108

Hours: Tuesday–Saturday,
9:00 a.m.–6:00 p.m.;
Sunday, noon–6:00 p.m.

www.mountainrise.com

Mountain Rise Organics

William Jennings Bryan described Naples, New York, as "a spread of poetry written by the Great Author of the Universe." It was the poetry of this place that lured an RIT-trained engineer and his wife to a hillside farm near Grimes Creek in the town of Naples.

The story of how Glenn and Marcia Litwiller became successful entre-preneurs is one of formidable challenges and fortuitous events. The couple moved onto six acres of land and tried to scratch out a living by selling organic fruits, vegetables, and herbs at the local farmer's market. But, at an elevation of 1,300 feet, early frosts roll off the hills and settle in their hollow, so growing season on the farm is painfully short. In their second year, with very little to bring to market, they decided to bake Marcia's original recipe for granola and pack it into jars to fill the space on their table. The granola quickly sold out each week, and the next thing they knew they were installing a commercial oven in the kitchen to meet demand.

Over the next few years, the Litwillers' granola business grew by leaps and bounds. They began selling to small groceries through a health food distributor, and, when the newly bag-packed product was introduced to Wegman's, our Finger Lakes–based supermarket chain, it became a sta-ple in all their stores. Then, in 2001, a crew from Food Network showed up at the farm to feature Mountain Rise granola in a segment called "Food Finds," and it wasn't long before the upstart cereal had achieved cult status.

The certified organic granola is handmade daily on the farm. Whole wheatberries are freshly milled for each batch, retaining all of the nutri-tional benefits of whole grain and then mixed with rolled oats and cornmeal. Natural vanilla is added for flavor, and fresh organic eggs from the farm's free-range hens are used as a binder. Organic sugar cane juice gives it just a bit of sweetness. It's baked to a light to medium toastiness for a chunky texture, broken into pieces by hand, and finished in the convection oven.

Although the granola adventure occupies most of their time and energy, the Litwillers still grow a wide range of organic vegetables, including Moskovich tomatoes, heirlooms from Eastern Siberia; Fortex pole beans, a stringless variety that grows nearly a foot long; and nar-row, finger-shaped Russian Banana potatoes. A delightfully fragrant herb garden fills the air with rich aromas.

The charming farmstead radiates "old vineyard" charm from an iso-lated, pastoral setting, and the sturdy house, built by a nineteenth-century craftsman, is embraced by old larch and sugar maple trees. It's a place where you can breathe fresh air, stroll the farm, and eat fresh-baked gra-nola right out of the bag.

Springwater Sprouts

In the 1970s, eating sprouts was still associated with the counterculture, part of a diet adhered to only by flower children and health food fanatics. But, on a visit to California, Bill Nies observed the movement toward mainstream vegetarianism, and he suspected that fresh sprouts might not be a fad food after all. He returned home to Springwater, New York, and within five years became a commercial grower. Today, Springwater Sprouts has expanded from the kernel of a small family business to become the leading supplier of hydroponic greenhouse produce in the Finger Lakes.

Sprouted foods are seeds that have been moistened with water and have begun to grow into a plant. To meet its needs, Springwater buys seeds that have been selected for sprouting purposes from around the world, including mung beans from China, alfalfa from Australia, and broccoli from Louisville, Kentucky. "Our products are only as good as the seeds we start with," explains Bill.

As sales grew in the 1980s, Springwater acquired new and improved equipment and eventually built its existing facility in Honeoye Falls in order to draw water from pristine Hemlock Lake. Greening seeds are additionally "sanitized" in a 5 percent solution of calcium hypochlorite, then rinsed and placed in chain-driven rotary incubators made of food-grade plastic. As the drums slowly turn beneath full-spectrum lighting, stainless-steel heads spray 68-degree water to stimulate germination at set intervals. After ninety-six hours, the sprouts are harvested, agitated to remove hulls, spun to remove excess water, packaged, and before they're shipped, tested to ensure a product free from any bacterial contamination. "This stuff is alive," says Bill. "It gains in weight even after it's packed."

The company has developed private label programs with Tops Markets and Wegman's, the two dominant retailers in the region, offering varietal packets and a "Sprout Garden" mix of alfalfa, Chinese cabbage, mung, broccoli, lentil, adzuki, and radish sprouts. Products are harvested in the morning, packaged, and delivered directly, often appearing on supermarket shelves the same day.

Mung bean sprouts, harvested separately for up to a week, supply Asian foods markets and currently account for highest sales; however, Bill expects that to change dramatically. New research has discovered that broccoli sprouts (labeled as "Broccosprouts") contain the same powerful cancer-fighting antioxidant found in fully mature broccoli, but in a more concentrated form. The advantage of eating plants in the sprout stage is that you can eat more individual sprouts than you can mature broccoli. You would need to eat over a pound of broccoli to receive the same amount of antioxidants as just one ounce of sprouts provides.

Every week of the year, the folks at Springwater, led by Bill Nies, his father, Herm, and food safety specialist Steve Horan, provide the Finger Lakes with 5,000 to 6,000 pounds of safe, healthy, pesticide-free sprouts

4 High Street
Honeoye Falls, NY 14472
(585) 624-1234

Hours: By appointment

*www.shoprochester.com/
springwater/index.htm*

at the peak of freshness. Each variety of these delicate threads of life offers its own distinct flavor to a range of dishes, such as soups, salads, sandwiches, and stir-fries.

RESTAURANTS

8613 Cohocton Street
Naples, NY 14512
(585) 374-8010

Hours: Lunch daily, 11:00 a.m.–5:00 p.m.; Dinner, Friday and Saturday, 6:00 p.m.–9:00 p.m. (April through November)

www.rcgolf.com

The Creek Café

Surrounded by the gentle, glacier-carved hillsides and nourished by Canandaigua Lake lies the village of Naples, a dignified community, except, perhaps, for its obsession with grape pies. Naples is where grape fanatics and pie pilgrims come to stuff themselves silly with traditional Concord grape pies every year during the last weekend of September.

If you don't play golf, you might never discover the Creek Café on your own. But local folks who know something more about good food than grape pies will send you to a small family restaurant at the Reservoir Creek Golf Course for the best meal in town.

The Creek Café, located at the halfway point of the eighteen-hole course, provides a golfer's lunch of comfort food with a flair. Salads include Classic Caesar, Chicken Waldorf, and Seared Tuna with house-made kimchee; a Corned Beef Reuben features house-made sauerkraut; burgers are served on house-baked pretzel buns, and even the relish is made from house-cured pickles. The made-from-scratch preparations lure a steady stream of patrons, even those who don't know a five iron from a steam iron. A talented craftsman has made his restaurant part of the community.

Born in New Orleans, Tim Trojian "meandered up to Canada," as he says, and went to work for chef-farmer-guru Michael Stadtländer of Ontario's Eigensinn Farm, who taught him to use genuine techniques and fresh, indigenous ingredients. After stints with a variety of proficient culinarians at several different establishments, Tim followed his family to the Finger Lakes.

The restaurant is a cross between an oak-paneled tavern and your grandmother's dining room, installed in an old farmhouse with seating on an outside deck for warm spring and summer days and evenings. Its location places the Creek Café in close proximity to small farmers who provide Tim a "restaurant garden" with a wide range of vegetables and small fresh fruits. "We use what's here and now," he explains. "Tomatoes that arrive in my kitchen are still warm from the sun."

With the assistance of his wife, Shauna Smith, who studied at the Cooking and Hospitality Institute of Chicago, the chef prepares weekend dinners with no two menus ever the same. Offerings might include a Smoked Duck Salad with roasted beets, brie, local apricots, and a vinaigrette made with Widmer's Pale Dry Sherry or a Nut-Crusted Breast of Chicken with a sauce of Arbor Hill Traminette and cream. Desserts are inspired by whatever happens to be in season at nearby Jerome's U-Pick; the chef picks his own strawberries, blackberries, raspberries, and blueberries for the café's pies and tarts, and, of course, house-made ice creams are served alongside.

The gifted Mr. Trojian is obsessive about the integrity of his ingredients, and he compares his craft as a chef to that of a winemaker. Part of his recipe for success is a deep respect for local producers, and the wine list is an almost priestly expression of his view. Although selections are rotating, you can depend on personal favorites, including Standing Stone Chardonnay, Heron Hill Riesling, Hazlitt Merlot, and the range of extraordinary Brickstone wines, produced just up the road a piece.

CONCORD GRAPE PIE

Makes one 9-inch pie

The local tradition of purple pies began sometime in the 1960s with Al Hodges, who commissioned Irene Bouchard to make a unique grape dessert for the Redwood Restaurant in Naples. Forty years later, thousands come to the village of Naples to celebrate the grape harvest and sample the native grape pies. The robust flavor of Concord grapes makes this unusual pie a treat. You will have to peel each grape, but the delicious results are well worth the effort.

▚▚▚▚▚▚▚

To make the pie crust, mix together the flour and salt in a bowl. Using a pastry blender or a fork, cut in the butter and shortening until the mixture resembles coarse meal. Sprinkle the water over the mixture a tablespoon at a time, mixing lightly after each addition, until the dough can be formed into a ball. Divide the dough into two pieces, form each piece into a ball, and allow them to rest for 15 minutes before rolling out.

To make the filling, slip the skins off the grapes and reserve them. Put the grape pulp in a saucepan and simmer over medium-low heat just until soft enough to release the seeds, about 8 minutes. Push the grape pulp through a wire-mesh strainer to remove the seeds. Combine the pulp in a bowl with the reserved grape skins.

Roll out each ball of dough on a well-floured board until they are 10 to 11 inches in diameter. Line the bottom of a 9-inch pie pan with a round of dough. Preheat the oven to 450°F. Mix the sugar, salt, and tapioca together in a bowl and spread about half of the mixture onto the bottom of the crust. Mix the remaining tapioca mixture with the grapes and add the lemon juice. Pour the pie filling into the crust and dot with the butter. Cover with the top crust and crimp the edges to seal. Bake for 10 minutes, and then lower the temperature to 350°F and bake for another 25 to 30 minutes, until golden brown. Remove from the oven and cool for 30 minutes before serving. If not serving immediately, warm the pie in an oven set on the lowest temperature for 10 minutes before serving.

PIE CRUST

2½ cups all-purpose flour, sifted

1 teaspoon salt

½ cup unsalted butter, chilled and cut into small pieces

½ cup vegetable shortening, chilled and cut into small pieces

6 to 7 tablespoons cold water

FILLING

4 cups Concord grapes

1 cup sugar

⅛ teaspoon salt

2½ tablespoons tapioca

1 tablespoon freshly squeezed lemon juice

1 tablespoon unsalted butter, at room temperature

8

Routes 5 and 20
Bloomfield, NY 14443
(585) 657-7120

Hours: Lunch,
Tuesday–Saturday,
11:30 a.m.–2:00 p.m.,
Dinner, 5:00 p.m.–9:00 p.m.;
Sunday, noon–7:30 p.m.
(April through November)

www.thehollowayhouse.com

The Holloway House

U.S. Route 20 begins in Boston, Massachusetts, and ends in Newport, Oregon. The historic road is over 3,200 miles long and winds its way through twelve states. During the Revolutionary War, what is now Route 20 was traveled by George Washington and Paul Revere, and afterwards it became a stagecoach route to the expanding West.

In 1808 a local blacksmith by the name of Peter Holloway established a tavern along Route 20 in Bloomfield, New York. Weary travelers took respite in his tavern for food and drink while the stagecoach operators changed horses. A few tables and many chairs filled the barroom, and meals were served from a large open hearth outfitted with a Dutch oven. Holloway House has been a welcome site for hungry and thirsty transients and local citizens ever since.

By the time Mr. and Mrs. Frank Munson purchased the property at the turn of the nineteenth century, it had evolved into a bastion of luxury for persons of wealth and privilege. Known then as Locust Lawn, its menu offered pheasant under glass to guests from nearby estates while chauffeurs cooled their heels outside. In 1939, the Seel family renamed it Holloway House and set it upon its present course as a destination for home-style meals.

Today, Steve and Dawn Wayne have preserved the lovely old place, which is appointed with four-legged maplewood tables and Mottville chairs, not only for the ladies who lunch, but for anyone who appreciates wholesome and soul-satisfying comfort food, made stylish by the setting. This is a great place to enjoy fresh, slow-roasted Tom Turkey with all the trimmings; Chicken Holloway, a sautéed boneless breast over stuffing with a fruity cranberry glaze; or pork tenderloin, sliced and served with local apples in a light maple-mustard sauce. Lunch offers an abbreviated version of the dinner menu along with Turkey Pot Pie, Turkey à la King, and Chicken and Biscuits—nearly forgotten classics, delivered by servers in Colonial-era long-sleeved, ankle-length dresses.

Sally Lunn bread, a semisweet, yeasty egg bread, baked in a cake pan, is a house specialty, served warm from the oven. And a meal here wouldn't be complete without a delicious old-fashioned dessert from skillful pastry chef Pamela Graham. Her fresh-baked pies are filled with handpicked seasonal fruit from White's Farm in nearby Ionia, and her Strawberry Shortcake is legendary.

Wines are a strong suit here, thanks to Steve's educated palate and his belief that local wines go with local foods. Drawing on his expertise as a wine judge, he has assembled the best bottles from his neighbors along the Canandaigua Wine Trail, as well as an eclectic mix of other Finger Lakes wines. Familiar Rieslings from Arbor Hill, Heron Hill, and Dr. Frank seem right at home with the restaurant's cooking.

Holloway House delivers a compelling restaurant experience that seems to belong to another era. It's refreshingly down-to-earth, and a real, authentic gem for those fed up with ever more superficial and cloned restaurant chains.

SALLY LUNN BREAD

To accompany the fine and fancy food at Holloway House, there has always been Sally Lunn bread. The recipe dates back to Colonial America, although history tells us there was actually no one named Sally. The words may be a corruption of sol et lune, *French for sun and moon, probably used by French immigrants to describe the round shape of the buns, similar to brioche. Sunday suppers in Bloomfield wouldn't be the same without it.*

Dissolve the yeast and 1 tablespoon of the sugar in the warm water and let the mixture foam. In a bowl, add the shortening to the warm milk.

Meanwhile, using an electric mixer with the paddle attachment, beat the eggs on high speed. While beating, gradually add the remaining ²/₃ cup sugar and beat until thick and lemon colored.

Change the attachment on the mixer to a dough hook. Add the dissolved yeast and the shortening mixture to the egg mixture and combine on low speed. Gradually add the flour and salt to the mixture. When all of the flour is incorporated, beat the dough on high speed for about 5 minutes, until the dough is firm but stretchy.

Pour the batter into a large bowl, cover with a kitchen towel, and let rise in a warm place until doubled, about 1¹/₂ hours. Punch the dough down, cover with the kitchen towel again, and return it to the warm place. Let the dough rise until doubled again, about 1 hour.

Preheat the oven to 350°F. Grease 2 angel food cake pans. Punch down the dough again, divide it into 2 equal pieces, and place the pieces, uncovered, in the greased pans. Set the pans in a warm place and let the dough rise to the top of the pans, about 30 minutes.

Bake for 30 to 45 minutes, until the top is golden and the loaf sounds hollow when tapped. Remove the pans from the oven, let the loaves cool for 2 minutes, and then remove from the pans. Slice the bread into 1-inch-thick slices and serve warm with butter.

Makes 2 loaves

2 packages active dry yeast

²/₃ cup plus 1 tablespoon sugar

1 cup water, lukewarm (90°–100°F)

¹/₂ cup shortening

1¹/₃ cups milk, warm

6 eggs

8¹/₄ cups all-purpose flour

1 tablespoon salt

Note: This bread is allowed to rise three times, resulting in very light bread. This process takes time, so allow approximately three hours for this recipe, with more than two of those hours being inactive time.

7

4356 East Lake Road
Canandaigua, NY 14424
(585) 394-4868

Dining Room Hours:
Call for hours
**Boathouse Hours
(casual dining):** Daily,
noon–10:00 p.m. (May
through October)

thendarainn.com

Thendara Inn

It was late in the nineteenth century, and next to Governor Teddy Roosevelt, John Raines of Canandaigua was the most powerful politician in New York State. He fought in the Union Army during the Civil War, became a lawyer, served, first in the State Assembly, then in the State Senate. As Republican leader of the Senate and political boss, he drafted legislation that became known as the "Raines Law," granting the state sole authority to issue saloon licenses.

The Senator loved to hold picnics and clambakes at Lincoln Wood landing, a steamboat stop and loading dock on the lake's Eastern shore, and he eventually purchased a nine-acre parcel of nearby land called "Thendara," the Seneca Indian word for "meeting place." It was on this bluff overlooking Canandaigua Lake that he would build a dignified, fourteen-room Victorian cottage, designed by John Handrahan, landscape architect of Sonnenberg. Thendara, the name he kept for the estate, had a billiard room, two bathrooms, and seven bedrooms, in addition to a large living room, dining room, three fireplaces, a wraparound porch, and a distinctive boathouse.

Senator Raines died in 1909, before Thendara was completed; however, the mansion was used by his children and grandchildren until the 1940s. At one time it served as the home of the Canandaigua Yacht Club, but for most of the last fifty years it has operated as a guesthouse and restaurant.

Today, Thendara Inn offers overnight stays in the stately guest rooms and serves casual lunches and dinners at the Boathouse and more formal meals on the mansion's enclosed porch to the annual tide of vacationers that washes into the area.

Chef Steve Maynard plies guests with a range of American dishes, including lusty Greens and Beans, escarole and white beans sautéed in a light chicken stock with Asiago, and a Harvest Salad of seasonal greens, tart apples, candied walnuts, blue cheese, and grilled chicken. Cumin-Dusted Grilled Veal Chop is served with black beans, sweet corn ragu, and crème fraiche; Veal Oscar, with lobster medallions and asparagus, is finished with béarnaise sauce.

The finesse that characterizes Steve's veal preparations is complemented by the Rieslings of Glenora, Heron Hill, and Hermann J. Wiemer.

While dinner in the mansion is glamorous, it has trouble competing with a visit to the Boathouse and the experience of dining on the deck to the music of gently lapping water. The place is full of friendly locals and tourists who come here for clam chowder, onion rings, Cobb salads, and beer-battered fish fries. If you want to splurge, order the Boathouse "Surf and Turf": a dozen chicken wings, a dozen steamed clams, and a bottle of Dom Perignon for $175. And, if you time it just right, you'll get to watch an incredible sunset across beautiful Canandaigua Lake while you sip.

Thendara, one of the most spectacular pieces of property in the entire Finger Lakes region, is a noteworthy destination on the culinary map, whether for fancy dining or something casual. Folks who find it get the best of both worlds.

KEUKA
LAKE

('kyü-kə)

THIRD LARGEST OF THE FINGER LAKES in size, Keuka is twenty miles long, two miles wide, with a maximum depth of 187 feet, holding 390 billion gallons in volume. Known as the "crooked lake" because of its unique "Y" shape, Keuka truly provides visitors one of the most beautiful destinations in the United States.

The scale of giant Birkett Mills dominates historic Penn Yan, and pleasing aromas from ovens that roast buckwheat into kasha waft through a downtown lined with mom-and-pop stores. Dairy and other types of farming, agriculture, and a lively tourist trade are the backbone of an area where you share the road with horses and buggies of a thriving Mennonite community.

Picturesque Hammondsport, on the south end of the lake, has a long history as a vintner's enclave. The first cultivated grapes in the Finger Lakes were brought here in 1829 by William Bostwick, minister of St. James Episcopal Church, and commercial wine production began here in 1860. Many of the fine homes along Lake Street were built by winery owners and winemakers during the second half of the nineteenth century.

The enchanting Keuka Lake area offers a panorama of lush fields with row after row of well-manicured fruit of the vine. The eye of the traveler is treated with picture-postcard views, while the palate is treated to small-production artisan wines.

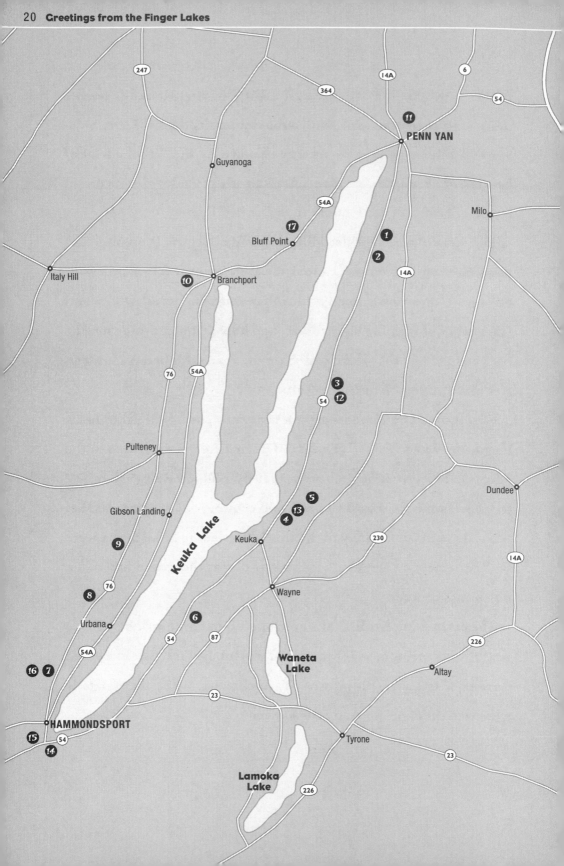

Wineries

1 Keuka Spring Vineyards *(PENN YAN)*

2 Rooster Hill Vineyards *(PENN YAN)*

3 Barrington Cellars *(see Buzzard Crest Vineyards, PENN YAN)*

4 McGregor Vineyard Winery *(DUNDEE)*

5 Keuka Overlook Wine Cellars *(DUNDEE)*

6 Ravines Wine Cellars *(HAMMONDSPORT)*

7 Bully Hill Vineyards *(HAMMONDSPORT)*

8 Heron Hill Winery *(HAMMONDSPORT)*

9 Dr. Frank's Vinifera Wine Cellars/Chateau Frank *(HAMMONDSPORT)*

10 Hunt Country Vineyards *(BRANCHPORT)*

Farms/Food Producers

11 Birkett Mills *(PENN YAN)*

12 Buzzard Crest Vineyards *(PENN YAN)*

13 Pa'tridge Run Farms/Fall Bright, The Winemakers Shoppe *(DUNDEE)*

Restaurants

14 The Village Tavern *(HAMMONDSPORT)*

15 Pleasant Valley Inn *(HAMMONDSPORT)*

16 Bully Hill Restaurant *(see Bully Hill Vineyards, HAMMONDSPORT)*

17 Esperanza Mansion *(BLUFF POINT)*

WINERIES

Barrington Cellars

See Buzzard Crest Vineyards (page 39) . . . .

Bully Hill Vineyards/Bully Hill Restaurant

8843 Greyton H. Taylor
Memorial Drive
Hammondsport, NY 14840
(607) 868-3610

Winery Hours:
Monday–Thursday,
9:00 a.m.–6:00 p.m.;
Friday–Saturday,
9:00 a.m.–9:00 p.m.;
Sunday, 11:00 a.m.–
6:00 p.m.
Restaurant Hours: Lunch
daily, 11:30 a.m.–4:00 p.m.;
Dinner, Saturday, 5:00 p.m.–
9:00 p.m.

www.bullyhill.com

It's hard to overstate the eccentricity of Bully Hill. The winery, situated on a terraced hillside overlooking Keuka Lake, is the inspiration and creation of a charismatic showman, who turned disdain for his family's business into one of the Finger Lakes' most popular destinations.

Walter Stephen Taylor was the grandson of the founder of the Taylor Wine Company of Hammondsport. An eager provocateur, Walter railed against the "wine factory" the company had become by the time it was swallowed up by Coca-Cola in 1977. He lambasted not only its dependence on labruscas and the addition of water and corn syrup to its wines, but also the undermining of local growers with juice delivered by tank car from California. Walter's family helped him repurchase his grandfather's original farm, called Bully Hill, and he set out on his own to make what he called "honest wines."

He hired a German winemaker by the name of Hermann Wiemer and cast his lot with nontraditional French-American hybrids, crosses between vinifera and native American labruscas. Combining cold-hardiness and higher quality, Walter's wines surprised the industry—and caught the attention of Coca-Cola. Since Coke had purchased the Taylor Wine Company lock, stock, and barrel, it was unhappy about Walter's use of the Taylor name on his bottles of Bully Hill wines. In a classic battle of Goliath versus David, the Coca-Cola Company sued Walter for trademark infringement.

A Barnum-like ability to capture public attention came naturally to Walter. After all, he was a distant cousin of Phineas Taylor (P.T.) Barnum, the man who built a circus empire with outrageous promotion and guile. When the court sided with Coke and enjoined him from using the family name on his labels, Walter started calling himself "Walter S. Blank." A talented artist, he drew his own winkingly irreverent labels, products of an idiosyncratic imagination. His most famous label was an image of a billy goat with the slogan, "They have my name and my heritage, but they didn't get my goat." Walter once appeared at my restaurant for a wine-tasting event with a live goat in tow.

Among the dizzying array of wines, goat labels are Bully Hill's best sellers. Love My Goat Red is primarily a blend of Baco Noir and Marechal

Foch, which comes in midway on the winery's dry to sweet scale. Le Goat Blush is a rosé-style blend of Seyval, Aurore, Vidal, and Colobel Noir for color. Greg Learned, winemaker at Bully Hill since 1981, still relies on French-American hybrid grapes for most of his wines, both estate-grown and purchased from as many as thirty-eight Finger Lakes growers.

Walter Taylor was a larger-than-life character in a big, sweeping epic charged with romance and tragedy. He married Lillian Rakic, a charming Croatian émigré, but six years later his van was rear-ended on a Florida highway, leaving him a quadraplegic on life support systems until he died at age sixty-nine. If her husband was the Baron of Bully Hill, as he liked to call himself, she is indeed the Baroness. Under Lillian's guidance, Bully Hill has not only stayed the course, but outpaced the growth of the wine industry in the region.

Bully Hill houses an informal restaurant where you can savor a glass of wine paired with roasted local garlic cloves, Lively Run goat cheese, and toasted baguette. Goat cheese also appears in a delicious combination of smoked salmon, greens, red onion, capers, and fresh dill, wrapped in a flour tortilla. Sip on Bully Hill "Iced Tea," a chilled white wine with mulling spices, or Bully Hill "Cylinder Head" grape juice, a refreshing blend of unfermented Concord, Ives, and Delaware juices. The inside dining room is adorned with Walter's artwork; the outdoor deck provides a picture-postcard view of Keuka Lake.

While the colorful figure of Walter Taylor is gone from his beloved winery, his antiestablishment wine making and off-the-wall labels have earned him hero's status in the Finger Lakes. He was a marketing genius whose sense of humor was the perfect antidote to wine snobbery.

Today, 150,000 visitors a year make the pilgrimage to Bully Hill; production exceeds a quarter of a million cases annually; mostly from the French-American hybrid grapes Walter championed; and the once-tiny winery is now the largest family-owned winery in the region. As P.T. Barnum once said, "Every crowd has a silver lining."

Dr. Frank's Vinifera Wine Cellars/ Chateau Frank

Willy Frank is the guardian of a revered legacy at this historic winery. This is where his father, Dr. Konstantin Frank, produced fine wines from grape varieties that were believed to be ungrowable in our region of the United States. The elder Frank's work enabled his family to achieve extraordinary results, not only for Vinifera Wine Cellars but for the viticultural progress of the entire Finger Lakes.

A Ukrainian-born professor of plant science, Konstantin Frank emigrated to the United States in 1951, settling in New York City, after having successfully nurtured wine-producing vines through some of Ukraine's nastiest winters. His belief that the same vinifera plantings

9749 Middle Road
Hammondsport, NY 14840
(800) 320-0735

Hours: Monday–Saturday, 9:00 a.m.–5:00 p.m.; Sunday, noon–5:00 p.m.

www.drfrankwines.com

could do no worse in upstate New York fell on deaf ears, including those of the experts at Cornell who, when he arrived at the Agricultural Experiment Station, handed him a hoe and sent him into the blueberry field. He was correct, of course, but it was not until he met Charles Fournier, winemaster of Gold Seal Vineyards, that he would be given the opportunity to prove it. The two men collaborated on an experimental Pinot Noir vineyard near Hammondsport, and, heady with success, Dr. Frank established his own winery in 1962.

He planted as many as fifty different varieties, including Riesling, Chardonnay, Pinot Noir, Gewürztraminer, Cabernet Sauvignon, and Rkatsiteli, a favorite grape from his native country, at what grandson Frederick describes as "Dr. Frank's own experiment station." It was the wellspring of the Finger Lakes' modern wine industry.

Although cold winters posed a problem, Dr. Frank knew it could be overcome by picking the best microclimates along the shores of the lakes. He was more concerned with phylloxera, a pest that attacks the roots of grapes and for which vinifera plants had no defense. So, one by one, he painstakingly hand-grafted each plant onto a resistant American rootstock. He would "hill-up" the vines with twelve inches of soil before the onset of winter, to protect that sensitive graft union, and then remove the mound of soil in spring.

To his credit, Dr. Frank never kept secrets. He passed on his intimate knowledge of the grapes and their different needs and inspired a generation of disciples—fellow vintners who believed in him, learned from him, and bought grafted vines from him. These people became pioneers within their own respective regions.

The winery itself has been a training ground for some remarkable and talented winemakers, including David Munksgard of Iron Horse in Sonoma County, Eric Fry of Lenz in Long Island, Peter Bell of Fox Run, Johannes Reinhardt of Anthony Road, and Frederique Perrin of Belhurst Winery in the Finger Lakes. Today, the winemaking team includes internationally educated enologists Morten Hallgren (Montpellier), Mark Veraguth (UC Davis), and James Radcliffe (University of Adelaide, South Australia), some of the best technical minds in the industry.

The global range of perspectives is part of the philosophy here, and, according to Fred, it was the reason Willy sent him off to Geisenheim, the venerable wine institute of Germany, to study winemaking. "Then," he explains, "my father borrowed an old European proverb and told me 'you should learn to shave on another man's beard,' so I prepared to take over the family business by working for Banfi Wines."

Fleur de Pinot Noir is a reliable nonvintage wine produced from younger plantings of Pinot Noir grapes. It has a lovely garnet color, aromas of plums and cherries, bright, ripe berry-cherry flavors, toasted almond, white pepper, and a long, dry finish with a little heat. Since young vines produce grapes with lots of fruit flavor and little tannin, it's immediately accessible and reminiscent of Beaujolais.

Interestingly, in an analysis conducted by Cornell University Professor Leroy L. Creasy, Dr. Frank's Fleur de Pinot Noir contained the highest resveratrol content of any wine ever encountered in his studies. Resveratrol, a chemical compound found primarily on grape skins, has been proven to contain cancer-inhibiting properties and is also known to aid in combating heart disease.

Johannisberg Riesling, however, may be the grape that best defines the winery. You will rarely find a semi-dry, Spätlese-style wine so light and delicate. This lovely wine has aromas of ripe peaches and honey combined with a nectarine, lemon peel, and mineral-rich personality that is both complex and elegant on the palate. Because of the wine's ability to retain classic Germanic characters and greatness with age, Willy Frank calls this his "Marlene Dietrich wine."

The Frank family is the closest we have to royalty in the Finger Lakes. Willy, the company chairman; son Fred, president and general manager; and Willy's nephew Eric Volz, vineyard manager, work tirelessly to preserve the historical accomplishments of Konstantin Frank. Willy, nearing eighty years of age, operates a sister winery, Chateau Frank, which is dedicated to producing outstanding sparkling wines from Pinot Meunier and other classic varieties. His brut is the Veuve Cliquot of our region, medium-bodied, nutty, honeyed, and round on the palate, with tight bubbles and a delicate mousse.

Dr. Frank was a man of vision, integrity, and stature. Those of us who had the uncommon experience of meeting and talking with him in his later years will always remember his passion and especially the pride he took as an immigrant in having his wines served in the White House.

Nearly everyone achieves a certain degree of success in a lifetime. Success for Dr. Frank came not just because he was the first to make Finger Lakes wines from vinifera grapes, but because he understood the implications of his accomplishment. He promised, somewhat grandiosely, a revolution in the industry, and he went right ahead and delivered it.

Heron Hill Winery

As children of the sixties, John and Josephine Ford Ingle (she is the great-granddaughter of Henry Ford) took a philosophical approach to life that emphasized freedom, peace, love, and a respect for others and the earth. "It was a beautiful period in American history," says John.

In 1971 the young couple moved to a property at Seneca Point on Canandaigua Lake, where, in a retreat from convention, they lived in a rustic, two-room cabin without running water, heated only by a woodstove. Their next-door neighbor, Verne Morgan, was a grape grower and an early mentor. He invited John and Jo to pick grapes during harvest, and he encouraged them to turn their abandoned orchard into a vineyard. It would become the alternative lifestyle the Ingles were seeking—living on a farm, raising a family, and doing something they loved.

9301 County Route 76
Hammondsport, NY 14840
(800) 441-4241

Hours: Monday–Saturday, 10:00 a.m.–5:00 p.m.; Sunday, noon–5:00 p.m.

www.heronhill.com

While Verne was content to grow labrusca varieties, John somehow knew this hillside property, looking across the lake to Vine Valley, had potential for greatness. He began planting Chardonnay and Riesling, determined to prove the naysayers wrong. When he sought support for his vinifera ambitions, he found a kindred spirit in Peter Johnstone, who had already achieved some success with European varieties on Keuka Lake. The two impassioned men joined forces in a venture that would turn grapes from both vineyards into fine wine. It was called Heron Hill, and it played an important part in the formative years of the Finger Lakes wine industry.

When a winery has matured and achieved success in the marketplace, it can undertake some changes that are a little daring. In 2000, John brought architect Charles Warren of New York City to Hammondsport to transform the Heron Hill facility. The result blends elements of the region's history into bold shapes with interesting materials, and it looks like nothing the Finger Lakes has ever seen. Dramatic stonework was inspired by the cobblestone homes built by masons who came to the region to build the Erie Canal, and the rounded, vaulted ceilings of the tasting room are suggestive of a giant wine barrel. "It's a concept of imagination and creativity, reflecting the tradition of wine culture," explains John.

Creative intervention did not stop there. The following year, John recruited a superbly trained winemaker by the name of Thomas Laszlo, born in Canada in 1968 of parents who escaped Hungary during the 1958 revolution.

He studied at the University of Guelph and made his first wines at Henry of Pelham Winery in Ontario. In 1997 he joined Chateau Pajzos and Chateau Megyer in the wine region of northeastern Hungary, where he helped to restore the wines of his ancestral home to their former glory.

This change is not a subtle one for Heron Hill. Thomas brings a pool of knowledge that reflects both the art and science of his profession. His arrival prompted the purchase of cutting-edge crushing and pressing equipment, including a new six-ton Bucher press. Since Bucher makes the most gentle and delicate press for crushing grapes, wines are less impacted by mechanization and retain more aspects of terroir.

Grapes used to fashion the intriguing Riesling Reserve come from the winery's two main locations. At the Heron Hill site, "stressed" vines grown in shallow topsoil over layers of shale and slate produce well-structured wine with citrus and mineral characters. Low yields from the Ingle vineyard's gravelly loam and rocky soils produce opulent, melon flavors. This Riesling is an industry benchmark.

Creation of ice wine may be the most magical process in winemaking, and Thomas has now made these much-sought-after wines in three different countries. "Ice wines," he contends, "are about pure fruit expression and contrast of acid and sugar, sweet and sour." He is delighted by the peculiarities that the Keuka Lake site provides for the pristine, botrytis-free Heron Hill Riesling Ice Wine, in his words, "a wine that screams *Riesling*."

What began as the "joyously undertaken" farming endeavor of John and Josephine Ingle has become one of the Finger Lakes' most prominent wineries. With a supply of exceptional fruit, a state-of-the-art facility, and a formidable winemaker in the cellar, it is obvious that Heron Hill is destined for continued greatness.

Hunt Country Vineyards

Branchport was already established as a farming community when Adam Hunt moved from the Hudson Valley and settled here in 1815. He built a simple but solid log cabin, took up residence, then planted fruit trees and grapevines on the rolling hillside. The farm has remained in the Hunt family for six generations and is now home to eighty acres of native, French-American hybrid, and vinifera wine grapes.

4021 Italy Hill Road
Branchport, NY 14418
(315) 595-2812
(800) 946-3289

The winery was established by Art and Joyce Hunt in 1981, first as Finger Lakes Wine Cellars, then renamed Hunt Country Vineyards. Over the years, the vineyard has expanded, the wines have evolved, and a definitive style has reached maturity.

Hours: Monday–Saturday, 10:00 a.m.–6:00 p.m., Sunday, noon–6:00 p.m. (July through October); Monday–Saturday, 10:00 a.m.–5:00 p.m., Sunday, noon–5:00 p.m. (November through June)

The advantageous site has a wide diversity of rich soils deposited by glaciers, which passed over the area thousands of years ago, but the keystone of this property's intensely fruity wines is its microclimate. The combination of warm, sunny days and very cool nighttime temperatures creates, ideal conditions for aroma and flavor development in the ripening grapes, and it's uniquely captured in the wines.

www.huntcountry-vineyards.com

Maximum intensity of fruit also depends on the age of each plant and its vigor, explains Art. Vines have to grow in the grid where they are planted until roots have thoroughly permeated the soil and the only place additional energy can go is into the fruit. "It takes eight to ten years before that happens," he explains.

The Finger Lakes provide one of the few locales in the world ideal for producing late harvest wines and practicing the art of sculpting frozen fruit into ice wine. Hardy Vignoles grapes are left on the vines past traditional harvest time so more sugar and interesting characters can develop. They produce a wonderful dessert wine with mouth-filling texture and hints of apricot and tropical fruit.

When left to hang on the vine even later into the season, the Vidal grapes become dried and shriveled and condensed with sugar. When temperatures drop to 20 degrees or below, water in the grapes freezes, but sugar, acid, and flavor extracts remain unfrozen. The grapes are quickly picked by hand, carried to the winery, and pressed immediately, as juice is separated from skin and pulp, drop by drop. The viscous, concentrated juice is fermented to produce a luscious, elegant, honeyed nectar that dances on the palate.

Proper etiquette calls for serving ice wine in a small glass that narrows toward the rim to focalize the bouquet, but this Vidal has such powerful aromatics, any glass will do. Although it's frequently served with cheesecake or another rich dessert, I prefer to savor the precious liquid as a dessert by itself. When served at cool room temperature, the wine retains maximum balance and complexity.

Vignoles produce excellent wines of many different styles, and the Hunts' semisweet version displays peach, pineapple, and citrus aromas, then bursts with flavors of tangerines, pears, apricots, green apples, and grapefruit, and finishes with notes of honey and raisins. Full bodied, with just the right amount of natural acidity, the wine makes a convivial apéritif.

While Seyval Blanc is a variety that commands little respect among many of the region's producers, Hunt Country has remarkable success with grapes from the nearby Morse Vineyard. This vineyard-designated Seyval is pale gold, with a slightly herbaceous, grassy nose; the palate is vivid and juicy with lots of crisp lemon, grapefruit, and bright citrus notes; a long, smooth finish hints at toasted oak.

Art's more ponderous utterances are reserved for "Foxy Lady," a series of red, white, and blush blends that he refers to as "fun wines, as opposed to serious wines." Entry-level drinkers seem to enjoy the "foxy" notes of native varieties, especially when they are toned down with compatible hybrids, so the blush version, for instance, blends Delaware, Cayuga, and Seyval grapes. What started out as fruity picnic wine for summer tourists now accounts for one-third of total production at Hunt Country. Who knew?

The Hunt estate is part of Finger Lakes agricultural history, and, in true farm family fashion, young Jonathan Hunt is being groomed to be the next generation entrusted with the legacy. He studied viticulture and enology at Cornell, then joined St. Francis Winery in Sonoma Valley, California, as an intern before returning to the historic homestead to continue family tradition.

PORK STEAKS IN SPICY CAYUGA SAUCE

Serves 4

Cayuga White is an easy-to-like, food-friendly wine, unique to the Finger Lakes region. Joyce Hunt was inspired by the Riesling-like characters in her family's Cayuga, and she developed a German-inspired dish to match the local wine.

Bring a large pot of salted water to a boil over high heat. Add the fettuccine and cook until al dente according to the package directions.

In the meantime, melt the butter in a large frying pan. Sauté the garlic, onion, and mushrooms with the Worcestershire sauce over medium heat, stirring constantly, until the onions caramelize, about 8 minutes. Remove from the pan and set aside.

Return the pan to stove, add the pork steaks, and cook over medium heat for 4 minutes on each side to brown. Add the wine and simmer over medium-low heat for 25 minutes, turning the steaks occasionally. Remove the steaks and add the heavy cream to the pan. When the cream is hot, whisk in the cornstarch solution and add the onion mixture.

Place a pork steak over individual portions of fettuccine and pour the wine cream sauce over the top.

1 pound dried fettuccine pasta

2 tablespoons unsalted butter

1 large clove garlic, minced

½ cup minced Spanish or sweet onion

½ cup sliced mushrooms

1 teaspoon Worcestershire sauce

4 (½ pound) pork steaks, trimmed of fat

½ cup Hunt Country Cayuga White

½ cup heavy cream

1 tablespoon cornstarch mixed with 1 tablespoon cold water

Salt and freshly ground black pepper

Note: Serve the leftover chilled Hunt Country Cayuga White with the meal. The light, fruity Cayuga wine goes well with the subtle spiciness of the pork steaks.

Keuka Overlook Wine Cellars

Every summer, the hill towns above Keuka Lake fill up with vacationers and visitors of every description, and, while there is a wide range of types of overnight accommodations, few of these spots have a working winery on the property. When making a weekend of it, a farmstay at Keuka Overlook B & B Inn may just fit the bill.

As corporate professionals based in Cleveland, Ohio, Bob and Terry Barrett became amateur winemakers, making regular pilgrimages to the Finger Lakes for each season's grapes. On a visit here in 1987, they found a unique property in the heart of wine country. It included a Victorian house, a humble old barn, and sixty-seven acres of highlands overlooking Keuka Lake from one view and Waneta Lake from another. During the next half-dozen years they spent every vacation and every weekend renovating the place, turning the barn into a practical winery and the house into a charming bed and breakfast. Together, Bob and Terry form a complete partnership, husband and wife, winemaker and innkeeper.

5777 Old Bath Road
Dundee, NY 14837
(607) 292-6877

Hours: Daily, 11:00a.m.–5:00 p.m., year-round (closed on major holidays)

www.kcukaoverlook.com

Guests at Keuka Overlook combine the best of these two worlds. Choose from four rooms, individually furnished and decorated, inspired by seasons of the year. Your early morning breakfast might include pancakes or waffles with fresh local fruit, quiche, or frittata with local vegetables, and Terry's Red Raspberry Shortcake, served over fresh-from-the-oven chocolate-zucchini bread, is an obligatory dessert. On Friday night, an informal pasta dinner is served, and on Saturday, Bob and Terry team up for a multicourse feast that includes an appropriate wine match with each dish. After dinner, the wide, wraparound porch provides a dreamy setting for sipping a glass of sweet mulberry wine while watching the sun dip into the lake. Bob turns the darkest and ripest berries from two mulberry trees resting behind the house into a fragrant, port-like dessert wine with deep, smokey, blackberry-honeysuckle characters and a long, seductive finish. Those trees happen to provide the only estate-grown fruit on the property.

With its high elevation, the site is not suited to temperature-sensitive vines, but Keuka Overlook is blessed with neighboring growers who regularly supply the winery with high-quality grapes. Vincent D'Ingianni delivers Cabernet Franc from his vineyard, and Tom Mitchell, a neighbor down the road, contributes Cabernet Sauvignon and Merlot from Pa'tridge Run Farm for an exemplary Meritage called Triumph. Bright garnet in the glass, this wine has a knockout nose that explodes with boysenberries, blueberries, and plums, then on the palate it's fruit-soaked with flavors of concentrated cherries, cranberries, and it winds up with a dusting of cinnamon and cocoa. The wine can be a bit youthful, but it is elegantly appealing and a very lovely wine to savor slowly. A reserve bottling of Chardonnay has a rich but lean profile of apple, pear, and honey notes with buttery, smoky, minerally undertones and faint oak and nutmeg flavors on the finish.

The Barretts preside over their lofty enterprise with a sense of pride and continuity that has resulted in a roster of guests who visit year after year. For travelers anxious for some honest wine country hospitality, this is one place that should not be overlooked.

Keuka Spring Vineyards

273 East Lake Road
(Route 54)
Penn Yan, NY 14527
(315) 536-3147

Hours: Monday–Saturday,
10:00 a.m.–5:00 p.m.;
Sunday, 11:00 a.m.–5:00 p.m.

www.keukaspringwinery.com

Len and Judy Wiltberger have had an intimate relationship with Keuka Lake for over three decades. In 1973 the couple purchased a summer cottage on Keuka Lake as a Thoreau-inspired retreat from their careers, Len as a technician at Eastman Kodak and Judy as a teacher in Rochester's inner city. Rather than simplifying their lives, as it turned out, they began growing grapes, and, in 1985, they decided to have a go at the wine business.

Years of work transformed an overgrown property into a prizewinning vineyard, named for the meandering spring that provides natural irrigation to ten acres of vines. Seyval Blanc, Vignoles, Chardonnay, and

Riesling—all white grapes—were the first plantings, and early successes of these varieties in wine competitions attracted attention to the winery. Then, over the next five years, they were able to slowly expand the production of red varieties, and, under the guidance of Keuka Lake's finest wine consultants, Lemberger and Cabernet Franc became the primary focus.

The stylish Keuka Spring Lemberger is a cold-hardy Austrian variety that dates back to the days of Napoleon Bonaparte and Otto von Bismarck, both of whom enjoyed the wine. The Wiltbergers' rendition is ruby-purple in color, velvety in texture, and it explodes with scents and flavors of rich, ripe berries and currants and finishes with hints of toasty oak and spices.

The winery earned the Governor's Cup for its 1998 Cabernet Franc, with a style that has remained consistent in successive vintages. The elegant wines deliver more and more with every sip, sneaking up on you with sweet, spicy blackberry and currant fruit overlaid with floral layers that linger on a polished finish.

The agrarian, wooden winery fits comfortably into the rural setting, and a pergola and terrace with picnic tables offer an unobstructed view of the vineyard and across the lake to Keuka College. Inside the bright and airy tasting room you'll find a knowledgeable and friendly staff happy to pour samples of wines that are fruity, balanced, food-friendly, and delicious.

You might say that Len and Judy have become like some of the wild geese that choose to live on the lake all year instead of migrating. Their lives are as rich as the land they farm and the wines they make.

McGregor Vineyard Winery

One of Keuka Lake's most venerable producers is indisputably McGregor Vineyard, practicing the art of winemaking here since 1979. The rustic winery, vineyards, and adjoining picnic grounds attract a year-round flow of visitors to this 1,200-foot perch overlooking Bluff Point at the widest expanse of the lake.

5503 Dutch Street
Dundee, New York 14837
(607) 292-3999

Before he became a wine grower, Bob McGregor was a systems engineer for Kodak and founding member of the Rochester chapter of the American Wine Society, a group of folks who believe that drinking wine is one of the most civilized things in the world. With encouragement from this network of vinophiles, including Walter Taylor of Bully Hill, Bob decided to grow grapes in a place he found, in his words, "by pure serendipity." But while most of his brethren were content with hybrid varieties, Bob and his family began planting the vinifera varieties he loved, conventional wisdom be damned.

Hours: Daily, 10:00 a.m.–
6:00 p.m. (April through
November);
Daily, 11:00 a.m.–5:00 p.m.
(December through March)

www.mcgregorwinery.com

The combination of cool temperatures and significant "lake effect" winds on the steep, north-facing slope stresses the vines, produces smaller yields, and results in more mature and concentrated flavors in the grapes. Mineral deposits in the heavy clay soil impart distinctive flavor profiles. Even in the early days, the intensity and complexity of fruit warranted a special vineyard designation on bottles of wine Glenora made from McGregor's harvest. Eventually, Bob became so enthralled with the wines others were making from his grapes, he left Kodak to start a winery of his own.

Finger Lakes Chardonnays are typically aged in oak, to impart flavors of vanilla and butterscotch, although, in some cases, character nuances of the grape are lost beneath the wood. McGregor offers a range of Chardonnays, including excellent barrel-fermented versions; however, the "Unoaked Chardonnay" is an expression of fruit rather than tree. Derived from a Muscat clone native to the Macon region of Burgundy, the wine is balanced and fresh, with subtle Muscat characters and herbaceous, grassy notes both on the nose and on the palate. The texture is delicate yet ample, with crisp, flinty, refined tropical and mineral flavors that carry into a subtle buttery finish. The style dates back to some of the vineyard's first-released wines, at a time when there was not a single oak barrel at the winery, and pure stainless steel provided a neutral, sterile environment during fermentation.

Bob McGregor has made his mark on Finger Lakes viticulture with much-publicized plantings of rare, Eastern-European wine grapes, propagated from a mother lode of cuttings that originated in the former Soviet Republic of Georgia. Two hardy varieties with noble bloodlines, Saperavi and Sereksiya Charni, are married to produce an audacious red wine called Black Russian. The deep scarlet–colored wine has aromas of blackberry and charcoal on the nose, while a powerful fruit-dominated palate bursts with concentrated ripe blackberry-blueberry, prune-plum, intense blackcurrant, and suggestion of burnt coffee. It's a full-bodied, eminently drinkable blend, comparable to Merlot, but with more complexity. Black Russian is vinified traditionally; it spends twenty months in American oak and a further six months in the bottle before release.

Success with these grapes inspired a unique blend of white Russian varieties, Rkatsiteli and Sereksiya Rosé, compellingly constructed with muted aromas of apricot and anise and a complex, herbaceous palate with notes of strawberry, baked apple, and sour/citrus, and a long, spicy, off-dry finish.

Jeff Dencenburg is the one who crafts these extraordinary wines for the McGregor clan. He is a protégé of Steve Reeder, winemaker at McGregor in the mid-1980s, who left to join Kendall-Jackson and, eventually, Chateau St. Jean in Sonoma Valley. Besides the grand experiment with curious Russian varieties, Jeff shows a firm hand with Chardonnay, Riesling, Vignoles, Cayuga, Muscat Ottonel, and Pinot Noir. His bottles capture the character and nuance expressed in the vineyard. And what a beautiful vineyard it is.

Ravines Wine Cellars

This winery takes its name from the numerous narrow ravines formed by small tributary streams that break up the declivities along Keuka Lake. In fact, the vineyard landscape is bordered by two such ravines.

Morten Hallgren, a Danish-born, French-trained winemaker, was already making wine directly across the lake at Vinifera Wine Cellars when he discovered this undeveloped property, ideal for his personal vision of a winery. The endeavor began when he and wife Lisa built a handsome chateau-style home that rises dramatically from a newly planted vineyard and established a tasting room to sell wines they bottle under the Ravines label.

A childhood spent playing in the cellars of his family's winery, Domaine de Castel Roubine, proved the perfect training ground for Morten. He moved into full-time winemaking after initially studying astrophysics, then eventually went on to earn a master's degree in oenology at L'Ecole Nationale Supérieure d'Agronomie. After an internship in Medoc, he landed at Ste. Genevieve in Fort Stockton, Texas, founded by French wine giant Domaines Cordier, then moved to Biltmore Estates Winery at George Vanderbilt's 250-room chateau-turned-tourist attraction, located on 8,000 acres in Asheville, North Carolina, and touted as the most visited winery in the country, before coming to the Finger Lakes.

Even more impressive than his resume, however, are his results. Since overseeing the winemaking, enology, and quality control departments at Dr. Frank's Vinifera Wine Cellars, beginning in 1999, he has been responsible for an array of extraordinary wines and dozens of gold medal awards in competitions. Willy Frank calls his winemaker "one of the finest young talents of his generation."

While other wineries have burst upon the industry like a skyrocket, Morten is content with the humble beginnings of Ravines as he sets out on his own path. He presently buys most of his fruit from local growers Steve Shaw and Sam Argetsinger, and he rents a facility for pressing grapes and storing wine. The ratio of estate to purchased grapes will increase in the next few years as newly planted acres of Pinot Noir begin producing fruit, but, according to Morten, he plans to limit total production to 5,000 cases annually.

"I'll never try to make a wine something that it isn't," says Morten, whose French education taught him that quality fruit needs little intervention to become a classic wine. In his opinion, blockbuster styles are not appropriate in the Finger Lakes. Instead, he strives for balanced, elegant, food-friendly wines—dry, but not harsh or astringent. With the careful application of time-tested winemaking practices, gentle handling, and fining, he produces wines that offer easy-drinking richness, even in their youth.

14630 State Route 54
Hammondsport, NY 14840
(607) 292-7007

Hours: Monday–Saturday, 10:00 a.m.–5:00 p.m., Sunday, noon–5:00 p.m. (April through November); Saturday, 10:00 a.m.–5:00 p.m., Sunday, noon–5:00 p.m. (December); Closed January through March

www.ravineswinecellars.com

Morten's approach to Chardonnay is unique in the Finger Lakes. He takes a portion of the harvest; sorts through the grapes cluster by cluster, removing individual berries that have a mold or a flaw; and places single layers of the good clusters in shallow trays. After two weeks, the grapes partially shrivel and dehydrate. This technique, known as *passito* and native to Northern Italy, concentrates the sugars, acids, and flavors. These grapes account for up to 20 percent of the fruit in a sophisticated Chardonnay.

Light yellow-green in color, with aromas of green apple and pear, this handcrafted wonder is rich and evolved with attractive butter, tropical, and mineral notes; honeydew, pineapple, hazelnut, and candied fruit characters; and just a touch of toasted oak. The wine holds and develops, and, after a while in the glass, it expands and shows more weight and energy in a persistent finish.

With fruit sourced from Keuka, Seneca, and Hobbit Hollow Farm on Skaneateles Lake, and from grapevines ranging in age from five to twenty years, the tantalizing Ravines Pinot Noir has aromas of red stone fruits and rose petals ringed with toasty oak notes. The palate has layers of sweet, ripe, strawberry fruit and spice with notes of lime and mint. It shows perfectly expressed yet restrained fruit with the structure and elegance more often associated with French wines.

It takes confidence and perseverance to build a business on your own preferences and require customers to fall in line, but Morten is determined to model Ravines, as he says, "in the spirit of those wines I have seen and loved in Provence."

While he concedes that Pinot Noir is the biggest challenge to winemakers in the Finger Lakes, Morten is determined to make the variety a centerpiece of his venture. He insists that our region is capable of turning these grapes into wines that have more in common with Burgundy than with West Coast Pinot Noirs. The fact that his wines have already acquired a cult following proves he is on the right track.

489 Route 54 South
Penn Yan, NY 14527
(315) 536-4773

Hours: Monday–Saturday,
10:00 a.m.–5:00 p.m.;
Sunday, noon–5:00 p.m.

www.roosterhill.com

Rooster Hill Vineyards

In 2002, when seven acres of overgrown grapevines on Keuka Lake came up for sale, David and Amy Hoffman traded in their business suits and briefcases for overalls and work boots, filled with the romantic notion of living and working in wine country. David Hoffman was a personal financial planner in Costa Mesa and Amy Hoffman a marketing vice president at Ingram Micro in Santa Ana, California. Together they left the fast track to restore a long-neglected vineyard on Keuka Lake and build a modern winery of technological efficiency. Rooster Hill Vineyards is a whole new challenge.

David and Amy had already discovered the pleasures of fine wine in California, and, upon return to their native New York, they were intent on channeling their passion into a commercial enterprise. Once they owned the property, they were smart enough to turn to a neighbor for guidance. That neighbor, as it turned out, was Lance Fullagar, a third-generation grower with a 170-acre vineyard of his own.

Convinced of their sincerity, Lance took the couple under his wing. He convinced them to purchase the adjacent twenty-eight-acre lot, as this was more in keeping with the scale of their ambition. He was influential in planning the new vineyard, testing the soils, and marking the field; he lent his planters and taught the Hoffmans about tying and spraying. Most important, he helped recruit an innovative winemaker.

After earning a degree in enology from Fresno State, Barry Tortollon became a laboratory consultant and research technician at commercial giant Italian Swiss Colony in Madera, California, before making his way east for stints at Fulkerson Winery, Fox Run Vineyards, and Glenora Wine Cellars in the Finger Lakes region. He brings a wealth of experience in small- and large-scale fermentations, cold sterile bottling, shipping and warehousing, product and process development, and vineyard management to the project.

A tireless worker, Barry set rigorously high standards at Rooster Hill. His first effort at Cabernet Franc is a graceful and satisfying young wine with nuances of licorice, clove, and dried figs, followed by spiced chocolate on the soft finish.

With an abiding belief in blending for the production of ready-to-drink table wines, Barry created "Silver Pencil," its name inspired by a breed of English hen. Vidal, Seyval Blanc, and Cayuga grapes, purchased from the Fullagar farm, combine to produce a pale yellow wine with tender sweetness and acidity in harmony, mild aromatics of green apples, bright citrus, pears, pineapple, and melon notes on the nose and palate. Bring out a bottle of this charming wine and serve it as a dinner party apéritif.

The Hoffmans have planted the Savina Vineyard with Cabernet Franc, Riesling, Pinot Noir, and Lemberger. Named for Amy's Tuscan-born great grandmother, Savina Volpona Garbarino, the lot will soon yield its first estate-grown fruit. Catherine Vineyard, honoring Savina's daughter, was planted at a slightly higher elevation in Cabernet Franc, Riesling, Gewürztraminer, and Lemberger. Estate wines will have single-vineyard designations.

Italian heritage inspired the decidedly European tasting room. The interior is tastefully decorated with straw-colored walls surrounded by copper molding; the space is highlighted by an oval bar that cleverly provides a lake view to every wine taster. The adjacent patio is fitted with a wood-burning pizza oven for weekend picnics and special events.

Unwavering devotion of two ardent enophiles has spawned a state-of-the-art winery, the promise of exceptional craft, and one of the prettiest tasting rooms in the Finger Lakes. Keep an eye on Rooster Hill. I am convinced that it will soon be a great source for small production, high impact wines.

MUSHROOM BRUSCHETTA

Serves 4 as an appetizer

Cabernet Franc, with origins in the Bordeaux region of France, is rapidly gaining recognition as a definitive Finger Lakes red. The wine's dark fruit and spice act as liaison between the tomato/garlic flavors and the earthy mushrooms.

CROUTONS

1 French baguette, sliced diagonally into 8 thin pieces, each 4 to 6 inches long

4 tablespoons unsalted butter, melted

½ cup freshly grated Parmesan cheese

2 tablespoons chopped fresh herbs (such as rosemary and thyme)

MUSHROOMS

2 teaspoons olive oil

8 ounces mixed wild mushroom (such as shiitake, oyster, and chanterelles)

2 cloves garlic, minced

1 sprig fresh sage, stemmed and chopped

2 tablespoons Rooster Hill Cabernet Franc

Salt and freshly ground black pepper

4 ounces fontina cheese, diced into small cubes

2 roma tomatoes, peeled, seeded, and diced (½ cup)

To make the croutons, preheat the broiler. Place the sliced bread on a baking sheet. Brush the tops with melted butter. Sprinkle the slices with the cheese and herbs. Place under the broiler for 2 to 3 minutes, or until the cheese melts. Remove from the broiler and leave bread on the baking sheet to crust up.

To make the mushrooms, heat the oil in a pan over high heat. Add the mushrooms, garlic, and sage. Sauté just until the mushrooms are hot, and then add the wine. Lower the heat to medium and continue to cook until the liquid is reduced, 5 to 7 minutes. Season with salt and pepper to taste.

Before serving, heat the broiler. Place the mushroom mixture on a heatproof plate. Place the fontina cheese on top of the mushrooms and heat under the broiler until the cheese is soft.

Spoon some diced tomatoes on top of each of the croutons. Arrange the croutons around the mushroom mixture on the plate and serve.

FARMS/FOOD PRODUCERS

Birkett Mills

The village's unique name derives from an early settler, Philemon Baldwin, who observed that about half of the inhabitants of the community were "Penn-sylvanians" and the other half were New England "Yan-kees." He proposed the name of Penn Yan, and so the village was christened.

The outlet that carries water along the 274-foot drop between Keuka and Seneca Lakes was formed by a ground fault in the Tully limestone. In 1789 a dam was built in Penn Yan to harness its waterpower for the operation of a grist mill, the only mill in the county for many years and the town's center of activity. The mill received grain from growers who wished to have it ground into flour for home use. The miller's toll was one pound for every ten pounds ground, and accumulated tolls of flour were offered for sale in the company store.

Nearly a century later, the mill was acquired by an Englishman named Clarence Birkett, who rebuilt and enlarged it, taking advantage of innovations in technology to change the operation into a merchant mill that purchased grain outright for cash from many producers and sold the flour in neighboring villages and cities.

Birkett's buckwheat flour took First Prize at the Paris Exposition of 1887, prompting expansion of distribution to wholesale grocers throughout the country. Quaker Oats, Pillsbury, Aunt Jemima, and other smaller companies purchased pure buckwheat flour for their pancake mixes.

Once a staple breakfast in farm and boardinghouse kitchens, the popularity of yeast-raised buckwheat pancakes declined in the industrial age, and the market for buckwheat flour diminished. Birkett's competitors either went out of business or converted plants to wheat flour production, and, by the time the mill retired its water turbines in 1947, it had become the preeminent buckwheat flour producer in the country.

Today, Birkett Mills contracts for 15,000 acres of buckwheat from the agriculturally rich Keuka Lake basin, throughout the Northeast, and up into Canada. Organically certified growers adhere to strict specifications, raising a recently developed buckwheat variety called Koto, which produces larger groats and better yields. Since these groats are more uniform in size, they are better both for milling and cooking, and, with a higher concentration of nutrients than other varieties of grains, buckwheat is now marketed for its healthful properties, including reduction of cholesterol and lowering of blood pressure.

The grist mill was an important cornerstone in the settlement of the Finger Lakes, and tradition is still carried on at venerable Birkett Mills, not only with production of its robust buckwheat flours, buckwheat pancake mixes, cream of buckwheat, and roasted buckwheat (kasha), but with wheat bran, wheat germ, whole wheat cereal, and soft wheat pastry flours for industrial bakers.

163 Main Street
Penn Yan, NY 14527
(315) 536-3311

Hours: By appointment

www.thebirkettmills.com

BUCKWHEAT PRETZELS

Makes 12 to 16 pretzels

3½ cups all-purpose flour

²/₃ cup buckwheat light or whole flour

2 teaspoons salt

2 eggs plus 1 egg white, lightly beaten

1 cup milk

Coarse salt, for coating

Sesame seeds or poppy seeds, for coating

Pretzels are probably the best snack to enjoy with beer, and if you're a fan of stout, these pretzels are an especially winning partner. The Pennsylvania Dutch brought their love of pretzels to Penn Yan, where Birkett Mills still turns out the dark, gritty buckwheat flour that gives handrolled pretzels a distinctive, nutty flavor. Since these pretzels don't require yeast or rising time they can be made very quickly, so start this recipe when hunger strikes. Caution: Baskets of these pretzels served with a peppy horseradish mustard will make you drink more than you may have bargained for.

In a large bowl, mix together the all-purpose and the buckwheat flours and the salt. Break the eggs into a small bowl and beat lightly with a fork until they form one color. Add the eggs and the milk to the flours and stir with a wooden spoon to form medium-soft dough.

Knead the dough by hand on a floured board for a few minutes and then place the dough into a sealed container or sealable plastic bag and let rest for about 20 minutes at room temperature.

Preheat the oven to 425°F.

Cut the dough into 12 or 16 pieces, depending upon which pretzel size you prefer, medium or large. Roll each piece into a rope and twist into the desired shape.

Place the pretzels on one or two lightly oiled baking sheets and brush with the egg white. Sprinkle with the coarse salt and the sesame or poppy seeds.

Bake the pretzels for 15 to 20 minutes, until golden brown. Serve warm.

Note: Pretzels taste best the day they are made. When stored, the salt may dissolve.

Buzzard Crest Vineyards/Barrington Cellars

A small ad in the *Rochester Democrat-Chronicle* attracted the attention of Ken and Eileen Farnum back in 1971. It offered a small farm on Keuka Lake, with twelve acres of grapes, and, although the shack that came with it wasn't exactly a dream house, they were certain it was where they wanted to settle down. Turkey buzzards that roost in nearby Eggleston Gully inspired a name for the farm.

After the first harvest it was obvious that what Taylor Wine Company was willing to pay for their fruit wouldn't be enough to support a family, so Ken took on work as a rural mail carrier and the couple began to make other plans. They made a transition on the farm from wine grapes to table grapes, since Mel Nass of Venture Vineyards would pay more for handpicked native varieties, especially Concords. The Farnums survived by expanding and diversifying.

Upon purchase of a nearby vineyard, the Farnums were able to plant additional seedless varieties and were now working fifty acres of grapes. With that harvest and with a harvest of exceptional table grapes, they decided to sell the fruit directly through the New York City Greenmarkets. Every Friday they drove down to the city, towing an insulated trailer full of grapes. Ken dropped off Eileen and the trailer at Union Square, while he sold at Borough Hall and Prospect Park markets.

They picked up quite a head of steam in the city, but, after a few years, it became clear that customers were more interested in organically grown table grapes. Buzzard Crest responded and converted to an organic farm.

Without synthetic and systemic pesticides, the vineyards now had to be kept as clean as possible, eliminating anything that might serve as a host for fungal disease spores. Weeds are controlled with sprays of hot water and vinegar; trellis wires are cleaned of tendrils; and any accumulation of pruned canes, thinned grape clusters, or leaves must be removed.

Buzzard Crest has sold organic Concord, Delaware, Niagara, and Caco grapes, as well as seedless Marquis, Himrod, Lakemont, Canadice, Glenora, and Mars varieties at the greenmarkets since 1984. Each week, from September through December, only the amount they expect to sell over the weekend is picked, and, since the Farnums have been doing it so long, they count on experience. "City folks have never tasted anything like Finger Lakes seedless grapes," says Eileen. "California grapes are 7 to 8 percent sugar; our grapes come in at 18 to 20 percent."

Grapes are harvested, trimmed, and packed directly from the vine, limiting damage to berries and loss of protective waxy bloom. Packed boxes are left under the vine, and a tractor forklift with pallet is used to collect the fruit and deliver it directly into the cold room. Only attractive bunches that have good eating, shipping, and keeping qualities make it to market. Fruit that is rejected for table grapes is fresh-pressed and cold filtered into full-strength grape juice with all of the natural enzymes,

2690 Gray Road
Penn Yan, NY 14527
(315) 536-9686

Wine Shop Hours:
Monday–Saturday, 11:00 a.m.–5:30 p.m., Sunday, noon–5:30 p.m. (Memorial Day through November 1); Weekends only in winter; Friday Sunday in spring.

www.barringtoncellars.com

vitamins, and nutrients intact. The juice is volatile since it has not been pasteurized, so it is frozen and sold directly from the freezer.

The Farnums added winemaking to their repertoire in 1995 with the founding of Barrington Cellars and production of Concord, DeChaunac, Delaware, Isabella, and Baco Noir varietals. The wine made from organically grown Baco Noir is deep colored and juicy and acidic in character, with black cherry and cedar flavors, toasty oak overtones, and a dry, lightly oxidized finish. This is a well-balanced wine, combining funky flavors with interesting complexity and good food compatibility, even if it lacks some finesse.

In the face of a tidal wave of change in the region, the Farnums have persevered. Their long days of hard work produce sweet, succulent table grapes, and turn fragile fruit into delicious grape juices and agreeable wines. We owe them a debt of thanks.

CONCORD GRAPE TAPIOCA PUDDING

Serves 2 to 4

1/4 cup granulated tapioca

1/4 cup sugar

2 1/2 cups Buzzard Crest Vineyards Grape Juice

Whipped cream (optional)

Tapioca pudding is an old-fashioned fuddy-duddy of a dessert. But substitute the rich, distinctive flavor of Concord grape juice for milk in real homemade pudding, and the result is a neighborly Finger Lakes version of the classic. You'll never look at tapioca the same way again.

Eileen Farnum prepares this dish for visitors to Barrington Cellars during Keuka Wine Trail holiday events.

Combine all of the ingredients in a large saucepan and mix well. Cook over medium heat, stirring constantly, until the mixture comes to a boil, about 15 minutes. Remove from the heat and let cool at room temperature for 20 minutes, stirring once. Spoon into individual dishes and chill in the refrigerator until the tapioca sets, about 45 minutes.

Top with whipped cream, and serve.

Pa'tridge Run Farms/
Fall Bright, The Winemakers Shoppe

The name Fall Bright, inspired by the Old English term for clarity in wine or beer, is a familiar one to amateur winemakers in the Finger Lakes. From an elevated vineyard on Pa'tridge Run Farms, the Mitchell family business has provided high-quality grape juice and winemaking supplies to local enthusiasts for the past twenty-five years.

In 1977 Thomas Mitchell gave up a career with the U.S. Fish and Wildlife Service and joined his wife Marcelle's family on one of the oldest continuously worked vineyards in the Finger Lakes. With plantings of Concord, Niagara, and Delaware, some dating back to 1865, they supplied wine grapes to the Canandaigua Wine Company and table grapes to Venture Vineyards, but Tom soon realized the farm was out of step. "We just didn't have the varieties winemakers wanted," he says. So they decided to do something about it.

A massive pull-out followed, reducing thirty-six acres to five acres, and they replanted new varieties, which would eventually include eight premium viniferas, fourteen French hybrids, and five native wine grapes, as well as New York Muscat, Alden, Yates, and seedless Canadice table grapes. The transformed vineyard sold fruit to Heron Hill and a few other wineries early on, and then Tom and Marcy formally opened Fall Bright in 1982 and began offering grape juice to home winemakers.

There was a lot of new equipment to install, and, in order to pay for it, Tom was forced to take the vineyard manager's job at Gold Seal Vineyards for several years while Marcy worked as a dental hygienist. Together, with sacrifice and diligence, they built a business and a reputation for gorgeous fruit that rivals their neighboring wineries. They take pride in the grapes that amateurs have turned into award-winning wines, more than once capturing "best of show" at the American Wine Society's annual national competition.

The grapes are picked both by hand (for grape orders) and by machine, then crushed, destemmed, and pressed with a four-ton bladder press. From there juice flows into refrigerated bulk tanks for chilling, settling, and filtering, then is pumped into tanks in a walk-in cooler to hold for pickup.

Nothing feels as satisfying and authentic as making your own batch of wine from fresh juice and cultured yeast, and Marcy has stocked the shop with everything you need to get started. A hydrometer ranks right at the top of the list, essential for measuring sugar levels and indicating when fermentation is complete. You'll also need glass carboy containers, fermentation locks, sanitized bungs, plus racking wands and plastic tubing to transfer the fermenting wine away from sediment.

It takes eighty-five to ninety pounds of fresh grapes to make five gallons, or about twenty-five bottles, of wine, and every grape has its own personality. Among red varieties, customers are loyal to Chancellor, and Seyval Blanc ranks high among the whites, although folks haven't lost

10110 Hyatt Hill
Dundee, NY 14837
(607) 292-3995

Hours: June to harvest:
Tuesday–Saturday,
10:00 a.m.–4:00 p.m.;
Harvest (September and
October): Tuesday to Sunday,
10:00 a.m.–5:00 p.m.;
November through May:
Tuesday–Friday,
10:00 a.m.–4:00 p.m.;
weekends by appointment

www.fallbright.com

sight of Diamond grapes for making a traditional favorite. According to Tom, Vidal is a foolproof variety, "a wine that tends to make itself." As a blending recommendation, he suggests Chelois and Chancellor, "since each of them seems to have something the other lacks."

If you visit the farm, don't expect shades of Provence. Fall Bright's longtime home is a glorified packing shed filled to the rafters with tools of the winemaking craft, alongside a loading deck, bladder press, and cooler and framed by the hardworking vineyards. It's nothing fancy, but from this hillside perch you can catch a glimpse of Keuka's version of the Côte d'Azur.

RESTAURANTS

16

Bully Hill Restaurant

See Bully Hill Vineyards (page 22) . . . .

17

Esperanza Mansion

3456 Route 54-A
Bluff Point, NY 14478
(315) 536-4400

Hours: Lunch,
Monday–Saturday,
11:00 a.m.–2:30 p.m.;
Brunch, Sunday,
11:00 a.m.–2:30 p.m.;
Dinner, Monday–Thursday,
5:00 p.m.–9:00 p.m.,
Friday and Saturday,
5:00 p.m.–10:00 p.m.

www.esperanzamansion.com

There is a little piece of heaven sitting astride the Keuka highlands—a Greek Revival mansion fully renovated to its nineteenth-century splendor. Before Esperanza Mansion became a luxury hotel and fine dining establishment, it was a lot of other things, and its history is worth a slight detour.

John Nicholas Rose, the son of Robert and Jane Rose, journeyed to the Finger Lakes region from the family plantation in Stafford County, Virginia. He purchased 1,000 acres of land and completed construction of the home he called "Esperanza" (derived from the Spanish word for "hope") in 1838. Esperanza was the largest house on the lake at the time, and its rectangular form, balanced proportions, and classical details were firmly rooted in Greek Revival tradition. The two-story ionic columns at its entrance were built around giant tree trunks encased in brick and stucco. In this bucolic setting, John Rose raised English-bred Saxon sheep and profited handsomely from selling high-quality wool.

Over the years, Esperanza has served as headquarters for a vineyard operation, supported a 1,000-acre farm, been home to several distinguished families, provided a link in the Underground Railroad, acted as the Yates County Poorhouse, and contributed to the character of the developing region as the Chateau Esperanza Winery.

Energy behind the latest incarnation of Esperanza comes from David and Lisa Wegman, who brought together a longheld dream of a hotel on the lake and turned the storied estate into one of the most extravagant resorts in the region. Rooms are furnished with reproduction antiques, each with private bath and a different set of amenities ranging from fireplaces to private porches, and the ground floor has been converted into an 88-seat restaurant, tavern, and banquet center with patios and verandas that provide an expansive, twenty-one-mile-long view of

Keuka Lake. An additional winery-theme cottage houses twenty-two deluxe guest rooms, also overlooking the lake.

Esperanza's chef, Korey Goodman, who once steered the kitchens of Fairport's Lodge at Woodcliff and Geneva on the Lake, tries to get his produce from local or regional providers and uses organic ingredients when sensible. His "regional with global influences" philosophy is expressed in sumptuous plates of escargots swimming in butter, Hunt Country Chardonnay, garlic, and herbs; an almond-crusted chicken breast deglazed with Frangelico liqueur and served with sautéed Empire apples; vegetables from local Amish farms rolled in flaky layers of phyllo dough and baked to golden brown, then finished with a roasted yellow bell pepper cream sauce. If you skipped dessert you would miss Chocolate Oblivion, a rich flourless chocolate cake with a Cabernet Sauvignon glaze.

At lunchtime, casual dining on fine food is the theme. Try the grilled fillet of mahi-mahi with double-smoked bacon, sliced tomato, and greens on a toasted Kaiser roll with lemon, horseradish, and herbed goat cheese spread, or a charbroiled Black Angus burger with slices of portobello mushrooms, grilled sweet onions, and pepper jack cheese, served with a pile of sweet potato fries. The colorful and textural Faith Salad includes mesclun greens and romaine tossed with toasted pecans, golden sweet raisins, crumbled feta cheese, shredded carrots, red cabbage, and Glenora Champagne vinaigrette. The Finger Lakes–focused, sixty-bottle wine list is far-ranging and whimsical, with choices that highlight the inn's neighboring wineries.

Esperanza Mansion offers a link to the past along with what has got to be the most spectacular view in all of the Finger Lakes. It's a romantic getaway and a must-visit for the discerning gastronomic pilgrim.

Pleasant Valley Inn

15

Before the village was named for early settler Lazarus Hammond, it was known as Pleasant Valley for its fertile farmland and pristine view of Keuka Lake, sheltered from the outside world by lush, green hills.

An 1848 Italianate manor nestles at the edge of the peaceful hamlet, originally part of the 400-acre Brundage farm, later a boardinghouse, a chicken dinner restaurant, and an antique shop. The peach-blossom–painted homestead planted among the vines began welcoming guests as the Pleasant Valley Inn in 1983, providing a cozy tavern with inglenook fireplace, beautifully appointed dining rooms full of character and charm, and overnight accommodations in four guest rooms.

7979 Route 54
Hammondsport, NY 14840
(607) 569-2282

Hours: Thursday–Sunday,
5:00 p.m.–9:00 p.m.
(Mother's Day weekend to
the weekend before
Thanksgiving)

www.pleasantvalleyinn.com

Today, there are a sociability and conviviality here that suggest this is a family concern. Restaurateurs Tom and Marianne Simons, who acquired the landmark in 1991, operated restaurants in northern Pennsylvania before settling in Hammondsport. As practiced chefs, they have developed a personal style of cooking that centers on what Tom describes as "focused flavors." He says they believe in treating food and flavors in a straightforward style, enhancing them to the point of harmonizing, but never further.

Pleasant Valley Inn strikes just the right note, from Grapevine-Smoked Salmon served with dilled Dijon sauce to a Toasted Goat Cheese Salad with roasted local tomatoes over fresh-picked baby greens in a light vinaigrette. Entrées include two dishes cooked with local Chardonnay, a Rosemary Dijon Chicken, and "Swimming Tigers," jumbo shrimp in a pool of pan garlic butter, finished with the wine.

Tom and Marianne share a deep passion for fresh local ingredients, and they depend on nearby Amish markets to supply components for many of their most popular dishes, including Bacon and Sweet Corn Chowder, Tenderloin Medallions with Local Asparagus and Hollandaise, and, of course, seasonal fruits for Marianne's cobblers and cheesecake toppings. "I hope that a little bit of that passion rubs off on every person who dines with us," says Tom.

The wine list has always featured unusual and eclectic wines from around the world, with a strong emphasis on the Finger Lakes, supporting the local wine industry in the same way the owners support local farmers. Keuka Lake Rieslings dominate the list, with exceptional bottles from Heron Hill, Bully Hill, Salmon Run, Keuka Overlook, Keuka Springs, and Dr. Konstantin Frank.

When folks come to wine country, they anticipate a little magic. They expect to find picturesque settings, regionally influenced cuisine with exciting wine pairings, and gracious hospitality. Every expectation is fulfilled at the Pleasant Valley Inn.

30 Mechanic Street
Hammondsport, NY 14840
(607) 569-2528

Hours: Lunch, 11:30 a.m.–3:00 p.m.; Dinner, 5:00 p.m.–9:00 p.m. (weekdays), 5:00 p.m.–10:00 p.m. (weekends)

www.villagetaverninn.com

The Village Tavern

Hammondsport is a throwback to a more gentle time in American life, a setting right out of a Norman Rockwell painting. There's a pavilion bandstand in the middle of Pulteney Square, and the village green is surrounded by a drugstore, ice cream parlor, post office, and the Village Tavern—all just a block away from Keuka Lake. Whatever else you do, don't visit quaint Hammondsport without stopping by the old, reliable Tavern for a bite to eat and a local wine to wash it down.

It's the latest in a succession of notable watering holes to roost at the corner of Mechanic and William Streets. The place is flush with great characters and stories dating back to the early 1900s, when Pietro "Pete" Grimaldi opened the original beer parlor on this spot. It became an "ice cream parlor" during Prohibition, but it's said you could nonetheless satisfy your thirst for a mug of brew in the back of the joint.

Today, under the stewardship of a bon viveur by the name of Paul Geisz, you'll still find plenty of "pub" ambiance, a beehive of activity with the sound of clinking glasses, rushing waiters, and lively conversation. Quintessential dark-wood paneling is a reminder of the tavern's early days; walls are lined with remnants of Hammondsport's aviation history; comfortable captain's chairs adjoin glass-top tables, which are illuminated by hurricane lamps. The long and accommodating bar attracts a cheerful and mixed crowd for a range of cocktails, beers (bottle or tap), and a blackboard list of three dozen local wines by the glass, while a rear dining area provides a more sedate environment than the main bar room.

One of the thrills of eating at the Village Tavern is the opportunity to browse through the encyclopedic, all–Finger Lakes wine list, novel for both its breadth and entertainment value. The thoughtful selection of nearly 200 different wines proves that you can offer a complete range of prices and taste profiles without having to go out of the region. Particularly impressive is the opportunity to savor as many as ten successive vintages of Dr. Konstantin Frank Riesling, all aging gracefully in a stone-wall cellar that maintains ideal temperature and humidity year-round. The Tavern's wine list is the governing dynamic of the restaurant, reflecting not only Paul's friendships with the local vintners, but his belief in the ascendancy of the region's wines.

While the wine list ensures that you will drink locally, the kitchen sees to it that you eat globally. Chef Richard Lerman's menu is surprisingly diverse, perhaps a bit pretentious for a neighborhood place, and it's all over the culinary map. There seems to be something for everybody, from smoked local farm-raised trout to a bouillabaisse overflowing with fresh seafood. While the regular menu seems to be priced for tourists, the "bistro menu," served between lunch and dinner and then again in the late evening, is an attractive alternative. Best choices are the Tavern Mixed Green Salad, Smoked Seafood Sampler, and Pesto Grilled Chicken. I can't imagine a better match to Bully Hill's "Love My Goat" Red (from just up the road) than the Tavern Burger, one-third of a pound of lean ground beef with lettuce, tomato, and a slice of raw Bermuda onion.

The essence of Finger Lakes wine country is rooted in this small village at the southernmost tip of Keuka Lake, and winery folks have made the Village Tavern their central gathering place.

SENECA
LAKE

('se-ni-kə)

THIRTY-EIGHT MILES LONG, up to three miles wide, with a depth that reaches 630 feet, and holding 4.2 trillion gallons of water, Seneca is the deepest of the Finger Lakes and the second deepest lake in the United States. Its massive amount of water provides a temperature-moderating effect and a microclimate like none other. As a result, Seneca has more wineries than any of the other Finger Lakes.

Seneca Wine Trail is easy to navigate, hugging close to the lake line. Many visitors like to travel up one side of Seneca Lake, then take a second day to travel down the opposite road. It's a good strategy, along with a stay at the northern end of the lake, and historic Geneva, a cultural, agricultural, and academic center, provides an excellent selection of accommodations.

Routes 14 (west side) and 414 (east side) pass through wine country like two asphalt arteries, connecting boutique-sized vintners clustered along hillsides rising sharply from the lake. Good restaurants, most featuring locally produced wines, have emerged, particularly in the stretch between Lodi and Hector, and senses are heightened during autumn harvest season, when the trees in nearby Finger Lakes National Forest paint the landscape in dazzling colors.

Watkins Glen, at the southern tip of Seneca Lake, is home to one of the best-known state parks in the world, with dizzying rock formations and a gorge trail along, above, and behind nineteen waterfalls on its course. NASCAR and Grand Am events are still part of this historic racing town, just a short side trip away from the world-famous Corning Museum of Glass.

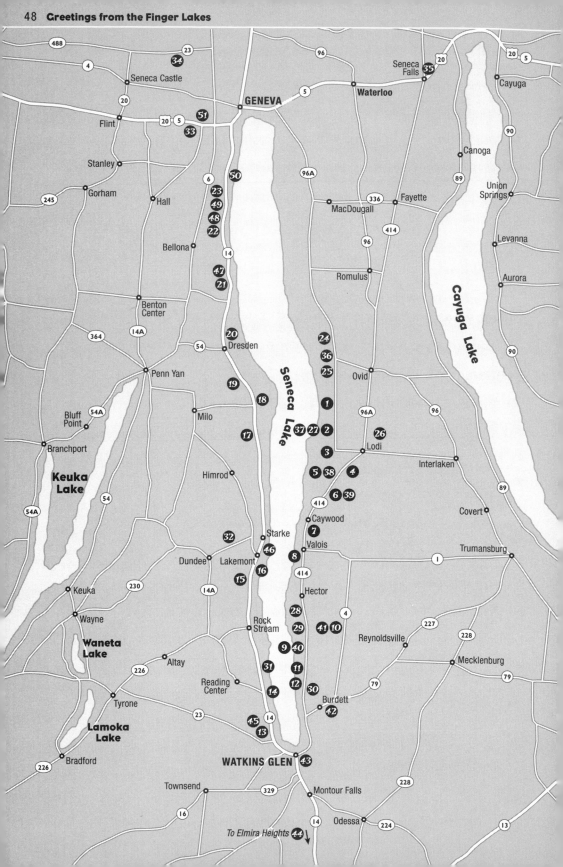

Wineries

1 Lamoreaux Landing Wine Cellars *(LODI)*

2 Wagner Vineyards *(LODI)*

3 Silver Thread Vineyard *(LODI)*

4 Shalestone Vineyards *(LODI)*

5 Standing Stone Vineyards *(HECTOR)*

6 Logan Ridge Wine Cellars *(HECTOR)*

7 Hazlitt 1852 Vineyards *(HECTOR)*

8 Leidenfrost Vineyards *(HECTOR)*

9 Bloomer Creek Vineyards *(HECTOR)*

10 Red Newt Cellars *(HECTOR)*

11 Chateau Lafayette Reneau *(HECTOR)*

12 Atwater Estate Vineyards *(HECTOR)*

13 Castel Grisch Estate Winery *(WATKINS GLEN)*

14 Lakewood Vineyards *(WATKINS GLEN)*

15 Fulkerson Winery *(DUNDEE)*

16 Glenora Wine Cellars *(DUNDEE)*

17 Hermann J. Wiemer Vineyards *(DUNDEE)*

18 Miles Wine Cellars *(HIMROD)*

19 Prejean Winery *(PENN YAN)*

20 Anthony Road Wine Company *(PENN YAN)*

21 Fox Run Vineyards *(PENN YAN)*

22 Billsboro Winery *(GENEVA)*

23 Belhurst Winery *(GENEVA)*

Farms/Food Producers

24 Blue Heron Farm *(LODI)*

25 Venture Vineyards *(LODI)*

26 Meadowsweet Farm *(LODI)*

27 Wagner Valley Brewery
(see Wagner Vineyards, LODI)

28 Sawmill Creek Vineyards *(HECTOR)*

29 Wickham's Twin Oaks Farm *(HECTOR)*

30 Glendale Farm *(BURDETT)*

31 Organic Cornucopia *(ROCK STREAM)*

32 Master's Touch Coffee Roasters *(DUNDEE)*

33 Red Jacket Orchards *(GENEVA)*

34 Pedersen Farms *(SENECA CASTLE)*

Restaurants

35 Henry B's *(SENECA FALLS)*

36 Suzanne *(LODI)*

37 Ginny Lee Café
(see Wagner Vineyards, LODI)

38 Smokehouse Café
(see Standing Stone Vineyards, HECTOR)

39 Petioles
(see Logan Ridge Wine Cellars, HECTOR)

40 Stonecat Café
(see Bloomer Creek Vineyards, HECTOR)

41 Red Newt Cellars Winery & Bistro
(see Red Newt Cellars, HECTOR)

42 Grist Mill Café *(BURDETT)*

43 Wildflower Café *(WATKINS GLEN)*

44 Pierce's 1894 *(ELMIRA HEIGHTS)*

45 Castel Grisch Winery Restaurant
(see Castel Grisch Estate Winery, WATKINS GLEN)

46 Veraisons
(see Glenora Wine Cellars, DUNDEE)

47 The Café at Fox Run
(see Fox Run Vineyards, PENN YAN)

48 Ports Café *(GENEVA)*

49 Belhurst Castle
(see Belhurst Winery, GENEVA)

50 Geneva on the Lake *(GENEVA)*

51 The Cobblestone *(GENEVA)*

WINERIES

20

1020 Anthony Road
Penn Yan, NY 14527
(800) 559-2182

Hours: Monday–Saturday,
10:00 a.m.–5:00 p.m.;
Sunday, noon–5:00 p.m.

www.anthonyroadwine.com

Anthony Road Wine Company

John and Ann Martini settled on 100 acres of farmland on Seneca Lake in 1973, where they planted grapes and raised their family. But selling grapes to the Taylor Wine Company didn't provide a livelihood, so in addition to his work in the vineyard, John held a research position at the New York State Agricultural Experiment Station.

In the late 1980s, John and Ann joined with Derek and Donna Wilber to form the Anthony Road Wine Company, and the venture's first bottle of wine was released in 1990. A decade later, when Derek left to become winemaker at Swedish Hill, the Martinis persuaded a young German winemaker by the name of Johannes Reinhardt to accept a position. The rest, as they say, is history.

Johannes was born in the sleepy German village of Franconia, near Wurtzburg, where his family has tended vineyards and produced native "Frankenwein" since 1438. Groundwork at the side of his father and grandfather led to formal schooling in viticulture and enology. After making wines in his own village for two years, he worked at Estate Kistenmacher-Hengerer, then at Hartmann Dippon Castle Estate, before coming to America as an intern at Dr. Frank's Vinifera Wine Cellars in Hammondsport.

You can take the man out of his German wine cellar, but you can't take the German influences out of his wines. Through experience and training, Johannes has come to believe that great wines begin in the vineyards, then, at harvest, as he says, "I listen to what the fruit tells me." Johannes's convictions are best expressed in a series of reserve wines designated "Martini-Reinhardt Selection," crafted from selected vineyard blocks and managed throughout the growing season to optimize fruit quality. These limited offerings, made by the hundreds of cases, not thousands, include Chardonnay, Riesling, Pinot Gris, Vignoles, and Cabernet Franc and are subject to successful growing seasons.

The spirit of innovation and inquiry that punctuates every aspect of Johannes's winemaking is evident in his precious Rieslings. The tightly structured, focused Dry Riesling has an attractive floral nose, with succulent, concentrated lemon, lime, and tropical fruit flavors, finishing dry with notes of honey. In contrast, the aromatic Semi-Dry Riesling is rich with ripe apricot, green apple, peach, and pear on the palate. The fruit and sweetness are balanced by the crisp, clean structure one might find in a classic German Kabinett.

Vignoles, a French-American hybrid that Johannes calls "a big brother to Riesling," might be considered the signature variety at Anthony Road. In his semi-dry version, he coaxes the exotic personality out of Vignoles. With flavors reminiscent of apricot, grapefruit, dried pear, and spice, this wine has noticeable sweetness complemented by a solid back-bone of acidity.

The Martini-Reinhardt concept showcases Veritas Trockenbeeren, a provocative late-harvest Vignoles. Gorgeous aromas of lemon zest, orange peel, and warm cinnamon are followed by peach, pear, apricot, sweet apple, and mandarin orange in an addictively creamy palate, with hints of spice and honey in the lingering finish. This wine is made only in years when the vineyard is blessed with an extended, warm and dry fall sea-son. After the grapes ripen, they hang a bit longer on the vine, creating a raisining effect that concentrates the flavors and sugars.

Some winemakers demonstrate their art in a masterly achievement with one or two varieties; some devise imaginative blends. With Johannes Reinhardt, the young man who lends his efforts to this crusade, his wines are consistently well made across the board, and nearly all are ready to drink when released. "I love *all* my babies," says the winemaker.

A footnote about Anthony Road: in a historic collaboration, the win-ery has committed to a joint project with the Robert Young family of Sonoma County, California, on a 100-acre Seneca Lake dairy farm. John Martini will manage and harvest a vineyard of Riesling, Gewürztraminer, Pinot Gris, and Merlot, then purchase the fruit for Anthony Road wines.

Atwater Estate Vineyards

12

In an earlier life, the property was called Rolling Vineyards, character-izing one of the most stunning landscapes on Seneca Lake's eastern shore. When Ted Marks, a Corning, New York, businessman, teamed up with Phil Hazlitt, scion of the legendary grape growing family, to purchase the eighty-four-acre estate in 1999, they ushered in a new direction at the winery.

5055 Route 414
Hector, NY 14841
(607) 546-8463
(800) 546-8463

Family ancestry inspired a new name for the venture, memorializing Rachel Atwater, who married James Hazlitt, the first in a lineage of pio-neer vineyardists in the region. Phil is Rachel's great-great-great grandson, and his expertise in wine growing was essential to the genesis of Atwater Estate Vineyards.

Hours: Monday–Saturday, 10:00 a.m.–5:00 p.m.; Sunday, 11:00 a.m.–5:00 p.m.

www.atwatervineyards.com

While nurturing the property's original vines of Chardonnay, Riesling, and Gewürztraminer, Phil planted new acreage of Cabernet, Merlot, and Syrah on the hillside he believes is blessed with exceptional terroir. Excellent drainage on the slope means less vigorous vines that produce smaller berries with more intense flavors.

Winemaker Vinny Aliperti set his sights on a winemaking career early on. His training includes work with two disciplined German winemakers, first with Roman Roth at Long Island's Wolffer Estate, then with Hermann J. Wiemer across the lake. At Atwater, he is the beneficiary of working under Phil's wing, and, now that he has taken charge, he uses the apprenticeships to back up his talent and ambition.

With the good fortune of several acres of three-decade-old Gewürztraminer vines, Vinny has crafted a wine that captures their maturity and vitality. He has a true appreciation for the dry Alsacian style, and his wine takes on many of the noble characteristics of its European counterpart.

Its exotic perfume is reminiscent of litchi, honeysuckle, and clove spice, with delicate, ripe pear fruit in the background. On the palate, the wine shows an oily-rich viscosity and full-body texture that are characteristic of the best Alsatian Gewürztraminers, balanced by firm acidity. The deep, spicy apricot-citrus and honey flavors are delicious and lead to a dry, spicy finish with notes of white peppercorn.

This textbook Gewürztraminer is but one of fifteen vinifera and hybrid varieties he makes according to what Vinny calls "rustic viticultural practices"—when the vineyard produces distinctive fruit, according to his theory, all you need is nuts and bolts winemaking. He'll be the first to admit that his wines are directly linked to where and how they are grown, and, as the vine roots grow deeper into the hillside, Atwater is destined for even greater wines.

23 49

4069 Route 14 South
Geneva, NY 14456
(315) 781-0201

Winery Hours:
Daily, 10:00 a.m.–8:00 p.m.
Restaurant Hours: Lunch,
daily, 11:00 a.m.–2:00 p.m.;
Dinner, 3:30 p.m.–9:00 p.m.

www.belhurst.com

Belhurst Winery/Belhurst Castle

Carrie Harron Collins was a direct descendent of Henry Clay, the senator from Kentucky, Speaker of the House, and secretary of state under President John Quincy Adams. In 1885, Mrs. Collins hired an architect and a crew of fifty laborers to begin work on a fairy-tale castle set amid twenty acres of forest on the shore of Seneca Lake. Four years later, Belhurst, the three-story, turreted, red-stone curiosity, was completed.

In the years since, Belhurst Castle has been at various times a private home, casino, speakeasy, guesthouse, and restaurant, but it was not until 1992 that the property came into the hands of a developer whose vision was on a scale worthy of its history. In addition to restoring fourteen period bed chambers, six dining rooms, and a spacious ballroom, Duane Reeder constructed the Vinifera Inn, an adjacent twenty-room luxury hotel with meeting and banquet facilities and a visitor's center. He also acquired a sister property, White Springs Manor, a Georgian Revival farm mansion on the grounds of historic White Springs Farm.

The farm property is now the site of sixty acres of newly planted grapevines, which will supply vinifera fruit to Belhurst Winery, a collaboration between Reeder and Carl Fribolin, owner of White Springs Farm. An existing slate-roof barn on the property is set to become the winemaking facility, and, in keeping with the importance of this project, Reeder hired Fredrique Madeleine Perrin, a remarkable French winemaker with experience on three continents.

Frederique's grandfather, who died just before she was born, had amassed a cellar full of some of the most outstanding chateau wines, and she grew up drinking these incredible wines at holidays and birthdays. By the time she was eighteen, the cellar was empty, and all that was left was her grandfather's notebook, filled with the names of his favorite wines. Prominent on the list were the treasured bottles of Michel Juillot, whose family has produced wines in Burgundy's Côte Chalonnaise since 1404, so when Frederique needed to secure an internship at school, she contacted Monsieur Juillot and asked for his help. He remembered her grandfather and accepted her as a trainee.

For her second year of training, Frederique says she wanted to work "with her feet upside down," as she nurtured a dream of going to Australia. Again, with the intercession of Juillot, she landed at Leeuwin Estate, a former cattle farm on Australia's Margaret River and producer of some of the best wines on the other side of the world. With her accomplishments there, it became clear that winemaking was far more interesting, exciting, and potentially rewarding than anything else she could think of. "It was then I decided to follow my passion and pursue a career in the wine industry," says Frederique.

After receiving her master's degree in oenology and viticulture from Ecole Nationale Superieure Agronomique in Montpellier, she worked as assistant winemaker at Chateau Yquem in Sauternes, Dr. Frank's Vinifera Wine Cellars in the Finger Lakes, then at Craggy Range Winery in New Zealand before joining the Belhurst team in June 2003.

With the invaluable experience garnered from each of her positions, at Belhurst she was given the opportunity to design her own facility, complete with all the tools, equipment, and state-of-the-art technology. "Mr. Reeder and Mr. Fribolin wanted to have wine, and they told me to make it happen," says Frederique. She explains that while she could visualize what an ideal winery should look like, eventually she had to put it down on paper. "That little piece of paper that I drew it on at the beginning is now being built," she proudly declares.

With varieties of Riesling, Chardonnay, Pinot Gris, Sauvignon Blanc, Gewürztraminer, Pinot Noir, Cabernet Franc, Cabernet Sauvignon, Lemberger, and Merlot in the ground, Belhurst expects to crush its first fruit in the fall of 2005, and, until then, Frederique has contracted for grapes and winemaking facilities.

Belhurst "Traditions" Chardonnay, labeled with a Seneca Lake appellation, exhibits caramel aromas and silky-textured fruit flavors, with layers of complex nuances from the wild yeast fermentation. Barrel fermentation and aging in new French oak integrate creamy vanilla tones, while spicy apples lift the finish.

Dry Rosé, in seductively curvaceous bottles imported from Provence, was made from Cabernet Franc and Cabernet Sauvignon fruit, crushed and macerated, its "free run" juice fermented in stainless steel. Salmon in color, simple but refined in style, the delicate wine awakens the taste buds, sip by sip, with elegantly mature strawberry fruit and a lovely creamy texture.

Frederique's entire portfolio of wines seems to prove the "view of the painter" perspective she learned at Domaine Michel Juillot. The winemaker wishes that, like an artist, she had total control and could employ the perfect "colors"—just the right sunlight and raindrops, some dimension here and intensity there. Winemaker and painter may both suffer through the process, but, in the end, Frederique's wines are masterpieces.

The castle's gorgeous, over-the-top interior is an appropriate setting for both Frederique's wines and the big, bold flavors of chef Casey Belile's cooking. The restaurant called Edgar's is a maze of lavishly striking rooms, appointed with crystal chandeliers; cherry, oak, and mahogany paneling; rich artwork; stained-glass pieces; mosaic-tiled fireplaces; beamed cathedral ceilings; and exotic balustrades. The opulence of the age in which the mansion was constructed has been preserved to provide the most enchanting ambiance for a special-occasion dinner, certainly in the Finger Lakes, and, perhaps, anywhere in America.

Casey earned his culinary wings in Pennsylvania Dutch country, and he has turned Edgar's in a carnivore's cathedral, featuring Flat Iron, Porterhouse, and New York strip steaks, filet mignon, roast prime ribs of beef, veal, lamb, pork, and a signature dish he calls the "Sportsman's Trilogy"—lightly peppered boar, elk, and venison medallions, pan-seared and finished with a demi-glace of Cabernet Sauvignon. For dessert, there's a deep-fried hunk of cheesecake with graham cracker crust, served with a compote of seasonal local berries. Like the décor, the food is robust and adventurous.

If all of this sounds exorbitant, a more sedate lounge called Stonecutters offers soups, sandwiches, or a Pub Steak Salad of sliced Angus beef, chopped romaine, red onion, blue cheese, sweet red peppers, and walnuts with Merlot vinaigrette. Frederique's wines match up well with either experience.

This place so overwhelms the senses you almost miss Seneca Lake in the background. It reminds me of Thoreau's counsel to advance confidently in the directions of dreams and to put foundations under castles in the air. This castle is a culinary dream come true in the Finger Lakes.

Billsboro Winery

4760 Route 14
Geneva, NY 14456
(315) 789-9538

Hours: Tuesday–Sunday,
noon–6:00 p.m.

www.billsboro.com

The Agricultural Experiment Station, established by an Act of the New York State Legislature, dates back to 1880. A site in Geneva was chosen, and researchers began concentrating their efforts on dairy, horticulture, and evaluation of varieties of vegetables and field crops. In 1887, the program was broadened to include work on beef cattle, swine, and evaluation of fruit varieties. Originally the unit of a state agency, the Station became part of Cornell University in 1923, animal research was moved to the Ithaca campus, and the Geneva Station developed into a true horticultural research institute. It has since evolved into one of the country's leading centers for the study of production, protection, and utilization of fruit and vegetable crops, including a wine research and analysis lab, forty acres of land devoted to test plots and teaching vineyards, and an extension program to transfer university-generated knowledge to the state's farmers, grape growers, and wine producers.

Dr. Robert Pool, the Station's esteemed professor of viticulture, hails from a family of peach farmers in California's Sacramento Valley. His career began with a scholarship to study enology at the University of California at Davis. During summer vacations he worked for Allied Grape Growers, then went on to earn his master's degree in winemaking. While conducting problem-solving viticultural research, he worked closely with growers and gained a great deal of experience in an advisory capacity. Graduating at the top of his class with honors, he was asked to join Fresno State as professor of enology and viticulture.

In 1971, the young man moved east and entered the doctorate program at Cornell, earning his Ph.D. in 1974. But before he could pack his bags for the return to California, Cornell offered him a position at the Experiment Station—at an interesting time for the Finger Lakes. A pioneer named Konstantin Frank was producing extraordinary wines, previously unheard of in the region, and that was enough to convince Dr. Pool of the quality potential here. Not only did he become part of the burgeoning wine industry, but, over the years, his work with the mechanization of pruning, crop level related to grape and wine quality, rootstock effects on cold hardiness, and vine productivity contributed greatly to its success.

Longing to apply his vast knowledge to a retirement project, in 1998 he began planting grapevines near his lakeside home in the village of Billsboro, ten miles south of Geneva. "I felt the time was right," he says. "I was at a certain age. I had thought a lot about wine growing, and I was determined to retire *to* something and not *from* something." The professor examined his own viticultural roots and found things he could do, perhaps better than anyone else. On a modest scale, with slow, gentle winemaking, his commercial venture is truly unlike any other winery found in the Finger Lakes.

Dr. Pool points out the similarity between the growing climate of Burgundy and this region, and he is energized by the challenge of working with the ever perplexing but rewarding Pinot Noir, a variety he spent years trying to understand. Using the experience of three decades of research, importing and testing French and American Pinot Noir clones, he combines both Old and New World approaches with the sole objective of maximizing quality. His ruby-colored Pinot offers black cherry and blackberry aromatics, with a thick, medium-bodied character, loads of chewy, dark cherry fruit as well as a beautifully ripe and structured finish. With extended bottle age it blossoms into a powerful, extroverted, and flavorful wine.

His relationship with the Experiment Station and access to small plots of unusual materials give Dr. Pool the opportunity to display the viticultural diversity of the Finger Lakes. A palette of varieties that includes Rkatsiteli, Viognier, Chenin Blanc, Pinot Gris, and Sauvignon Blanc combines for a perfectly quirky white table wine he calls "Eclectsia." Take one sip, and you recognize the apples and melon of Chenin Blanc; take another and savor the citric, grassy notes of Sauvignon Blanc. Rkatsiteli provides structure, while Viognier contributes to a long, minerally finish.

The red version of Eclectsia is constructed of Cabernet Franc, Syrah, Sangiovese, Barbera, and Pinotage, a blend that ensures structure and complexity. The principal component is berry-rich Cab Franc, but Syrah adds luscious aromatics and cassis characters. The accent of soft plummy fruit and earthy, dusty notes comes from Pinotage, while acidity from Sangiovese and Barbera gives the blend a vital Italian character on the finish. A mixture of American and French oak is used to age what might be the region's richest, craziest, tastiest red wine.

The professor admits that he was drawn to winemaking because he loves the opportunity wine affords to combine one's analytical skills with sensory evaluation. After all, winemaking requires proficiency in many different disciplines. His reflective approach adds an element of quiet power to the wines he helps to craft.

Bloomer Creek Vineyards/Stonecat Café

The best example of the synergy between fine wine and good food in the Finger Lakes might be here at the shared quarters of Bloomer Creek Vineyards and the Stonecat Café. Winemaker Kim Engle and chef Scott Signori have presided over this kitschy former fruit stand since 1999 with separate but extraordinarily compatible enterprises.

5315 Route 414
Hector, NY 14841
(607) 546-5000

Hours: Call for schedule

www.stonecatcafe.com

The winery takes its name after the rivulet that feeds Cayuga Lake from a spring at the old Bloomer family farm. It cuts right through the center of a ten-acre benchland vineyard where Kim practices low-impact farming and manages low crop yields, ensuring that each handpicked cluster of grapes is ripe with intense varietal character.

By his own account, Kim has worked for practically every grape grower on Cayuga Lake, and by the early 1990s he began cultivating his own vines on a modest property he named Bloomer Creek Vineyards. Well over a mile from the protective effects of the lake and with a challenging variation of soil types, he planted each variety, in his words, "slowly and reluctantly," settling on Riesling and Cabernet Franc, with smaller blocks of Pinot Noir and Gamay Noir on a south-facing hillside above the creek.

Kim is firmly anchored in his own terroir. A small, isolated planting of Cabernet Sauvignon along with part of the Cab Franc is reserved for "Block 97," a particular patch of lean soil with heavy clay that consistently produces low yields of small berries, resulting in excellent concentration of bright, pure flavors in the food-friendly wine.

Growing up in an Italian household and part of a family of food lovers shaped Scott Signori's palate and started his quest to find the perfect place in the world to live and explore the craft of cooking. While coming of age in the kitchen of Escape Café in Washington, D.C., he met Greg Sandor, a vineyardist who had started a winery project on Cayuga Lake's Sheldrake Point. Scott was invited to join the team, and by 1997 he was remodeling an old tractor shop into a café. It was here that he first came into contact with the bounty of local farms.

Kim happened to be managing Sheldrake's vineyards at the same time Scott was turning out distinctive fare, and it wasn't long before the two men were making other plans. Doug Bond's old fruit stand in Hector was up for sale, a space big enough for both a winery tasting room and a restaurant. Kim and Scott gutted the building and put it back together as a joint venture of Bloomer Creek Vineyards and Stonecat Café.

At Stonecat, named for the local stonehead catfish (excellent live bait for trout fishing), Scott's food is inspired by the region's abundance of locally grown fruits and vegetables, as he creates his own brand of wine country cooking. Each plate is its own culinary universe of regional, cross-culturally influenced sauces, temperatures, and textures. Wild Mushroom Ravioli is served with sorrel pesto in the spring, when sorrel's flavor is mildest and lemony in flavor. Housemade Maple Juniper Sausages are finished with a mustard-thyme cream sauce and served with herbed spaetzle and organic sauer reuben. The flavorful junipers are harvested in the fall from local red cedar trees. When seedless Himrod and Reliance grapes grown on an adjacent property are harvested in early fall, Scott turns them into a memorable grape and cream pie.

"Every season is unique," says Scott, whose greatest enjoyment is creating a dish that makes his customers aware of what's in season. He changes the printed menu every three weeks, but runs daily specials that depend on what comes in from nearby Blue Heron Farm, his primary supplier. When the seasons for strawberries and arugula overlap, Scott offers a smoked duck salad with strawberries, arugula, and cashews with a strawberry-balsamic reduction.

Scott goes out of his way to foster relationships with a variety of growers, and wherever he finds the best ingredients, he brings them in and marries them to big flavors. He burns the applewood and grapewood that local growers pile up at his back door to smoke wild Alaskan salmon, served chilled over organic greens with capers, red onions, and dill cream cheese; local pork is slow-smoked for eight hours to develop layers of flavor, then marinated in a "Carolina-style" or vinegar-based sauce and served with cornbread and black-eyed peas.

Scott may be at his best with Peter McDonald's pasture-raised chicken and a blazing fire. I'm thinking specifically of his "Chicken Under a Brick," a lightly smoked leg and breast that he brines overnight, then grills to order under a hot fire brick, skin side down, searing both sides simultaneously. It's tender and moist inside, seared and crisp outside—he has refined the technique, and the result is sophisticated comfort food. In rhubarb season, expect your chicken slathered with the chef's "rhubarbeque" sauce and served alongside rosemary mashed potatoes and fresh dill slaw.

The kitchen thrives on invention, and the food, in turn, finds some of its best matches when it also stays close to the vine. Kim's blend of Chardonnay and Cayuga, a fruit-forward wine called Stonecat White, is an easy partner with many of Scott's dishes. Its floral, honey nose paves the way to crisp melon and lively citrus flavors with a finish of complexity and grace.

The Bloomer Creek–Stonecat collaboration has a well-deserved local following as a destination for visitors seeking excellent wine and exquisitely prepared food in a wine country setting. The match was made in foodie heaven.

RHUBARB-EQUE SAUCE

Local rhubarb season overlaps with strawberry season in the Finger Lakes, and that's enough to fire both the imagination and the grill at Stonecat Café. Culinary wizard Scott Signori slathers this unique sauce over Peter McDonald's pasture-raised chicken and suggests washing it down with Ithaca Nut Brown Ale.

In a medium saucepan over medium heat, add the rhubarb, strawberries, water, and brown sugar and cook until soft, about 10 minutes.

In a separate pan, heat the peanut oil and onion over medium heat. Add the garlic and ginger followed immediately by the fennel, cardamom, coriander, cayenne, chili powder, and hot sauce. Stir into a paste and cook for 1 minute.

Add the rhubarb mixture to the spice paste and reduce for about 15 minutes or until it reaches a desired consistency, stirring frequently. After the sauce has cooled sufficiently, taste and adjust seasoning, adding more hot sauce to taste. Serve over smoked or grilled chicken.

Yield:
Approximately 8 cups

5 pounds fresh rhubarb, peeled and cut into 1-inch pieces

1 pint fresh strawberries, hulled and sliced

¼ cup water

½ cup brown sugar

1 tablespoon peanut oil

1 small yellow onion, peeled and diced

2 cloves garlic, finely chopped

½ tablespoon finely chopped fresh ginger

1 teaspoon ground fennel

1 teaspoon cardamom

1 tablespoon coriander

Dash of cayenne

1 tablespoon chili powder

1 tablespoon hot sauce, plus more to taste

Note: At Stonecat Café, the chef uses Scooter's Hot Sauce in this spicy sauce.

Castel Grisch Estate Winery/ Castel Grisch Winery Restaurant

Lush vineyards literally cling to the steep hillside, fanned by lively lake breezes; visitors enjoy a breathtaking view from the chalet while sipping estate-grown wines and feasting on bratwurst and strudel. If this sounds like a travelogue of Switzerland, then Castel Grisch has succeeded in bringing a bit of Alpine ambiance to Seneca Lake.

The winery was founded in 1982 by Aloise Baggenstoss, a chemist by profession, and his wife, Michelle, both natives of Switzerland. They fell in love with this property, it is said, since, when viewed from here, the lake resembles the Rhine River. The vineyard's first plantings of Riesling were, in fact, inspired by wines of the Rheingau, and culinary influence at the winery's restaurant was borrowed from the mother country.

Traditions continued when Tom Malina, a wine merchant, purchased the estate in 1992. The goal was (and still is) to maintain the size of wine production that can be sustained and hand-operated by the Malina family,

3380 Lover's Lane
(County Route 28)
Watkins Glen, NY 14891
(607) 535-9614

Winery Hours: Daily, 10:00 a.m.–5:00 p.m.
Restaurant Hours: Call for schedule

as well as keep it true to its roots. Currently, Castel Grisch enjoys a solid maturity, offering vintages of labrusca and hybrid "introductory drinking products," as Tom calls his everyday wines, and two versions of estate-grown Riesling.

The Johannisberg Riesling's striking characteristics include rich floral perfume, notes of ripe apricot, orange blossom, honeycomb, and tropical fruit, wonderfully framed by crisp acidity, and just a bit of perceptible sugar on the finish. This Spätlese-style wine has an easy drinking quality, less tiring to the palate than fuller bodied wines, yet with a fruit intensity that stands up to robust foods.

Winemaker Rick Evans has quietly established a reputation for luscious dessert wines, especially the prized Riesling Ice Wine, reminiscent of German Eiswein. Here, grapes are handpicked at the peak of ripeness and then immediately frozen for three months. Freezing turns their water to ice, and the resulting juice is much more concentrated and viscous. The sugar levels are also higher than normal, allowing for partial fermentation, and leaving behind some residual sugar. This intense nectar opens with inviting aromas of exotic fruit, fills the palate with bold flavors of oranges, pineapples, and peaches, and finishes with wildflower honey and rich Riesling fruit.

Wine and food make good partners at Castel Grisch. Patrons in the chalet's dining room savor classic Swiss fondue with squares of toasted rustic bread made on the premises, speared onto long fondue forks for dipping into the pot of bubbling Gruyère and Emmenthal cheeses and spiked with the winery's own Cuvée Chardonnay. Other dishes include bratwurst simmered in brown beer sauce, Black Forest ham, German chocolate cake, and warm, fresh-baked fruit strudels served with vanilla ice cream.

Every traveler finds little gems now and then. For wine lovers these are usually small family-run estates that are barely represented in tourist guides. Castel Grisch is such a gem.

Chateau LaFayette Reneau

5081 Route 414
Hector, NY 14841
(607) 546-2062
(800) 469-9463

Hours: Monday–Saturday,
10:00 a.m.–6:00 p.m.;
Sunday, 11:00 a.m.–6:00 p.m.
(April through October);
Monday–Saturday,
10:00 a.m.–5:00 p.m.;
Sunday, 11:00 a.m.–5:00 p.m.
(November through March)

www.clrwine.com

Richard Reno can trace his family tree all the way back to Louis Reneau, who was born in Paris and arrived in the New World in the early 1600s. Although the family name was Americanized by his father, when Dick needed to attach a name to his winery, he called it "LaFayette Reneau," honoring his grandfather, a gentleman farmer from Oneonta, Alabama.

Following a career in the printing business, Dick retired to an old dairy farm on Seneca Lake, with nothing more ambitious in mind than keeping a rocking chair in motion. But soon he was out pruning, tying, and restoring the abandoned Concord, Catawba, and Niagara grapevines he found on a corner of the property. One thing led to another, and soon, he and his wife, Betty, decided it might be fun to make their own wine.

The success of next-door neighbors at Rolling Vineyards provided some needed assurance that this was, indeed, an ideal location to plant vinifera grapes. In 1985 they converted the cow barn into a winery and transformed their sixty-three acres of land into vineyards of Chardonnay, Riesling, Pinot Noir, Merlot, Cabernet Sauvignon, and, in the lowest part of the property, a tiny plot of Malbec. Dick and Betty decided early on that, while the winery would produce a full range of varieties, the sizzle would come from small-lot, Bordeaux-style wines from estate-grown grapes.

To help carry their mission forward, the Renos employed two talented and zealous young winemakers—Rob Thomas for the first vintage, and then Dave Whiting. Both men recognized the potential of this vineyard to produce grapes that reflect all the best qualities of Cabernet Sauvignon. Their early efforts were handsomely rewarded with gold medals in competition, and, as each went off to start his own winery, the position was filled by journeyman winemaker Tim Miller.

Working closely with his vineyard manager, Tim hones the grapes to his vision of quality, which includes keeping the crop small, as is done in the best French vineyards. The goal is low yields (about three to four tons per acre), which they believe results in the most intensely flavored grapes. Reserve Cabernet calls for hand-picking ripe berry clusters from the oldest vineyard and two years of aging in small French and Hungarian oak barrels for complexity and structure. Addition of up to 5 percent of Merlot and Malbec softens the tannins and pushes the fruit forward. The goal is minimum intervention, allowing the fruit to express itself.

I can't think of a more irresistible invitation to visit Chateau LaFayette Reneau than an opportunity to taste the Owner's Reserve Cabernet Sauvignon. It's a bright, soulful wine, with true to varietal aromas of vibrant cherry, blackberry, and toasted oak, complemented by accents of cassis and spice. Extremely smooth and sumptuous on the palate, with notes of black cherry and plum fruit, the style is restrained and elegant, medium-bodied and mouth-filling, with a long, silky finish of dark chocolate and spice.

As if to offset the snob appeal of the Cabs, Lafayette Reneau also produces some of the Finger Lakes' best lighthearted quaffs. The Seyval-Chardonnay balances citrus zest from Seyval Blanc with tropical flavors from Chardonnay; Cuvée Rouge softens the tartness of Baco Noir with 25 percent Pinot Noir. These two ingeniously blended table wines ought not to be overlooked.

The reason the wines here are so good is because the owners have such a high regard for quality and tradition. Some might say that "Chateau Lafayette Reneau" is too assuming a name for a winery in an old cow barn, but, in this case, it reflects both an homage to the noble wines of France and a respect for French-American ancestry.

670 Route 14
Penn Yan, NY 14527
(800) 636-9786

Winery Hours:
Monday–Saturday,
10:00 a.m.–6:00 p.m.;
Sunday, noon–6:00 p.m.
Restaurant Hours: Daily,
11:00 a.m.–5:00 p.m.

www.foxrunvineyards.com

Fox Run Vineyards/The Café at Fox Run

Peter Bell, armed with a degree in enology from Charles Stuart University in New South Wales, and winemaking experience, first at Hunter's Wines in New Zealand and then at Dr. Frank's Vinifera Wine Cellars on Keuka Lake, was the logical candidate for winemaker at this ivory tower among the vines. Fox Run Vineyards is at the forefront of a small but influential corps of progressive wineries bent on transforming the image of the Finger Lakes.

An anthropologist, amateur chef, musician, teacher, and gifted winemaker, Peter's foremost passion is Pinot Noir. He modestly suggests that not much of what he does is different from other competent winemakers in the Finger Lakes as long as it includes respect for the fruit, less intervention, and more attention.

While it is often said that great wines are made in the vineyard, Peter suggests that's like saying, "Great works of art are contained inside tubes of paint."

Four specific blocks of Pinot on the Fox Run property are diversified by vine age and clones. They are hand-harvested and pressed separately, aged in individually selected oak barrels, and sequestered until he is ready to blend.

Peter's gorgeous Pinots start with a whiff of smoke and black cherry in the nose, then open up on the palate with earthy, truffley, raspberry, black cherry, plum, and bacon characters, and subtle spices like orange, clove, and cardamom. These are excellent wines of incredible length, with cherries and chocolatey oak lingering on the finish.

"Riesling is the one Finger Lakes variety that produces high-quality grapes every year, no matter what the weather," insists Peter. He also

believes that if you ferment a Riesling completely dry, all the fruit disap-
pears, and you are left with an austere, minerally, smokey wine with
perhaps a few wisps of lime. The trick, he explains, is to stop fermentation before complete dryness, and, since Riesling is naturally high in acids,
a bit of sweetness brings the wine into balance. He calls the contrast
between German and Finger Lakes off-dry Rieslings "amazing." "We have
greater aromatics, cleaner fruit, and more zing from higher alcohol."

Oftentimes a straight varietal wine may need a little fine tuning to
make it a great wine, and, while Peter found Lemberger intriguing, the
palate structure was lacking, the finish too abrupt. As a varietal it had
plenty of blackberries and fresh black pepper, but blending with up to
20 percent Cabernet Franc lengthened the finish, added a note of raspberry, and improved the aromatics, making it a more complete wine. He
suggests that a winemaker sees the needs of a wine as a chef sees the
needs of a sauce: "The character of the wine may be nearly the same,
but an extra component makes the difference between good and great."

For more than a century Fox Run was a dairy farm. The first grapes
were not planted until 1984, and the barn, erected shortly after the Civil
War, was restored and opened as a winery in 1990 by Larry and Adele
Wildrick. Three years later it was sold to Scott Osborn and investor Andy
Hale, drawn to the property for its promise of fine winegrowing.

As a student of international politics, Scott studied in Kenya, India,
Thailand, Japan, and England. He worked in real estate development on
the West Coast before his passion for wine led to an apprenticeship at
Konocti Winery in Northern California's Lake County. He went on to
guide the early efforts of Long Island's Pindar Vineyards as general manager before the purchase of Fox Run brought him to the Finger Lakes.

Scott explains that he was fortunate enough to put together a group
of talented people who not only share his vision but contribute the efforts
to make it a reality. Besides winemaker Peter Bell, Scott's dream team
includes John Kaiser, longtime vineyard manager, and CIA-trained chef
Frank Caravita, who oversees operation of The Café at Fox Run.

Tasty platters of food from the upscale cafeteria offer a platform to
showcase the food-friendly Fox Run wines. A sandwich of Genoa salami,
sopressata, cappicola, provolone cheese, and sun-dried tomato pesto on
cheese pizza bread is suggested with Merlot; portobello mushrooms,
roasted peppers, fresh mozzarella, and basil pesto on rosemary-garlic
focaccia bread with Pinot Noir; roast beef with artichoke and sundried
tomato–cream cheese spread on a tomato ciabatta roll with Lemberger;
and the flourless chocolate cake is just begging to be paired with a glass
of Fox Run port.

The soups, salads, sandwiches, and desserts make the most of local
produce, and an outdoor patio offers the opportunity to enjoy imaginative cuisine overlooking the lake.

With sixty acres of vines in production and an additional fifteen acres
coming on-line over the next few years, Fox Run is one of our most

influential enterprises, nourishing citizens and visitors to the region and helping to reshape the way the Finger Lakes approaches its crafting of fine wine.

5576 Route 14
Dundee, NY 14837
(607) 243-7883

Hours: Daily,
10:00 a.m.–5:00 p.m.;
Sunday, 11:00 a.m.–
5:00 p.m.

www.fulkersonwinery.com

Fulkerson Winery

Steeped in history, the Fulkerson farm is composed of vineyards, pastures, and ancient oak trees on rolling land that has been in the hearts and hands of the same family for 200 years. The property was purchased in 1805 by Caleb Fulkerson, a veteran of the Revolutionary War, passed down to Samuel, then to Harlan, Harlan Jr., Roger, and now to Sayre Fulkerson, the sixth-generation owner, who is charged with preservation of the family farm as an agricultural enterprise.

Fulkerson Winery is the culmination of the family's history of farming on a site that was cleared by the Indians and planted with black raspberries by the early settlers. The first grapevines appeared around the time of the Civil War, intended, not for wine, but for table fruit.

When management of the farm was handed to Sayre, he learned winegrowing literally from the ground up. When the grape juice plant expanded to include a winery in 1988, he assumed duties of both vineyardist and winemaker. With old-fashioned Dutch common sense and pragmatism, he believes that quality of farming is reflected by quality in the bottle. He respects his terroir and responds to it with some of the Finger Lakes' most profound wines.

Diamond is a rarely seen native American grape that seems to thrive in a section of the vineyard with clay-rich soil to produce a juicy, grapey, fruity wine with fully developed pineapple and pear characters. It so perfectly expresses the nature of this varietal that taking a sip is like biting into a fresh-picked grape.

Sayre makes a brave effort with Dornfelder, a robust grape from the German Rheinhessen, which we don't often see as an American varietal wine. It fully ripens in the vineyard to produce a wine of deep plum color, faintly earthy aromas, concentrated flavors of wild berries and cola with hints of cinnamon and clove, soft tannins, and a velvety finish. This is still a small-production wine here, but newly planted acreage promises more of the same.

St. Vincent of Saragossa, the patron saint of winegrowers, inspired a hybrid grape variety that bears his name. On the Fulkerson farm, Vincent (the grape) is planted where stony soil tends to keep the vines warmer and retain heat through the night. With less water availability, yields are lower, but flavors are more intense. Fulkerson's Vincent is plump and generous, and, while I enjoy its spicy, herbal, tomato-infused flavors, some are dismissive of this wine. Try it for yourself and decide.

A clever blend of varieties at Fulkerson's results in a wine that has probably given second thoughts to grape growers who've been busy uprooting their plantings of Catawba. Responding to the development of his customers' tastes, Sayre reversed a dwindling interest in Catawba by blending in 15 percent Rougeon, a French-hybrid variety. The addition of firm tannins and jammy, black cherry flavoring from the Rougeon is just enough to moderate the telltale muskiness of the native grape. Attaching the name "Red Zeppelin" assures that this wine will not be mistaken for anything other than a sweetly refreshing summer quaff.

Besides these oddities, the winery crushes an impressive complement of other grapes, with nearly half the juice sold to amateur winemakers and the remainder turned into about 10,000 cases of wine. During fall harvest, customers place their orders at least one day in advance and then bring containers to fill with freshly pressed juice. To assist with home winemaking, Fulkerson's stocks a full range of supplies, equipment, and yeasts appropriate to each variety.

Sayre has inherited his ancestors' reverence for the special qualities of this place. He is personally involved with every container of juice and every bottle of wine that leaves the winery, and he takes pride and joy in fulfilling the destiny of the family farm.

Glenora Wine Cellars/Veraisons

16 46

The Finger Lakes first set its sights on producing a pinnacle New World sparkling wine back in 1934, when Charles Fournier, the Champagne master at Veuve Cliquot in France, came to work for Gold Seal Winery in Hammondsport. Although progress was achieved, the goal was not ultimately realized until 1991, when Glenora Wine Cellars' 1988 production of Blanc de Blancs captured a Double Gold Award at the San Francisco Fair Wine Competition. This semi-legendary wine established the winery as one of the top sparkling wine producers in the country.

5435 Route 14
Dundee, NY 14837
(800) 243-5513

Winery Hours: Daily,
10:00 a.m.–6:00 p.m.
(May and June); Daily,
10:00 a.m.–8:00 p.m.
(July and August); Daily,
10:00 a.m.–6:00 p.m.
(September and October);
Daily, 10:00 a.m.–5:00 p.m.
(November through April)
Restaurant Hours: Call for
schedule

www.glenora.com

Glenora was the brainchild of three eminent grape growers, led by Gene Pierce, who, as a young man, studied agricultural economics at Cornell. In 1977, when passage of the Farm Winery Act handed grape growers incentives to become vintners, Gene and his pals Ed Dalrymple and Eastman Beers, relying on fruit from their own vineyards, got started in the wine business.

One of the first people they hired was John Williams, originally a dairy science major at Cornell. After a fortuitous work-study program at Taylor Wine Company, John entered the Enology and Viticulture Masters Program at UC Davis. The Davis degree and an apprenticeship at Stag's Leap Wine Cellars in Napa Valley gave him a leg up over other candidates for the winemaking position. Glenora's founding fathers reasoned that a California trained winemaker was essential to the start-up of an important venture, and, according to Gene, John set standards for the winery that are, for the most part, still in place.

Another California winemaker, Jim Gifford of Domaine Mumm (now Mumm Napa), who would join the merry band ten years later, made significant contributions to Glenora. He insisted on using only traditional vinifera grapes in the sparkling wine program, and he boosted production of the sparklers from 600 cases a year to 6,000 cases. Although Jim's whirlwind tenure was abbreviated, his cellar team, which included

a credentialed technician by the name of Steve DiFrancesco, remained dedicated to making great wines.

After a hiatus at Lucas Vineyards, Steve was appointed winemaker at Glenora, and, with the acquisition of Knapp Vineyards and the opening of Logan Ridge Wine Cellars, he is now at the helm of production for all three properties. Outwardly quiet and unassuming, Steve is fanatical about attention to detail, and he's got the crafting of sparkling wines down to a fine art. He nurses the yeast aging for Glenora Brut and fashions this beauty according to classical méthode champenoise. The blending of Pinot Noir and Chardonnay grapes provides full body and firm acidity in the assertive yet delicate wine. It's creamy on the palate, with elegant fruit and a profusion of tiny bubbles.

While Chardonnay and Pinot Noir grapes are cherished for the sparkling wines, Riesling has become especially important here. In fact, to fans of Riesling, the Glenora offertory is cause for celebration. Long skin contact (up to eighteen hours) after picking extracts the vibrant flavors on display in Dry Riesling. Unmistakable lime characteristics fill the palate, with hints of red apple skin and wildflower honey, and a savory finish of fresh mineral acids.

Protecting the grapes from oxidation during processing maintains a clean, vine-fresh taste in the Semi-Dry Riesling. Fermentation is stopped to retain residual grape sugars in the wine, and it's balanced by a clean, crisp acid finish. Savvy, sassy, and eminently likable, the wine has rich, honeylike notes and a musky lime, ripe pear, and toasty complexity.

Glenora Vintner's Select is a textbook Finger Lakes Riesling, produced from a special block of grapes on Glenora Farm. Its sweetness level falls in between the dry and semi-dry styles, and, with extra bottle age, this brilliantly intense wine shows a hint of the Riesling petrol note behind green apple, tangerine, and peach aromas. The palate is lean and austere, building slowly in the mouth, and delivered over a chalky backbone. Balanced with ripe apricot and a touch of mineral in the finish, it is rich and satisfying in every respect. These wines are not only good but, ounce for ounce, a real bargain.

The Glenora complex has expanded over the last quarter century and now includes a thirty-room inn and a 125-seat restaurant, both commanding a spectacular view of Seneca Lake. Veraisons is the winery restaurant, its name inspired by the time in the vineyard season when grapes change color. Its provincial dining environment is guided by an enthusiastic young chef, Arthur Kelly, who takes advantage of the region's artisanal cheeses, pasture-fed poultry, and organic produce.

Art has mastered the nuances of cooking with wines, and he is mindful of how his food pairs with Glenora wines. He has the luxury of tasting developing wines with the winemaker and then highlighting flavor profiles with whatever is fresh and in season. Signature creations include Cabernet French Onion Soup gratinée and "Trestle Creek" Salad of baby greens, grapes, roasted sliced almonds, and shredded ricotta salata tossed in raspberry-rose mignonette. Entrées are highlighted by the Regional Sword Skewer, a mixed grill of McDonald Farm lamb and veal, Fullview Farms ostrich, and Glenora–Maple Valley elderberry-sage sausage, paired with local vegetables. Chef Kelly goes an extra mile or two to be creative without wandering too far afield.

As the first of the "new" farm wineries, Glenora was a leader in spreading the revolutionary idea that our region's wines could compete with the likes of California and Europe. Today, it is a radiant and thriving symbol of the Finger Lakes renaissance as a wine-producing region and a quintessential wine country experience.

CALLEBAUT-CABERNET SAUVIGNON BEEF BOURGUIGNON

The concentrated, complex flavors of Cabernet Sauvignon provide a good match with chocolate. Chef Arthur Kelly Jr. has incorporated cocoa as a savory flavoring in a Finger Lakes take on the traditional French dish.

Marinate the beef in half of the Cabernet Sauvignon for at least 1 hour, or overnight, if possible.

Combine the flour with the salt and pepper in a mixing bowl and coat the marinated beef cubes in the mixture. Remove the coated beef cubes by hand. Reserve the unused flour mixture. Melt the butter in a saucepan over medium-high heat. Add the beef cubes and sauté until brown, about 4 minutes. Add the remaining flour and stir until there are no lumps. Add the remaining wine and all of the remaining ingredients to the pan and bring to a simmer, stirring constantly to prevent lumps from forming in the sauce. Simmer for 10 minutes. Decrease the heat to medium-low and simmer, uncovered, for 1 to 2 hours or until the sauce reaches a medium consistency, stirring occasionally. Spoon into bowls and serve hot with some crusty bread.

Serves 6 to 8

3 pounds choice top round, cubed

½ bottle (375 ml) Glenora Cabernet Sauvignon

¼ cup all-purpose flour

1 teaspoon salt

1 teaspoon freshly ground black pepper

½ cup unsalted butter

½ pound mushrooms, quartered

1 large yellow onion, cut in medium dice

¼ cup tomato paste

2 cloves garlic, chopped

2 tablespoons fresh thyme, chopped

½ cup unsweetened cocoa powder

1 (10.5-ounce) can beef stock

Note: Try this flavorful dish served over your favorite pasta.

Route 414
Hector, NY 14841
(607) 546-9463
(888) 750-0494

Hours: Monday–Saturday,
10:00 a.m.–5:00 p.m.;
Sunday, noon–5:00 p.m.

www.hazlitt1852.com

Hazlitt 1852 Vineyards

In October 2002, Hazlitt 1852 Vineyards & Winery founder Jerry Hazlitt died, at the age of sixty-four. Jerry was part of the fifth generation of his family to grow grapes and tree fruit on the eastern shore of Seneca Lake, and the name he and his wife, Elaine, gave the winery includes the year this prolific site was first settled by his ancestors.

A traditionalist in the vineyard and a bold experimenter in the cellar, his objective was always unwaveringly simple and straightforward: his winery would make products that reflected his family's proud heritage. Jerry and Elaine produced their first wines in 1985, and twenty succeeding vintages are testament to their success.

Born into their present roles, a sixth generation of Hazlitts continues the family enterprise, with Doug Hazlitt serving as winery manager and his sister, Leigh Hazlitt Triner, overseeing the tasting room operation. Together they head up a small team that includes winemaker Mike Sutterby and vineyard manager John Santos, and each plays a vital role in the winery's growth and evolution.

With century-old Catawba grapevines and eight acres of Baco Noir on the property, one of the first wines produced by the fledgling winery was a proprietary blend of the two. Combining both of these early ripening, high-acid varieties proved much better than either one on its own, especially with added sugar for balance. With an annual production of 60,000 gallons, the popularity of "Red Cat" has been explained as a beginning drinker's bridge between Coca-Cola and more serious wines. Perhaps because of the abundance of inexpensive Catawba grapes, the formula for this pop wine has since been widely imitated by other farm wineries in the region.

While Hazlitt 1852 Vineyards still calls itself "Home of the Red Cat," and fun-loving crowds who pack the tasting room can't seem to get enough of it, the estate can hardly be defined by this one wine. Rather, over two decades, Jerry developed an ambitious roster that includes Riesling, Chardonnay, Gewürztraminer, Pinot Gris, Cabernet Sauvignon, Cabernet Franc, and Merlot, all rich with varietal fruit that John Santos ascribes to the farm's remarkable terroir.

The vineyards are situated in what John calls Seneca Lake's "banana belt," consistently the warmest microclimate in the Finger Lakes as measured by Geneva Experiment Station thermometers planted throughout the region. From Peach Orchard Point north to Lodi Point on Seneca's eastern shore, the weather pattern keeps soil warmer into the fall. An extended growing season means the fruit has more time on the vine.

Depending on how you position those vines, according to John, you get more or less sunlight interception, which can have a big impact on the yields of the fruit or the potential wine quality. Canopy management is an important protocol of John's work in the vineyards, and he devised an original trellis system, the "Hazlitt Twin Tier," for Pinot Gris and Pinot

Noir. Since Pinot varieties are pendulous, his split wires encourage the vines to train down, exposing more sun.

Adding to the unique features of the vineyards are reddish colorings in the soil, a result of oxidized iron. The presence of iron and other trace minerals on this site ensures a steady diet of nutrients to the vines, gives a touch of color, and intensifies berry flavors. Hazlitt's best red wines come from plantings in a red pebbly hillside soil weathered from iron-rich glacial till.

Mike Sutterby loves Merlot as a stand-alone varietal, and he turns it into the fullest, most concentrated of Hazlitt's bottled varietals. On the nose, this wine entices the palate with aromas of black cherry and black pepper; in the mouth, it bursts with blackberry, currant, sweet oak flavors, and notes of coffee and olives, followed by lingering hints of licorice, leather, smoke, and chocolate. In addition to estate-grown grapes, fruit from Jim Hazlitt's Sawmill Creek Vineyards contributes to the compelling Merlot.

No winegrower can have a greater tribute to his memory than the living vines he nurtured and the wines they continue to produce. As the family continues the course set by Jerry, and, as vine roots reach deeper into the fertile soil on this glacial slope, there is little doubt that the winery is headed for greatness.

Hermann J. Wiemer Vineyards

He makes a particularly German contribution to the Finger Lakes, and a profound one. His wines draw connections to his homestead in Bernkastel, in the southern Mosel. Hermann J. Wiemer is descended from a long line of winemakers in a Riesling-producing region, so it seems quite natural that he makes prize-winning wines from Germany's "noble grape."

The self-portrait that emerges from the winery that bears his name is of an impeccable artisan with a deep respect for his profession and his heritage. He brings a strong sense of classical decorum to his operation and a remarkable measure of finesse and sophistication to the region. He is passionately and romantically involved in the life of his vineyard. So don't expect any frills or breathtaking lake views. It's all about great wine here.

A graduate of Geisenheim, the renowned German wine school, Hermann could have remained in Germany and grown old making fine Rieslings. Instead, he wandered over to the Finger Lakes. In 1968 he accepted a job making sacramental wine for the Roman Catholic Diocese of Rochester. After two years he felt isolated at the Conesus Lake winery, and he was ready to return home when he met Walter Taylor, the "bad boy" of the Taylor Wine family. Walter was estranged from his family's enterprise, intending to start his own winery at Bully Hill, and all he needed was the right winemaker. As they say, it was "the beginning of a beautiful friendship."

3962 Route 14
Dundee, NY 14837
(800) 371-7971

Hours: Monday–Saturday,
10:00 a.m.–5:00 p.m.;
Sunday, 11:00 a.m.–
5:00 p.m.

www.wiemer.com

Hermann managed the vineyards and made the wines at Bully Hill, while Walter shook up the establishment. Together they created New York's first "boutique" winery, a maverick adventure that built its reputation with French-American hybrid grapes such as Seyval Blanc, Marechal Foch, and Baco Noir, wines that hurtled past native varieties in quality. However, while Walter was content with this achievement, Hermann couldn't ignore the breakthroughs in vinifera by his neighbor, Konstantin Frank. "Walter drank his own wines," says Hermann with typical bluntness. "I didn't."

In 1973, with Walter's blessing, Hermann purchased 140 acres of Seneca Lake property on a shoestring. The land contract called for payments of $300.59 every month, with the seller holding title until the final payment was made. Hermann's upstart nursery of hand-grafted vinifera vines was a true pioneering effort, with a vineyard tended by hand and given personal attention.

Then, on Christmas Eve in 1981, while Hermann was visiting family in Germany, he received a telegram from Walter, who was terminating his position at Bully Hill. It was the result of an inevitable clash of egos. Hermann's "experiment," in Walter's opinion, had gone too far for his own good. It would be time for Hermann to strike out on his own.

Perhaps no other wine region is so driven by a single grape as Germany is by Riesling, and it was Hermann's passion for this hearty variety that defined his next move. While others in the Finger Lakes were eager to imitate California's success with Chardonnay, he knew instinctively that this was Riesling country. Despite lingering memories of the poor quality German imports of the not-too-distant past (Hermann calls it the "Blue Nun hangover") and little consumer demand, he made his beloved Riesling the focus of Hermann J. Wiemer Vineyards. With the first release of wines, it was clear that his challenge was well worth the toil.

Hermann makes his Rieslings with the confidence of Leonard Bernstein conducting the *Meistersinger Overture*. He proves that the variety can cover a wide range of sweetness and styles. He was the first to make a truly "dry" Riesling, and the first to put "Dry Johannisberg Riesling" on a label. True to form, the elegant, Kabinett-style wine is fresh, crisp, and beautifully balanced, with grapefruit and mineral aromas; notes of apricot, peach, and honey; and a clean, lingering finish.

Other versions of his firm hand with Riesling include the smooth and nicely balanced Spätlese-style Semi-Dry Johannisberg Riesling, a fruity, flowery, pleasantly sweet wine, bursting with pure peach, apple, and melon flavors and a note of citrus in a subtle, refined finish; TBA (Trockenbeerenauslese)-style Select Late Harvest Johannisberg Riesling displays sensual aromas of mint, eucalyptus, and thyme, and its well-framed palate of apricot, peach, orange, and smoke is magnified in an elegant, intense finish. Grapes from the oldest vines on the estate were handpicked for Ice Wine, a complex, powerful, and stylish nectar with dazzling, concentrated essences of sweet apricot, peach, honey, and notes of lemon-candy and caramelized apples that leave the mouth ringing with an extreme sensation of pleasure.

Hermann uses classic German bottles, German corks, even German capsules, yet he is convinced that his rendition stands out next to the European standard. The winery's other significant varieties include Chardonnay, Gewürztraminer, and Pinot Noir, but, as the translation of a German proverb explains, "Where your treasure is, there is your heart." Hermann J. Wiemer Riesling is a Finger Lakes treasure.

Lakewood Vineyards

The Finger Lakes' earliest wines were made from winter-hearty grape varieties such as Concord, Catawba, and Niagara. Over nearly a century of commercial production—all the way up to the 1970s—the industry depended on these wines, despite an aroma and flavor profile variously described as wild and musky. A wine writer once compared the sweet and "foxy" native wines to grape jelly with a shot of vodka.

4024 Route 14
Watkins Glen, NY 14891
(607) 535-9252

Hours: Monday–Saturday, 10:00 a.m.–5:00 p.m.; Sunday, noon–5:00 p.m.

www.lakewoodvineyards.com

Flash forward three decades. Christopher Stamp of Lakewood Vineyards is making wines not only rich in taste but rich in history. And even while he creates brilliant wines from some of the Finger Lakes' oldest varieties, Chris regularly produces some of the region's best wines from the noble grapes of Europe.

The Stamp family has farmed the picturesque western shore of Seneca Lake for three generations. In April of 1951, Frank Stamp packed his wife, Lucy, and their three children into the family Hudson and drove from Maryland to the piece of property he had purchased with his life savings. Within a year they had planted five acres of Concord grapes in the fertile soil, and the Stamps have been faithful stewards of these vineyards ever since.

Monty Stamp, the oldest son, enrolled at Morrisville College to study agricultural science, then returned to run the farm. After growing and selling grapes to the Taylor Wine Company for all of thirty-six years, Lakewood Vineyards became a winery in 1988. With the exception of some Concords they sell to Welsh's, all grapes on the estate are turned into Lakewood wines.

The sixty-five-acre site is divided into specialized vineyard blocks. Each specific location is chosen according to the depth, structure, and composition of the soil in order to promote the vigor of the grapes. Steeper elevations with better air drainage and higher levels of limestone are best suited to later-harvested varieties, according to Chris, so that's where he's planted Riesling, Cabernet Franc, and Catawba.

Chris, first-born of the third generation, earned a food science degree from Cornell, then served as winemaker at Planc's Cayuga Vineyard before joining the family enterprise. He holds the same passion for his region's indigenous grapes as he does for the top-flight varietals, and his wines are perfect examples of the heights to which labruscas can aspire when placed in the proper hands. He continues to set the pace in the region with his remarkable ability to coax flavor and finesse out of Concord, Catawba, Niagara, and Delaware.

The challenge with these varieties, acknowledges Chris, is making wines for a true wine lover, and what astonishes most is the way he respects honest flavor profiles. Matching the sweetness level to its fruity aromas, he makes a Delaware Ice Wine called Glaciovinum that transcends a more typical version of the wine with concentrated, complex tropical flavors in a luscious, syrupy nectar.

Over the years, the Stamps have added vinifera grape varieties such as Chardonnay, Riesling, Pinot Noir, and Cabernet Franc to supplement the farm's original plantings, and these wines are consistently among the top performers in competition. Chris's approach to the capricious Pinot Noir produces a silky, crimson wine, with characters of cherry and plum, hints of vanilla from the oak, and very light tannins in the lingering, faintly bitter, very pleasant finish. It was awarded a gold medal at the New York State Fair Wine Competition for the 1999 vintage.

Chris Stamp is a highly disciplined revolutionary, and his energy shines through in the Lakewood catalog of vinifera, hybrid, labrusca, ice wines, fortified wines, and honey mead. He has garnered the respect and admiration of his fellow vintners in the Finger Lakes and has worked relentlessly to help our regional wines get the attention and recognition they deserve.

PEACHY CHICKEN MARINADE

Serves 4

1/2 cup grapeseed oil

2 cups Lakewood Vineyards Riesling

2 tablespoons capers

1/2 cup freshly squeezed lemon juice

6 peaches, coarsely chopped

1/2 teaspoon chopped fresh thyme

1/2 teaspoon ground cumin

1/2 teaspoon marjoram

1/4 teaspoon cayenne pepper

4 (6-ounce) chicken or duck breasts

Note: For a pleasant smoke flavor, put grape cuttings into a charcoal grill while cooking the meat.

Flavor pairing comes naturally when using products that come from the same region, and Lakewood's assistant winemaker, John Damian, developed this recipe to prove it. The secret to a chicken dish that he guarantees will awaken sleeping taste buds is the combination of fragrant, flavorful local peaches and just enough residual sugar in the wine to give the marinade a lift.

Combine all of the ingredients except for the chicken or duck breasts in a blender. Blend until peaches are puréed. Place the breasts in the marinade in an airtight container and refrigerate overnight.

Preheat a medium-hot fire in a charcoal grill or preheat a gas grill to medium (about 450°F).

Place the breasts on the grill, reserving the marinade. Cook for about 8 minutes, turning halfway through, until cooked through but still moist. Keep warm.

Place the marinade in a saucepan and bring to a boil over medium-high heat. Reduce to a consistency that coats the back of a spoon. Place the cooked breasts on individual plates and drizzle the reduced marinade over the top. Serve warm with fresh vegetables.

Lamoreaux Landing Wine Cellars

During the nineteenth century, steamboats and scows collected fruit from growers around Seneca Lake and transferred the cargo to railroad cars for delivery to markets throughout the northeast. One stop, at the mouth of a creek on the Lamoreaux family property, was known as Lamoreaux Landing. Today that site is home to Lamoreaux Landing Wine Cellars, where Mark Wagner earns national acclaim for meticulous vineyards and handcrafted wines.

9224 Route 414
Lodi, NY 14860
(607) 582-6011

Hours: Monday–Saturday, 10:00 a.m.–5:00 p.m.; Sunday, noon–5:00 p.m.

www.lamoreauxwine.com

There are several novel aspects to this enterprise, not the least of which is the towering Greco-modern winery, designed by architect Bruce Corson and built in 1992. With a spectacular view of the vineyard hillside and lake, it suggests a cross between Greek Revival architecture, common throughout the Finger Lakes, and one of the region's field barns. In fact, it captured the attention of the American Institute of Architects, who named it one of the most notable buildings erected in New York State during the twentieth century.

The surrounding winery property is planted with uniformly spaced rows of Chardonnay, Riesling, Gewürztraminer, Pinot Noir, and Cabernet Franc, and the success of Lamoreaux Landing lies in those vineyards.

Mark's family grew apples, cherries, and grapes on a forty-acre property not far from Lamoreaux, so he was literally born to be a grower himself. Raised on the farm, he was fascinated from childhood by the way vines grow and what they do. "My mom kept me at her side while she worked in the vineyard," says Mark, "so I never needed a babysitter." He brings both a lifetime of experience and a deep reverence for the land to Lamoreaux Landing.

As one of the most-respected independent growers in the Finger Lakes, Mark supplied high-quality fruit to other wineries for many years before seeking another challenge. Since growing good grapes is only half of the equation, establishing a winery was his next logical step.

Soils are widely variable in the Finger Lakes, even contrary on a single farm. Mark grows five blocks of Chardonnay on three different soil types: Honeoye, very fertile silt and loam; Lansing, a rich, gravelly soil;

Conesus, a heavier soil with clay. He uses grapes from each of those blocks to create complexities he wouldn't get from a single source, nuances of terroir expressed in the different soil types. They are fermented separately so the winemaker can "build" a wine by blending the right characteristics at the right proportion. For example, grapes from the Honeoye lots usually dominate in the Reserve Chardonnay, since they develop more tropical fruit flavors and produce wines that stand up to extended oak age.

Rob Thomas, the first winemaker at Lamoreaux Landing, made his mark with a groundbreaking 1993 Chardonnay that bested 400 other American wines in the 1995 New World Wine Competition. The award catapulted Finger Lakes Chardonnay to the forefront of the industry and quickly established Lamoreaux Landing as a significant force in the region. After charting the course to produce wines of true varietal expression and flavor, Rob left full-time responsibilities at the winery to concentrate on his own venture (see Shalestone Vineyards), but continues his involvement as a consultant to the winemaking team now headed by Martha Gioumousis.

Special mention should be made here of a wine that emerged from Mark's curiosity about how Cabernet Franc, which he says "has the ability to produce consistently high-quality reds," would do without oak age. Taking inspiration from a common practice in the French Loire, the 2002 T23 Cabernet Franc matured in a specific stainless steel tank. With expressive aromas of raspberries, currants, and a hint of spice, this purebred wine offers elegance and harmonious layers of cherry, sweet berry, cut grass, and cassis. It is velvety and well-balanced on the palate with a long, graceful finish of berries and light caramel.

Mark Wagner quietly continues his proud heritage and artisanal approach to grape growing and winemaking—establishing a connection between the land and the wine. His wines have an extremely loyal following and are sought after by our best restaurants. Superlatives are part of any discussion of Lamoreaux Landing Wine Cellars and the impressive lineup of wines. And not without good reason.

5677 Route 414
Hector, NY 14841
(607) 546-2800

Hours:
Daily, 10:00 a.m.–5:00 p.m.
(May through November);
Saturday–Sunday,
noon–5:00 p.m. (December
through April)

Leidenfrost Vineyards

John Leidenfrost qualifies as one of the region's modern-day adventurers in a quest for the "holy grail" of red wine. His vision and determination not only proved that Pinot Noir is well-suited to his site, but he established a touchstone with a style that bursts with ripe black cherry varietal character. Robb Walsh, food and wine writer for the *Houston Press*, calls it "the best Pinot in the world under $15."

John's father, a shipbuilder by trade, moved the family to this lakeside farm just after World War II. Originally covered with peaches and apples, the property was replanted in grapevines, mostly Catawba, beginning in 1954. As a young man, John left the farm to study art history. After a few years in the teaching profession, he returned to the family homestead. It was his turn to manage the vineyards, and he set out to grow the grapes he loved.

Physically and temperamentally, the Leidenfrost property is different from some of its neighbors. Steep slopes supply good drainage, and the higher temperatures of well-drained soils assist ripening. Proximity to the lake provides a thermal advantage, especially on the eastern shore, where afternoon sun bathes the grapes and prevailing winds moderate temperatures. These conditions significantly extend the growing season, allowing grapes to hang on the vines longer and develop complex flavors while keeping their good acidity. Pinot Noir makes vastly different styles of wine on each plot of ground where it's grown, and, in nearly every respect, John's site appears to possess an ideal microclimate and soil structure for exceptional Pinot Noir.

John's grapevines struggle on the thin hill-slope soil, which is rich in clay and loam. Less vigorous growth and low rainfall inhibit overgrowth and produce much more concentrated flavors. North to south orientation of the vine rows not only reduces erosion but ensures that both sides of the vines catch every bit of sunlight from sun-up to sunset. Also in his favor, John separates the canopy into upward- and downward-positioned shoots using a training system called "Scott Henry," so that the vines have enough leaves for photosynthesis but are not so dense that the sun cannot ripen the grapes.

Older vines tend to yield less, and this is yet another advantage for John. His mature, quarter-century-old vines produce grapes with intense, concentrated flavors, and, since grapes are picked by hand, only the ripest, healthiest fruit is harvested. He is a stickler for hands-on quality control at every stage of winemaking. During fermentation he "punches down" the grapes, mixing juice and skins twice a day to extract maximum color and flavor. Then, up to two years of aging in small French oak barrels adds to the wine's intriguing complexity and depth.

Leidenfrost Pinot Noir creates a lasting impression on the palate. Its aroma is intense with violet, peppermint, and black cherry aromas. It is full-bodied, with green tea and herbal notes, and earthy, energetic fruit flavors. ("It tastes of the earth it came out of," says John.) Tannins are perfectly balanced between the sweetness of the fruit and the acidity. The wine has a soft, velvety texture, and its most appealing quality is the long, persistent finish, with subtle vanilla and toasty oak characteristics.

John, by the way, didn't end his pursuit of noble grapes with Pinot Noir. He also enjoys success with Cabernet Sauvignon, Cabernet Franc, Merlot, Chardonnay, Riesling, and Gewürztraminer. He designed and built the winery, grows the grapes, tends the vineyard, and handcrafts some of the best wines in the Finger Lakes. With his name on those bottles, his place in wine country history is secure.

3800 Ball Diamond Road
Hector, NY 14841
(866) 546-6486

Winery Hours:
Monday–Thursday,
10:00 a.m.–5:00 p.m.;
Friday and Saturday,
10:00 a.m.–6:00 p.m.;
Sunday, noon–5:00 p.m.
Restaurant Hours:
Lunch, Monday–Saturday,
11:00 a.m.–4:00 p.m.;
Dinner, Wednesday–Friday,
5:00 p.m.–9:00 p.m.;
Brunch, Sunday, 11:00 a.m.–
3:00 p.m.

www.loganridge.com

Logan Ridge Wine Cellars/Petioles

This winery is an offshoot of its parent, Glenora Wine Cellars, and sister winery to Knapp Vineyards. Originally the sprawling chateau of local contractor and Glenora co-founder Ed Dalrymple, Logan Ridge is perched high above Seneca's waters and rolling hillside vineyards. While Glenora and Knapp products have well-established styles and predictable profiles, it was anticipated from the beginning that this facility would take some chances. "This is a voyage of discovery," says winemaker Steve DiFrancesco. "We've got an opportunity to produce wines in nontraditional ways, yet on a commercial scale."

Horizons have expanded to include an innovative barrel-fermented Vidal, the Austrian-influenced hot-pressing of red wines, barrel aging in unique cooperage from a variety of sources, including American Appalachia and Russia, development of a nouveau-style Rougeon using carbonic maceration, and mastery of an apéritif-style rosé that has become Logan Ridge's signature wine.

In order to produce Rosé of Sangiovese, grapes are crushed and pressed as soon as they arrive in the cellar. The juice is left in contact with the grape skins for only a few hours, leaving hues of pink and rose, then cold-fermented and bottled early to retain its freshness of fruit flavors. The fragrant nose is reminiscent of mixed berries and vanilla; the softly balanced palate is packed with luscious, fresh-crushed strawberries and notes of lime and orange peel, well-balanced with good acidity and a long, lingering finish. Encouraged by the success of Rosé of Sangiovese, Logan Ridge has taken another leap with Rosé of Cabernet Franc, a sweeter wine that is more akin to the ubiquitous White Zinfandel.

Not every experiment succeeds. A blush wine produced from a blend of Cayuga White and seedless Reliant, Vanessa, and Lakemont grapes provided interesting berry flavors, but color was poor, and it didn't age well in the bottle. It was a trial run that Steve compares to taking a fall while learning to ski. "We just went too far out on a limb with that one," he admits. "I learned my lesson."

Guests who visit Petioles, the winery's restaurant, are in store for cuisine that's as edgy as the wine, this time from an adventurous, resourceful chef by the name of William Cornelius. He creates a personal style in a dining room that feels like an oversized ski lodge, and he produces big, bold flavors to match.

Teenage William enjoyed the attention he received cooking for his Boy Scout troop campouts, and he never looked back. Working with Parker Bosley, the legendary Cleveland restaurateur-chef, was instrumental, according to William, "in helping me find direction, focus, and refinement as I developed my skills." Bosley taught him to form relationships with local farmers so that he could maintain a consistent familiarity with the products he was purchasing.

VIDAL BLANC SCALLOP GRILL POUCHES

Serves 6 as an appetizer

Used correctly, wines should intensify, enhance, and accent the properties of a dish, not overpower it. With years of experience in winery kitchens, Chef William Cornelius has mastered the fine art of cooking with wine. Using Vidal Blanc as the key flavoring component, he adds a remarkable richness of tropical fruit and a slightly spicy finish to this preparation of bay scallops.

Prepare a medium-hot fire in a charcoal grill or preheat a gas grill to medium (about 450°F).

Cut six 18 by 20-inch pieces of heavy-duty aluminum foil. Mold each piece of foil around your fist to shape it into a bowl. In each of the foil bowls place 1/4 cup of the Logan Ridge Vidal Blanc, one-sixth of the sliced shallots, 1 tablespoon of the butter, and 1/2 teaspoon of the olive oil. Top each pocket with 1/3 pound of the scallops, 1/6 portion of halved tomatoes, 1/2 cup of the spinach, 1/6 portion of corn, and 1/4 cup of the basil. Season with salt and pepper to taste. Seal each foil bowl by folding the top of the bowl over itself two times.

Place the scallop pouches on the grill and cook for about 10 minutes. The steam inside will inflate the packs, and you will hear the juices bubbling. Remove the packages from the grill and use a knife to carefully (the steam is hot) cut open the top of each bowl. Transfer the contents of the packages to individual plates, add garnishes, and enjoy.

1 1/2 cups Logan Ridge Vidal Blanc

2 shallots, thinly sliced

6 tablespoons unsalted butter

1 tablespoon extra virgin olive oil

2 pounds bay scallops

1 pint grape tomatoes, halved

3 cups (about 2 ounces) loosely packed baby spinach

1 cup sweet white corn kernels

1 1/2 cups chopped fresh basil

Salt and freshly ground black pepper

Lemon slices, for garnish

Fresh chopped parsley, for garnish

Note: Along with the salt and pepper, Old Bay seasoning or any other seafood seasoning can be used to season the scallops before the pouches are sealed. Open the foil pouches carefully, letting the steam escape slowly. You can present this dish still in the foil bowl atop a plate or transfer the pouches' contents to soup bowls and garnish with fresh herbs and lemon slices.

After a position at the Wooster Inn in Wooster, Ohio, William took continuing education courses at the Culinary Institute in Hyde Park, New York, where he was invited to Pierce's 1894 Restaurant in Elmira Heights as guest chef for the 1997 Finger Lakes Barrel Dinner. He stayed on at Pierce's for a year before becoming executive chef at Wagner Vineyards' Ginny Lee Café.

Because of the colossal scale, it's difficult to find a cozy spot for dinner in the huge space, but ask for a table in the Library, a suspended level behind the massive fireplace. Choose from appetizers such as Grape Tomato Salsa and Fresh Mozzarella, bocconcini-style nuggets of cheese dressed with heirloom grape tomatoes in a balsamic reduction with virgin olive oil, fresh basil, and garlic, served between slices of an Alpine French roll. The same flavorful, zesty salsa fresca of sweet, vine-ripened tomatoes is served during lunch on brushcetta. Fresh, seasonal food is William's first priority, and he works closely with grower Modesto Cappelluti to incorporate local produce into the menu.

Entrées include Cappuccino Free-Range Chicken, a boneless, skinless breast served with an imaginative sauce of seasoned espresso flour, coffee brandy, and cream that adds smokiness and depth to the dish. "The sauce started out as an accompaniment to chocolate mousse," explains the chef. "I think it adds a playful touch to chicken."

He believes good cooks should pay attention to food-wine flavor matches, and he coaches his own waitstaff on suggested pairings with the winery's products. The combination of Triple-Chocolate Raspberry Torte and Logan Ridge Port, according to William, is "a way to warm your taste buds and your heart."

The Logan Ridge enterprise has, as one might say, put it all together. From producing innovative wines, to operating one of Seneca Lake's best tasting rooms, to serving creative regional fare, it is difficult to find anyone doing it better.

Miles Wine Cellars

18

168 Randall Crossing Road
Himrod, NY 14862
(607) 243-7742

Hours:
Daily, 10:00 a.m.–5:00 p.m.

www.mileswinecellars.com

No winery property in the Finger Lakes has more interesting history than Miles Wine Cellars. Originally a land grant from the King of England to the Rapalee family, its dock on Seneca Lake provided area farmers with access to the barges that moved their produce to the cities. An imposing house, built in 1802, was originally Federal-style in design, then converted to Greek Revival fifty years later by the Rapalees. It became a stop on the Underground Railroad, a shelter for runaway slaves as they made their way north and into Canada, where they could live as free citizens.

Doug Miles grew up in Stamford, Connecticut, but worked during summers for his uncle, Ed Dalrymple, a Finger Lakes grape grower and one of the founding partners of Glenora Wine Cellars. In 1978, with Doug in college, his folks bought the old Rapalee farm, including its remaining 115 acres of land; the twenty-room house, nearly in ruins since it was abandoned in 1929; and the Rapalee family cemetery.

If you were looking for ghosts, you would probably start your search in a cemetery or in an old, dilapidated house. Since this place had both, neighbors claimed it was haunted. Although the Miles family moved into the renovated mansion unfazed by the local ghost stories, strange noises, unexplained events, and actual sightings turned them into believers. They even hired a clairvoyant to confirm that as many as seven spirits are wandering the farm.

Ghosts or no ghosts, Doug switched his studies from architecture to viticulture, intent on developing a vineyard at what promised to be a nearly perfect site. Ties to Glenora provided his first market for the grapes, and, as the vineyard expanded, as many as seventeen wineries came to depend on the vineyard's fruit.

It was Doug's father, William Miles, who introduced his son to Chateau Petrus, Bordeaux's most intensely concentrated, richly flavored, and unique red wine. Grapes for this legendary wine are grown in a "buttonhole" of clay-rich soil, much like the soil near this part of Seneca Lake. Inspired by similarities in terroir with the vineyards of Pomerol, and using historic clones from that region, the two men established Miles Wine Cellars and set out on a mission to make Finger Lakes wines in the Petrus tradition.

"Milestone" represents the current progress in that effort. This blend of 80 percent Cabernet Franc and 20 percent Merlot has a dense, red-purple color; distinctive aromas meld wild blueberry, cassis, red cherry, violet, minerals, brown sugar, and a tobacco leaf note; accents of cassis, bitter chocolate, and white pepper are concentrated with layers of ripe, chewy, mouth-filling fruit. The Cabernet Franc component adds spice, garden-herb, and a tobacco-leaf note to the aroma of the wine; Merlot, especially affected by the clay, adds volume, silky-smooth tannins, and firmness to the finish.

As Cabernet Franc gains momentum in the Finger Lakes, Doug has taken a fancy to it as a varietal. His hands-on skills in the vineyard are on display with complex aromas of blackberries, black cherries, and a hint of eucalyptus; notes of burnt caramel, chocolate, cranberry, and spice predominate in the mouth; the smooth, smokey finish is long and lingering.

Easy-drinking Miles Chardonnay is approachable, versatile, and food-friendly. It begins with lemon custard aromas and toasted oak that give way to generous ripe flavors of pear and tropical fruit with a slightly sweet honeyed edge. It's nicely restrained with smoky notes backing up taut lemony fruit on mid-palate, leaving a long, fresh, precisely structured finish.

This is a vineyard-driven enterprise. As an experienced and respected grower, Doug devotes his full time to the grapevines and relinquishes winemaking to neighboring facilities. At harvest, he delivers his prime fruit to Fox Run and Lakewood Vineyards for custom winemaking in separate tanks and barrels, designated for Miles Wine Cellars.

The unique sense of balance and history makes this an important stop on any serious exploration of the Seneca Lake province. It's not only a picture-book vineyard, but you can taste handcrafted wines in a haunted lakeside mansion.

19

2634 Route 14
Penn Yan, NY 14527
(315) 536-7524

Hours: Monday–Saturday,
10:00 a.m.–5:00 p.m.;
Sunday, 11:00 a.m.–
5:00 p.m.

www.prejeanwinery.com

Prejean Winery

James and Elizabeth Prejean belong to the long list of city dwellers who sought a better life on the land. In 1978 they settled down on a farm near Seneca Lake, where they planted nine acres of grapes and eventually established an important winery. More vineyards were added through the years, to total the thirty-seven acres currently planted to Riesling, Chardonnay, Gewürztraminer, and Merlot, along with Marechal Foch, Cayuga, and Vignoles.

For most of its history, Prejean has made good but not particularly noteworthy wines. In recent vintages, however, quality has stepped up considerably. Tom Prejean, who has assumed management of the winery, credits Cornell and the Geneva Experiment Station for their research and development programs, and for making technical information available to the industry. He points to advancements in vineyard management, varietal selection, and winemaking technology for raising wines to a higher overall level. "They've turned grape growers into wine growers," says Tom.

Better farming practices, including shoot positioning, weed control, and environmentally friendly irrigation—not to mention maintaining the health and balance of the vineyard—are all factors. Tom attributes improvement in quality to the harvesting of grapes for flavor rather than ripeness parameters, and he is particularly proud of his distinctive Rieslings.

The Dry Riesling is a sleek, rich, and elegant wine, with aromas of peaches, pears, and honeysuckle. It's nearly dry on the palate with hints of spicy peach, apple, and lime, and a graceful, lingering finish.

Semi-Dry Riesling has a lovely confectionery bouquet and concentrated flavors of peaches, honey, and marzipan. This wine isn't a blockbuster, but it's elegant and refined nonetheless, with a wonderful sense of harmony and flavor.

Jim Zimar is a well-traveled winemaker who seems to have found a comfortable home at Prejean. Skilled and thoughtful in the cellar, he won't give in to the compromises that were made in the early years. With Riesling, he uses a direct-to-press method for small lots. When whole clusters are pressed, the juice has minimal contact with the grape skins, resulting in less extraction of bitterness from the tannins. And, since seeds are not crushed, their astringent characters don't end up in the wine. This gentle handling is common for Champagne grapes, but considered too meticulous and labor-intensive for most still wines. At Prejean, this minimalist approach preserves and expresses the true varietal character of the vineyard's Riesling.

Progressive and innovative, Prejean Winery has become a pacesetter in the Finger Lakes for its carefully cultivated grapevines and its integrated use of technology alongside good, old fashioned winemaking.

Red Newt Cellars/
Red Newt Cellars Winery & Bistro

This is all about one of the Finger Lakes' most talented husband and wife teams, David and Debra Whiting, and it began with good chemistry, or, perhaps, good biology. The couple met while she was conducting research in microbiology at Cornell and he was putting his own biology background into practice as a winemaker. When Debra changed careers and started a catering business, the path was set toward an extraordinary food and wine collaboration.

The couple's first home had a small pond, which, at springtime, teemed with a local species of the red-spotted newt. They called their place "Newt Puddle," and the little creature would eventually inspire a name for their dream venture. "Red Newt," besides its sense of place and graphic image, symbolizes the personal, unpretentious style of the winery and bistro David and Debra have run since 1999.

David's earliest experience was at Sayre Fulkerson's farm, pressing grapes during fall harvest. Next, he persuaded Bob McGregor to take him on at Keuka Lake's McGregor Winery, where he labored at cellar chores before assuming the responsibility for making wine. After three vintages, he joined Chateau Lafayette Reneau as head winemaker and then consulted on the development of Standing Stone Vineyard. When the old Wickham Winery property became available, it presented David with an opportunity to make his own wines.

One glaring oddity about Red Newt is the fact that they do not own their own vineyards and must purchase all of their grapes. However, long-term contracts with dependable grapegrowers provide exceptional fruit, including some rare Syrah from Jim Hazlitt's Sawmill Creek Vineyards.

David enjoys working with the Riesling grape, particularly, he says, since it is so perfectly suited to the region. Fermentation, in stainless steel, is stopped with some residual sweetness, an interpretation that shows lovely slate and lime notes and honeysucklelike scents. The rich fruit and juicy acidity capture, in his own words, the "quintessential personality" of Finger Lakes Rieslings. His Riesling Reserve is exquisitely dry and elegantly aromatic, with overtones of tangerine, apricot, and citrus fruit, finishing in long length and floral delicacy.

For production of Cabernet Franc, another good regional fit, David looks to the Burgundian model. Gentle crushing includes some whole

3675 Tichenor Road
Hector, NY 14841
(607) 546-4100

Winery Hours:
Monday–Saturday,
10:00 a.m.–5:00 p.m.;
Sunday, noon–5:00 p.m.
Restaurant Hours: Call for schedule

www.rednewt.com

clusters and stems; aging in oak cooperage encourages the development of complexities in the wine; small amounts of Merlot and Cabernet Sauvignon are utilized to fine-tune the finished blend. Red Newt Cabernet Franc somehow reminds me of walking through a garden of herbs and violets. Successive vintages display bright cranberry and raspberry fruit characters, a bit of green pepper and clove, and, buried deep within the palate, hints of cool mint and rich chocolate.

The lake-facing side of the facility provides a restaurant space for Debra, including an outdoor deck where you can contemplate a glorious sunset while dining on innovative wine country cuisine. Using an Alice Waters cookbook as her bible and the concept of Chez Panisse as her guide, Debra's menu is based on spanking-fresh local ingredients, and it changes every three weeks or so to stay in the rhythm of seasonal availability. She knows the provenance of every morsel of food she serves, and she keeps in close contact with local suppliers to stay abreast of what's ready to harvest on their farms.

Debra is well supported in her efforts by purveyors such as Organic Cornucopia, in nearby Rock Stream. She consults with owner Modesto Cappelluti in January to determine the mix of greens, vegetables, and herbs he will grow for the bistro in a designated section of his farm. McDonald Farm supplies pasture-raised chickens, Seneca Smokehouse supplies free-range Cayuga ducks, and chèvre from Lively Run Goat Dairy appears in one form or another on practically every menu. When it comes to desserts, Debra can point to "that orchard over there" as the place where the evening's cherries or peaches were grown—Twin Oaks Farm is just across the street from Red Newt. You can't get more local than that.

The Whitings' efforts go hand in hand. David's wines are food friendly, and Debra's menus complement his winemaking style. Together they create an honest expression of regionality and locality, whether on a dish or in a glass.

Silver Thread Vineyard

1401 Caywood Road
Lodi, NY 14860
(607) 582-6116

Hours: Saturday and Sunday, noon–5:00 p.m. (May through November); other times by appointment

www.silverthreadwine.com

The notion of organic wines in the Finger Lakes is not as obvious as it might seem. While organic produce flourishes throughout the region, winegrowers generally have been reluctant to farm organically. Besides intensity of labor, tonnage per acre is much lower, creating a need for higher prices to offset the yields, and wines are sometimes unstable and relatively short-lived. But Richard Figiel, the man whom *Wine Spectator* calls a "viticulture guru," is on a mission to prove that sustainable farming can produce exceptional fruit and superior wines.

Richard was a New York City journalist who, while reporting on breakthough vintages in the 1970s, was drawn to the promise of greater wines in the Finger Lakes. He moved his family upstate, where he planted grapes and worked as editor, first for *Eastern Grape Grower and Winery News*, then for *International Wine Review*, before setting out to make wines for a living. His pursuit became Silver Thread Vineyards, a small, ideologically driven winery committed to natural farming and conservation, and he has been swimming against the tide now for more than twenty years.

Since his earliest plantings in 1982, Richard has been the most radical proponent of change in Finger Lakes viticulture. He uses mulch and compost instead of chemical fertilizers and adds white clover as a cover crop between his vines to compete with weeds. (Clover adds nitrogen to the soil, essential for the growth of the stem and leaves, and eliminates the need to apply potentially harmful nitrates.) An old favorite tool, the French plow, is used to remove weeds from under the vine rows instead of using herbicides. As an alternative to herbicides or synthetic pesticides, only naturally occurring sprays, including elemental sulfur, seaweed extract, fish emulsion, and a tea made on the farm from local horsetail plants, are part of his intensively managed program.

Planned to the scale of his fifteen-acre vineyard, there is almost no aspect of the winery that escapes efficiencies. A low-tech cellar is set into the hillside for natural insulation and temperature control; water supply is gravity-fed from a spring next to the vineyard, and southern exposure provides natural heat and light to the tasting room. Small batches of grapes are pressed in a primitive basket. No chemical additives or processing aids are used in winemaking, with strictly natural materials employed for fining and filtration, and a minimal dosage of sulfur added for stability. Another technique is canopy management, in which the leaf and cane canopy is opened to bring in sunlight, to reduce the chance of mold and rot and eliminate the need for fungicides.

With silky-smooth texture and gobs of delicious fruit, Silver Thread's elegant Chardonnays are testament to the winemaking craft. Straw-gold in color, the wine is rich and ripe, but still balanced, with waves of pear tart, lime, honey, and tropical layers, creamy-buttery accents, and smoky, minerally undertones. A vibrant, juicy finish reveals hints of oak and vanilla.

Pinot Noir fruit is selectively hand-harvested in perfect condition, then fermented with wild yeasts. The indigenous yeasts add complexity, since they provide more complex organisms at work during fermentation. The resulting wine is light-to-medium bodied and Beaujolais-like, garnet red in color, with fresh, concentrated flavors of Bing cherry, cranberry, raspberry, strawberry, and cherry cola, and complex, savory notes in the bouquet. It's a good, sound, easy-drinking Pinot Noir, true to variety and region.

These wines have found niche markets, not only in some of our local restaurants, but in a handful of small, enlightened cafés in New York City's Soho and Greenwich Village neighborhoods. Still, your best bet is to follow the narrow, unpaved end of Caywood Road heading down toward Seneca Lake and take a look at this place for yourself. There you will see a beacon to the future of winemaking.

Standing Stone Vineyards/Smokehouse Café

9934 Route 414
Hector, NY 14841
(800) 803-7135

Winery Hours:
Monday–Friday,
noon–5:00 p.m.; Saturday,
11:00 a.m.–6:00 p.m.,
Sunday, noon–5:00 p.m.
Smokehouse Café Hours:
Friday and Sunday,
11:30 a.m.–5:00 p.m.;
Saturday, 11:30 a.m.–
6:00 p.m. (mid-June through
mid-October)

www.standingstonewines.com

Vintners and growers share the same concern—growing the right grapes in the right locations. Over thirty years ago, Charles Fournier and Guy DeVeaux of Gold Seal chose this site over a hundred others for their vinifera plantings, so, when Tom and Marti Macinski acquired the property in 1991, they inherited vineyards of exceptional pedigree.

What was originally an old chicken farm overlooking Seneca Lake was planted with four acres of Riesling in 1972, then with eight acres of Chardonnay in 1974. The old, sadly neglected Gold Seal "Area 13" was lovingly restored by the high-energy Macinskis, as they added Gewürztraminer, Vidal, Pinot Noir, Cabernet Sauvignon, and Merlot.

Tom is a senior engineer for IBM, and Marti is an attorney with a part-time practice in nearby Watkins Glen. The aura of the Finger Lakes and its winemaking traditions attracted the Binghamton natives to the project they named Standing Stone Vineyards, inspired by Indian legend. The earliest inhabitants of this region believed when you found the "standing stone," you found perfection. For Tom and Marti, it was indeed the perfect place to establish an important winery.

Winemaking facilities are housed in a barnlike structure standing among the original Riesling vines, and a dilapidated chicken coop was converted into a tasting room. The bright yellow color of the Standing Stone complex is a sure sign that something exciting is going on inside. The goal, to grow and produce distinctive wines from this coveted site, was realized as soon as the first vintage in 1993. With David Whiting (see Red Newt Cellars) guiding the winemaking team, Standing Stone came from out of nowhere to win a silver medal at the San Francisco International Wine Competition for Riesling and a gold medal at the New York Wine and Food Classic for Gewürztraminer. The following year, Cabernet Franc captured the New York State "Governor's Cup" as best in show.

Ironically, making the best wines sometimes means returning to some old traditions. When Russell Hearn, an Australian born and trained enologist, joined Standing Stone as consultant in 2000, he began to emphasize natural, uncomplicated winemaking practices. With the production of "unfiltered" wines, Standing Stone is moving increasingly in a rarefied direction. It's the first-ever attempt at commercial unfiltered bottling in the Finger Lakes.

Filtration occurs when wine is clarified before bottling, and many claim that heavy filtration can strip a wine of significant properties and flavors—

in effect, its personality. However, there are years when wines develop excessive levels of brettanomyces from residual yeast, and the unpleasant "horsey" characters must surely be filtered out. So, filtering decisions at Standing Stone are made vintage by vintage, variety by variety.

Hand-harvested grapes need only travel a few hundred feet from the vines to the winery, ideal for Pinot Noir grapes, since they are so sensitive to handling. Prior to the start of fermentation, the grapes are cold-soaked for three to five days, to gain maximum nonalcoholic extraction. Following traditional Burgundian farmyard techniques, they are fermented in small, open-top fermenters and pressed in a small, very gentle bladder press. The wine is aged in a combination of French and American (Missouri oak) barrels for up to twelve months, then bottle-aged for at least six months.

The unfiltered, handcrafted Pinot Noir displays heady aromas of blueberry, pepper, and violets, which unfold to lots of black cherry, plum, cassis, and spice. Its tapestrylike richness is supported by firm tannins and a long, refined finish with hints of underlying mint and cocoa, resulting in a concentrated yet sophisticated wine. Now and then, expect a bottle to throw a "noble" natural sediment sometime during its evolution, but that doesn't dissuade the band of followers who are extremely loyal to this wine.

Despite her genteel manner, Marti Macinski is known for her competitive nature, and she cites trailblazers Konstantin Frank and Hermann Wiemer as her models for a focused product line and consistently high-quality wines. She would be the first to point out that Standing Stone's success is linked to the winery's auspicious location, or what she calls "our unique patch of dirt." According to Marti, "The less we do with it and the more we maximize how well that dirt shows through, the more we're doing justice to where we are."

These rustic country wines provide an excellent match to the inspired food prepared and served by Christian and Elizabeth Chiron in the Smokehouse Café, a charcuterie (French-style deli) attached to the tasting room. Christian is a native of the French Loire region, where he studied the art of charcuterie-traiteur before plying his trade in America. His skills have been wonderfully adapted to picnic-style fare, like hickory-smoked rotisserie chicken, garlic sausages, housemade pâtés, and a delicious onion soup, spiked with red wine and topped with croutons and strips of Emmenthaler. A cheese board offers a selection of local and French cheeses with country breads from Grist Mill Bakery, and ingredients for generous salads are supplied by neighboring farms. Desserts might include toasted Apple-Walnut Cake, Black Cherry–Cabernet Sorbet, or Peach-Riesling Ice Cream.

Visitors to the winery may enjoy Smokehouse Café's offerings with Standing Stone wines by the glass on an open-air deck. Picnic tables, decorated with pots of fresh flowers, provide a view of vineyard and lake while you share some of life's glories.

9322 Route 414
Lodi, NY 14860
(607) 582-6450

Winery/Brewery Hours:
Daily, 10:00 a.m.–5:00 p.m.
Ginny Lee Café: Lunch,
Monday–Saturday,
11:00 a.m.–4:00 p.m.;
Sunday, noon–4:00 p.m.;
Brunch, Sunday,
10:00 a.m.–2:00 p.m.

www.wagnervineyards.com

Wagner Vineyards/ Wagner Valley Brewery/ Ginny Lee Café

The vineyards of Bill Wagner's youth were his playground. In later years, they would become his passion and his life's work. Bill returned home to the family farm at the end of World War II after service in the Navy, planted a vineyard in Lodi, and followed in his father's footsteps as a grape wholesaler. Three decades later, he decided to turn his grapes into wine. Today, the octagonal building that Bill conjured up to save space is a Finger Lakes landmark, housing an operation that has been on the leading edge of developments in wine country for the past quarter century.

A reserved man of quiet intensity, Bill Wagner has a demeanor that does not suggest an industry revolutionary. While entrepreneurs of his stature are often larger-than-life figures, he ambles around the complex with hardly a nod of recognition from the hundreds of guests who visit his winery every day.

The first crush in 1978 produced 50,000 gallons of juice, and the wines followed in 1979. It's not surprising that one of the first-released wines was a DeChaunac, since Bill was already growing this red variety for the Taylor Wine Company. As a stand-alone varietal, the French hybrid reveals inelegant portlike characters and puckery tannins, and, although practically everyone else in the Finger Lakes has given up on it, he has persevered. According to Bill, DeChaunac has better utilization of sunlight than any other grapevine, and by restraining its vigor and removing some of the junglelike foliage, he has coaxed aromas of peppers and eucalyptus from the grapes and rounded off hard edges in oak.

His winery now produces a total of thirty estate-grown wines, all from his 240 acres of vineyards, and all over the varietal map. Besides native Delaware and Niagara, and hybrid Cayuga, Vignoles, Seyval Blanc, and DeChaunac, the winery offers Gewürztraminer, Riesling, Pinot Noir, Cabernet Franc, Merlot, and Cabernet Sauvignon. But over the years, Wagner Vineyards has been best-known for rich and complex yet elegant and polished Chardonnays, beginning in 1980 with a wine that became a milestone for the fledgling industry. Unlike other Finger Lakes wineries still hand-picking their premium grapes, Bill produced this wine from mechanically harvested grapes, a method, he insists, that results in healthier fruit. Since then, barrel-fermented, stainless steel–fermented, and reserve versions of Chardonnay have been at the center of the Wagner portfolio.

An eminently quaffable "unwooded" Chardonnay, bright, fruit-centered, and balanced, with lovely aromatics and crisp acidity, reveals notes of lime, green apple, grapefruit, lemongrass, and a liquid mineral character.

Reserve Chardonnay shows a penetrating, aromatic bouquet of ripe tropical and exotic fruits marked by a pronounced fragrance of new oak and vanilla. The palate is packed with apple, peach, and tangerine fruit, concentrated and lush, with a rich, buttery, mouthfeel supported by crisp acidity, firm structure, and a lengthy finish of spice, toast, and smoky oak.

Behind these wines, two talented winemakers, John Herbert and Ann Raffetto, have worked as a team since the early days of the venture. "We know the vineyard well and know how to get the most from its grapes," says Ann, whose credentials include a degree from UC Davis. John, who claims his interest began when he received a home winemaking kit for his twenty-first birthday, explains, "Even when you make mistakes, you learn, and we've learned a lot together."

Bill has always believed that wine with food is one of life's most important alliances, and, in 1983, he built a café adjacent to the winery and named it after his granddaughter, Ginny Lee. CIA-trained executive chef Vachel Mitchell has devised a menu of salads, sandwiches, pizzas, and pastas, artfully prepared and influenced by the winery.

The chef's Reserve French Onion Soup is spiked with both red and white wines, topped with seasoned croutons and melted Provolone; the Grilled Chicken Sandwich is a boneless breast marinated in red wine and herbs, grilled, and served on a hard roll with lettuce, tomato, onion, and roasted garlic aïoli. Lunch on the deck overlooks a picturesque valley of vines.

"It takes a lot of beer to make good wine," insists Bill, who figured, since beer was part of winemaking culture, especially after long days during harvest season, maybe he ought to make his own. So he added a twenty-barrel, German-style brewhouse to the winery, with an annual capacity of 3,500 barrels, and hired brewmaster Andrew Cummings to create artisan-style brews. After five years, Cummings left Wagner Valley Brewery for a college teaching position and turned the job over to his able assistant, Bernie Hauf.

Sled Dog Doppelbock is a very malty, full-bodied lager brewed with Munich, dark caramel, and chocolate malts and Northern Brewer and Tettnang hops. Flavors start out with caramel and chocolate and finish with just a touch of hops. Sled Dog Trippel Reserve is a heavier, more concentrated dark lager, teeming with sweet, malty aromas. It's full of lush, fruity flavors and has a note of hop bitterness on the finish. Awards in competition, especially by the bock beers, are but another feather in Bill's cap.

I've known Bill Wagner for twenty-five years, and I am certain he has more ambition and more energy than many men half his age. He's approaching eighty, and he still plays racquetball every morning before coming to work. Although he has relinquished office management to daughter Laura and vineyard management to son John, Bill remains fully engaged with the continued growth of his company. His vision was to create wines in the Finger Lakes that belong in the company of the great wines of the world. By almost any measure, he has succeeded in making that vision a reality.

SLED DOG STEW

Serves 6 to 8

Sled Dog, a malty, full-bodied craft lager with notes of caramel and chocolate, is the key ingredient in Wagner Valley's version of Carbonnades Flamande, Belgium's rich national dish. The hearty stew is an excellent bracer against our cold, snowy winter days in the Finger Lakes.

½ cup all-purpose flour

1 teaspoon salt, plus more as needed

1 teaspoon freshly ground white pepper, plus more as needed

3 pounds beef chuck, trimmed of fat and cut into ½-inch cubes

2 tablespoons olive oil

¼ pound bacon, chopped

2 cloves garlic, minced

3 carrots, sliced lengthwise and cut into ½-inch dice

3 parsnips, peeled, sliced lengthwise, and cut into ½-inch dice

2 cups sweet corn kernels

3 bay leaves

3 cups beef stock

½ tablespoon chopped fresh thyme

2 cups diced russet potatoes

12 ounces Sled Dog Doppelbock, or another dark, full-bodied lager

2 cups pearl onions

Combine the flour, salt, and white pepper in a bowl. Toss the beef in the seasoned flour and shake off the excess.

Place the olive oil and bacon in a 1-gallon stockpot and set over medium heat. Once the bacon begins to render its fat, add the beef and sauté for about 5 minutes, stirring often, only until the bacon begins to crisp. Add the garlic, carrots, parsnips, sweet corn kernels, and bay leaves. Sauté for about 5 minutes. Add the beef stock, thyme, and potatoes and bring to a boil. When the stew boils, decrease the heat to medium-low, and add the Sled Dog and pearl onions. Cover the stockpot and simmer, stirring often, for 2 hours.

Remove from the heat, discard the bay leaves, and adjust seasonings to taste.

For a thicker stew, remove about 1 cup of the broth, place it in a bowl, and add some of the remaining seasoned flour, then add the mixture back to the stew.

Note: Enjoy this hearty stew with some warm biscuits and garlic mashed potatoes. For a complementary beverage, buy a 25-ounce bottle of Sled Dog Doppelbock, use half for this recipe, and drink the rest with the meal; or try the stew with a full-bodied red wine such as Wagner Vineyards Cabernet Sauvignon. Venison may be substituted for the beef chuck.

FARMS/FOOD PRODUCERS

Blue Heron Farm

A full-grown great blue heron is as tall as an eight-year-old boy and weighs as much as a human baby. It is four feet tall, with a wingspan that reaches nearly six feet. It fishes and hunts around Seneca Lake, patiently patrolling the water's edge, then lifts off into flight, wings flapping slowly and purposefully. The beautiful bird is a common sight near the farm Robin Ostfeld and her partner, Lou Johns, named for the native blue heron, an enterprise that has changed the way people eat around here.

1641 Shaw Road
Lodi, NY 14860
(607) 582-6336

Hours: By appointment

www.ithacamarket.com/ vendors.asp

The couple took a circuitous route to becoming inspirational Finger Lakes farmers. Following graduation from Evergreen State College in Olympia, Washington, where she majored in sociology and he in natural history, they started a truck garden on a patch of land in the Chehalis River basin, inspired by Robin's summer internship on a blueberry farm. After five years, they moved back East to be closer to family, purchased the old Hallet place near Seneca Lake, and started a diversified vegetable farm that adheres to ecologically responsible growing practices.

Close proximity to the lake provides more than the advantage of bird-watching. In spring and fall the ice-free lake moderates air temperatures along its shores, and the gently sloping landscape boasts fertile, gravel-laden soil that is ideal for farming. With the benefit of extensions on either end of the season, Robin and Lou have taken an additional step to reduce economic risk by diversifying their business. They grow forty different row crops to supply the Ithaca Farmer's Market, Greenstar Co-op, local restaurants, and a CSA (Community Supported Agriculture) program.

In a CSA, the farmer contracts directly with a group of consumers to grow their food. Consumers receive a weekly box of produce for a fixed price, paid at the start of the season. By eliminating the middleman, farmers receive enough compensation to sustainably produce foods in an alternative to commercial farming. While CSA members account for only 15 percent of Blue Heron's revenues, it's an important part of the operation, especially for continuity.

While most CSA farms run subscription programs during the summer, Blue Heron instituted a "winter share" CSA, which provides needed income during January, February, and March. Just over 100 members pay for shares in the fall, guaranteeing Robin and Lou a year-round livelihood, and payment in advance also eases their financial burden in the early growing season.

On alternate weeks, deliveries are made to distribution points in Rochester, Watkins Glen, and Ithaca. Throughout the winter, bountiful boxes may include carrots, potatoes, rutabagas, turnips, parsnips, onions, garlic, cabbage, winter squash, and pie pumpkins; if the weather cooperates, there might be early and late greens, including kale and collards. "We set ourselves the task of providing vegetables in winter because we didn't want to lose touch with our customers at the Farmer's Market after it closes in December," explains Robin.

Lou loves to grow heirloom varieties, but he insists they have some merit besides histories. He wants honest taste and reasonable productivity, and he is constantly experimenting with heirlooms to expand the storage varieties. A beautiful Italian eggplant, Rosa Bianca, light pink with shaded white stripes, has meaty texture and creamy, mild flavor, without a hint of bitterness; short, thick, rich-orange Chantenay carrots keep their crunchy, sweet flavor without becoming tough or woody; Gold Ball is a globe-shaped old English heirloom turnip with deep-yellow skin and flesh and a sharp, spicy flavor; oblong Irish Kennebec potatoes, outstanding in flavor, texture, and storage quality, tend to grow so big they are planted close together to keep the size down. What's most amazing is that we can eat these treasures all year long.

Blue Heron Farm, a successful example of organic agriculture, has been a fixture at the weekly Farmer's Market in Ithaca for nearly two decades. Tourists and locals flock to the produce with an almost religious fervor. Its permanent stall near the market's center provides a dependable source for so much of what is good about the regional food movement.

4590 Route 414
Burdett, NY 14818
(607) 546-8479

Hours: By appointment

Glendale Farm

A devout Christian and staunch prohibitionist, Dr. Thomas B. Welch objected to the use of wine in his church's communion service. In 1869, Welch and his son, Charles, gathered forty pounds of Concord grapes from the trellis in front of their house in Vineland, New Jersey. They cooked the grapes for a few minutes, squeezed out the juice through cloth bags, and poured the world's first processed fresh fruit juice into twelve quart bottles on the kitchen table. They called it "Dr. Welch's Unfermented Wine."

At first, the juice was donated to the church as alcohol-free sacramental "wine." Then, in 1892, Charles decided to test out his belief that the grape drink could be successful as a commercial product, and he set up a juice production facility on the family's property. To make his product more appealing to the general public, he changed its name to "Welch's Grape Juice," and soon the drink appeared at soda fountains alongside root beer and sarsaparilla. In 1896, Charles transferred juice production to Watkins Glen, New York, for access to a better supply of grapes.

Welch's eventually moved to Western New York and is today the world's largest processor of Concord grapes, pressing 300,000 tons a year into juice. But a few miles north of the old Watkins Glen juice plant, on a much smaller and more personal scale, Joe Ottati produces a high-quality, regionally expressive organic grape juice that has gained a loyal following in the Finger Lakes and beyond.

In 1977 the Patterson, New Jersey, native purchased Lester Funk's vineyard property on a beautiful slope above Seneca Lake, bordered by the trickling waterfalls of Fenton's Creek and the Lehigh Railroad right-of-way. He restored its overgrown vines and began pressing fresh juice from the grapes.

Fruit from the land dictates what Joe produces. While winemakers might fashion a wine with a skillful, carefully determined blending of grape varieties, Glendale Farm grape juice is the result of the "field blend," which means the components are assembled according to the proportion in which they grow in the vineyard. Joe inherited a vineyard that was two-thirds Concord to one-third Catawba, with small plantings of Delaware, Niagara, and Cayuga, so when he picks grapes for pressing, he picks two rows of Concord for every row of Catawba, then adds a smattering from the other varieties. Joe likens the process to making a sauce. Concord is the stock, the basic building block, and Catawba tempers the flavor and intensity to help build a better whole. The other varieties are considered just a pinch of seasoning that adds subtle spice to the recipe.

Concord and Catawba grapes are picked at the same time, which means that while the Concord grapes are fully ripe, the Catawbas are slightly underripe. Concord gives the blend its dark red-purple color; sweet, rich fruit; and generous mouthfeel; lower sugar and higher acid in the early Catawba grapes lift the flavors and add astringency, or "bite," to the character. The natural fruit acids also have a preservative effect on the juice.

For the first two years of operation Joe would harvest 800 to 900 pounds of grapes on a Friday morning, press on Friday afternoon, then sell fresh, unpasteurized juice at the Ithaca Farmer's Market on Saturday. In the early 1980s he found that New York City's Greenmarket customers would pay more for his juice, and he trucked half-gallon containers to the city every week throughout the season. "Grape juice is the hardest thing to make from grapes," he grumbles, since the unstable liquid is always on the verge of fermentation. In 1986 he decided to flash-pasteurize and bottle the juice at Royal Kedem Winery in Milton, New York, for more practical retail sale and distribution. At the same time, the vineyard obtained organic certification, and the grape juice found an important niche in the market.

Joe Ottati, it should be noted, wears many more hats than grape grower. His car repair shop keeps many of our aging Volvos on the road.

He is an antique car collector, an amateur race car driver, a metal sculptor and master welder, and a self-taught musician who regularly plucks his washtub bass in a local bluegrass band. But, all things considered, he is most passionate about his labors to produce the savory, satisfyingly sweet Glendale Farm grape juice and about the contribution he makes to the culinary riches of the Finger Lakes.

32

4484 Lakemont-Himrod Road
Dundee, NY 14837
(888) 874-1323

Hours: By appointment

www.masterstouchcoffee.com

Master's Touch Coffee Roasters

Wine drinkers favor varietal wines, such as Chardonnay, Cabernet, and Pinot Noir—each made from a single grape variety. Similarly, many serious coffee drinkers have embraced single-origin coffees from specific geographical regions. These pure, unblended coffees, each with a unique taste profile, are the passion of husband and wife team Borys and Karissa Polon, proprietors of Master's Touch Coffee Roasters.

Borys gave up a career in plant pathology and a position on the Cornell hydroponics research team for the coffee roasting business. When he and Karissa moved to a small farming community between Seneca and Keuka Lakes, they found the area awash in wines but without a drinkable cup of coffee. So, in 1993, they set out to provide premium, locally roasted coffees to cafes, restaurants, and gourmet groceries under the Master's Touch label.

Like our local wines, coffee beans get their distinctive character from where they are grown, and Borys allows each variety's signature flavors to take center stage. He considers himself a purist and insists that blending a variety like Ethiopian Harrar would mute its distinct blueberrylike aroma and wild, ambrosial flavors.

With a hands-on approach to microroasting, he considers the weight, volume, and water content of the bean, as well as the potential flavors he will derive from the degree of toastiness. He relies on meticulous notes from tasting trials to determine precisely when to remove beans from his small-batch drum roaster. Indeed, it takes surgical precision to release the proper intensity of flavor and individual properties of varieties such as Colombia Supremo or Tanzanian Peaberry.

Borys favors light to moderate roastness, which allows for the development of distinctive flavor notes and better mouthfeel. Lightly roasted high-quality beans exhibit increased body, low palate acidity, and a delicate nuttiness, while dark roasts are less lively and interesting.

Master's Touch supplies mostly single-origin coffees to coffee bars around the Finger Lakes, and Borys hand-tailors proprietary blends to restaurants like Suzanne in Lodi and Ports, Café in Geneva. When Jeff Ritter, co-owner of Ports, insisted on a distinctive coffee to complement his menu, Borys recommended Tanzanian Peaberry for its medium body, subtle brightness, and gentle winey tones. But many palates are sensitive to Peaberry's high acidity, and Jeff was not convinced. The solution was a fifty-fifty blend of Peabody and Indonesian

Sulawesi. The rich body of Sulawesi, with an earthy, spicy complexity, moderates the acids in Peaberry, and together they achieve a more complete coffee.

Since the intensity of the espresso brewing process can accentuate a bean's characters, blending is necessary to get a balanced cup. Borys blends his espresso from four carefully chosen varieties, each roasted separately according to a proprietary formula inspired by Northern Italian tradition.

Master's Touch espresso reveals a natural fruitiness; rich, full-bodied flavors with almost no acidity notes; and an excellent crema, the frothy top of espresso.

The Polons reveal a dedication to their artisan coffee operation that is unassuming and genuine. Each batch is a labor of love, elevating flavor consciousness to a higher level and satisfying even the most discriminating coffee drinker. They are bound and determined to make a mark in our region with the craft of small-batch roasting.

Meadowsweet Farm

26

The village of Lodi lies in prime dairy-farming country, with flat, low-lying, rich grassland. Meadowsweet Farm, grazed since the turn of the twentieth century, was dormant for about five years before Steve and Barbara Smith came to its rescue, utilizing modest yields of milk from a herd of twenty grass-fed cows to produce yogurt, kefir, and farmhouse cheeses.

2054 Smith Road
Lodi, NY 14860
(607) 582-6954

Hours: By appointment

www.meadowsweetfarm.com

Steve was working as a mission specialist for NASA and Barbara was a home-school teacher to their five children when they came across a magazine ad that offered a small, family-run yogurt company for sale. The opportunity to change their lives was irresistible, so they purchased the name, recipes, and equipment and moved the operation to the Lodi farm for its proximity to the Ithaca market. They started milking cows and delivered the first batch of Meadowsweet yogurt to Greenstar Co-op by the fall of 1995.

Their herd of gentle, light-brown Jersey cows are excellent grazers and produce nutrient-rich milk on a diet of nearly 100 acres of organic grass and clover pastures. Jerseys are known for creamy milk with a shade of yellow color from carotene in the fresh grass during spring and summer. Subtle variations in flavor take place throughout the year as their diet changes from dandelions and bluegrass, to orchard grass and timothy, to clover and alfalfa, and then to hay in winter.

Fresh whole milk is pasteurized at 185 degrees, cooled to 110 degrees, and then inoculated with yogurt cultures and allowed to thicken for three hours in a 100-gallon vat. Kefir follows the same process as yogurt but ferments overnight and at a lower temperature. Stirred-in flavors might include maple syrup from W. E. Allen's sugar maples, wildflower honey from Duane Waid's bees, or fresh-picked strawberries from nearby Blue

Heron Farm. No pectins, juices, or thickeners are added to dilute the natural taste.

Both products are delivered to stores in Ithaca within three days, ensuring fresh taste and live and active cultures. The number of these cultures decreases to one half of the original concentration in two weeks, so Meadowsweet buys back any yogurt or kefir past its prime.

Cheesemaking on the farm begins with gentle heating of the raw milk in a vat, then adding "starter" and vegetable rennet. This causes the milk to curdle, forming small grainy lumps (curds) within the residue (whey). When ready, the mixture is run off into shallow tubs, where the whey drains while the curds set together. After the curd is cut into manageable-size wedges, hand-turning, or "cheddaring," takes place before packing into cylindrical molds. The cheeses then go into a temperature-controlled maturing store, where they are gently aged for ten to fourteen months and regularly checked for developing flavors.

Barbara explains that raw milk cheese is linked to the old French farmsteads that made excellent, high-flavor cheese, yet couldn't afford pasteurization. Meadowsweet cheese has the natural, farm-fresh flavor of raw milk, more pronounced and complex than any Cheddar cheese I've tried before, full of bite and nuances and the natural golden color of grass-fed Jersey milk. It melts easily, so it's great for cooking, but I prefer simply to savor a wedge of it with a sociable pint of local ale.

Each week the Smiths handcraft about 100 gallons of yogurt, twenty-five gallons of kefir, and an eighty-gallon batch of hard cheese. Like fine vintage wines from a small vineyard, these single-herd products have special flavors with subtle qualities found only in a small local dairy.

31

96 Hunt Road
Rock Stream, NY 14878
(607) 243-3691

Hours: By appointment

Organic Cornucopia

For a Finger Lakes chef, purveyors like Organic Cornucopia are the next best thing to having a vegetable garden right outside the kitchen door. Good cooking begins with selection of ingredients, and, as interesting, freshly harvested local produce works its way onto the menus of progressive restaurants, the people who oversee the kitchens prefer to buy directly from someone they know.

Modesto Cappelluti descends from an Italian immigrant family that grew vegetables and peaches in the backyard of their home in Sheepshead Bay, Brooklyn, and he has been a gardener for as long as he can remember. During his student days at Brooklyn College he started the school's first gardening club and created a community garden on campus. When his efforts caught the eye of Mayor Koch, he was asked to lead a task force to develop "vest pocket gardens" on unimproved lots throughout the borough.

After they were married, Modesto and his wife, Gayle, packed up and moved out of the city and onto an old farmstead planted with a vineyard and sugarbush and overlooking Seneca Lake. Beginning in 1996, they cleared brush, tilled the ground, planted a variety of heirloom tomatoes and potatoes, and raised them organically. That year the entire crop was sold to Manhattan gourmet grocer Balducci's. Heirlooms sell at a higher retail price than standard varieties, and Balducci's was prepared to pay it.

But after a few years, regular deliveries to the city proved impractical, and besides, these varieties had not been bred for long-distance shipping. They really needed to be sold close to where they were produced, and opening up a local market for their specialty crops became the next challenge for the Cappellutis.

"The way I sell my crops," says Modesto, "is to get people to taste them." He found that once chefs taste an heirloom, they never go back to hybrids, and they appreciate quality produce when it arrives at their doors within a few hours after harvest. The farm's treasures include Purple de Milpa Tomatillo, which has a lovely lavender rather than green skin, and Turkish Orange eggplant. This is a tiny, brilliant orange fruit that looks like a mini-tomato/squash hybrid. It's less than an inch across and has a sweet, slightly perfumey flesh. Modesto experiments with the best place to grow each variety of tomato the way vintners find the best terroir for their wine grapes. His glorious selection includes distinctively spicy Brandywine, exceptionally sweet Sun Gold, and seedless Golden Nugget, a slightly oval fruit with a deep yellow color.

In early October, Modesto picks his four acres of organically grown Concord grapes. The best-looking fruit is sold as table grapes, and the rest is cold-pressed into fresh grape juice. Because it is unfiltered, there is still sediment at the bottom, but the flavor of this raw juice pulp is sweet, like plums, and balanced by a bracing berrylike acidity.

Chefs like Deb Whiting at Red Newt and Art Kelly at Glenora are always searching for novelties to satisfy restless foodies, and they depend on Modesto for ever more exotic ingredients. He and his restaurant clients comb through seed company catalogs at the beginning of each growing season to determine what crops they want him to grow and what quantities they expect to use per week. The newest focus is on mixed lettuce varieties such as mizuna, Tango, and Dark Lollo Rossa, and fresh herbs including summer thyme, orange thyme, and specialty mints.

"I'm in a partnership with the earth to grow the best food possible," says Modesto, who, like a botanist, cultivates more than two hundred herbs, vegetables, fruits, and flowers on the farm. As an urban gardener, he learned respect for the soil, efficiency of technique, and a methodical approach to growing. Today, his horn of plenty at Organic Cornucopia has achieved its own, quiet fame.

34

1798 County Road 4
Seneca Castle, NY 14547
(315) 781-0482

Hours: By appointment

www.pedersenfarms.com

Pedersen Farms

It seems like old times now that Rick and Laura Pedersen are growing hops in the Finger Lakes. A hundred years ago, hop fields covered over forty thousand acres of upstate New York farmland, producing nearly 22 million pounds of ingredient for breweries all over America—over 80 percent of the nation's crop. But the arrival of Prohibition in 1920 resulted in the demise of commercial hopyards in the state. By the time beer drinking was legal again in 1933, production had shifted to the Pacific Northwest.

Derived from the cones of a perennial climbing plant, hops give beer and ale their distinctive flavor, bitterness, and aroma, as well as provide a natural preservative to the drinks. Growing hops for beer is much like growing grapes for wine—the soil, the climate, and the farmer's care of the vines greatly affect the taste and aroma of the delicate hop flowers.

At Pedersen Farms, conditions are close to ideal. Although two varieties, Perle and Nugget, did not produce economically viable yields and were discontinued, Cascade, Mt. Hood, and Willamette varieties, from Washington State cuttings, yield 800 pounds of hops each season on the half-acre in current production. Since Rick had farmed that section before, he knew the hops would thrive in its deep, loamy, well-draining soil.

The hopyard consists of a sixteen-foot-high trellis system, planted three feet apart, with twelve feet between rows. Young vines are trained in May and bloom throughout the summer. As hops reach maturity, which begins in mid-August, vines are harvested by hand and then transported to a cleaning shed, where machinery separates leaves and stems from the cones. Next, they are dried with forced hot air at 120 degrees and carefully controlled to retain essential oils. From there, the hops are milled into pellets and packed in airtight bags for shipping.

At one time, Rick entertained the idea of starting his own microbrewery, but, as his farm operation expanded in scale, another venture was out of the question. Instead, he decided that the next best thing would be to grow some of the ingredients. The first crop of fresh hops was delivered to Ithaca Beer Company and used to brew an acclaimed Double IPA, and Wagner Valley Brewery now uses Rick's hops for India Pale Ale.

Iroquois communities once prospered in this area. They maintained herds of milk cows and raised hogs for meat; they planted fields of corn and gardens of vegetables. The Indians lived in handsome, multifamily houses, often called "castles," and the name Seneca Castle is derived from one such village.

Besides its small-scale production of hops, this Seneca Castle farm grows vegetables and field crops in the fertile soil, following in the footsteps of the original inhabitants. The Pedersens supply processors, wholesalers, farm markets, and grocery stores throughout the region. Asparagus and cucumbers are sold to Wegman's, cabbage and snap beans to Birdseye Foods, and a wide range of produce makes its way to the tables of restaurants through the Finger Lakes Culinary Bounty.

Red Jacket Orchards

Saguwatha, the famous orator of the Seneca Indians, was known as "Red Jacket" because of the colorful uniform jacket given him by the British troops during the American Revolution. His name inspired an apple orchard, originally planted along the rolling hills of Seneca Lake in 1917 and now stretching to over 500 acres of apple trees and summer fruits.

957 Route 5 (at Route 20)
Geneva, NY 14456
(315) 781-2749
(800) 828-9410

Hours:
Daily, 8:00 a.m.–7:00 p.m.
(June through December);
Daily, 8:00 a.m.–5:00 p.m.
(January through May)

www.redjacketorchards.com

Joseph and Emily Nicholson operated a large poultry farm in Bethpage, on Long Island, but in 1958 were forced to sell the property to make way for the Wantaugh-Oyster Bay Parkway. The Finger Lakes were familiar territory to Joe, since he regularly attended poultry clinics at Cornell. Shortly after responding to a newspaper listing for Red Jacket Farm, he purchased the upstate property, moved his family to Geneva, and began selling fruit at a roadside stand.

Today, the Nicholson family grows sixteen varieties of apples and four varieties of strawberries, as well as sweet and sour cherries; rhubarb; peaches; plums, including Greengage and Mirabelle, prized in Europe but unheard of in the United States; and apricots, which were thought to be impossible to grow on the East Coast. The operation has grown to include four different farms located along the rolling, glacially derived soils in the area from Geneva to Penn Yan.

Plantings include 375 acres of apples, mainly on dwarf rootstock that allows for planting up to 1,100 trees per acre (compared to the old standard of seventy-five full-sized trees to the acre). These smaller trees receive better sunlight and air movement to the fruiting wood, yielding larger and more colorful, flavorful apples while decreasing the need for excessive insect and disease control. When the orchards are in full bloom, it's one of the loveliest sights in the Finger Lakes countryside.

Brian Nicholson, one of four members of the family's third generation on the company payroll, is an outspoken proponent of Finger Lakes agriculture, and he delights in calling Geneva the "Silicon Valley" of apple growing. By happenstance, Red Jacket Orchards is located just down the street from Cornell's Agricultural Experiment Station, whose fruit-growing technology helped to develop Empire, Cortland, Jonagold, and Macoun apples, among others. The relationship between Red Jacket and the Station is important to production agriculture, providing links from research to orchard to consumer.

Our region's apples have a zest they get from the colder climate and high-acid soil, elevating malic acid, which gives the fruit its high-profile flavor. Red Jacket reserves a portion of its apples for ciders and juices, fresh-pressing whole fruit in small batches just as they have for over forty years. Juices of mainstays like Empire, McIntosh, Crispin, and Fuji apples are blended with other varieties, keeping tartness and sweetness in balance. Other seasonal products include rhubarb-apple juice, strawberry-apple juice, and cherry-apple juice. Varietal Fuji apple juice, with a unique pearlike aroma from the fruit's tannins and a complex sweet and tart, almost wine-like taste, is remarkably delicious.

Red Jacket is able to maintain fruit at the highest level of quality through vertical integration—they grow, pack, store, and transport all of their own products, managing each distribution channel, from grower to consumer. Final market destinations range from local farm markets, grocery stores, and, in the most unique part of their business, New York City. Red Jacket trucks deliver to the metropolitan area three to five days a week, with direct sales through the Greenmarket system, accounting for one-quarter of company business. Back-door deliveries are made to many of New York's finest restaurants, bakeries, and gourmet groceries, and total sales in the city make up a full 80 percent of the company's overall volume.

Pastry chef Pierre Reboul of Blue Hill, a favorite restaurant among members of New York City's slow food set, uses Red Jacket fruit in his stunning preserves and desserts. Closer to home, Red Jacket supplies the ingredients for some of our local fruit wines. Dave Peterson buys peaches for Swedish Hill, John Earle buys strawberries and apricots for Torrey Ridge, and Bill Martin buys blueberries, strawberries, and rhubarb for Montezuma Winery fruit wines. Each bite, each sip provides a reminder of the harvest and a connection to the orchard at its most bountiful moment.

Route 414
Hector, NY 14841
(607) 546-6777

Hours: By appointment

Sawmill Creek Vineyards

The creek at the boundary of Jim Hazlitt's property was named for the early sawmill that supplied much of the lumber used to construct the original buildings on this side of Seneca Lake. Over time, the creek formed Peach Orchard Point with deposits of rich, gravelly soil, the same soil that attracted Jim's fruit-growing ancestors here in 1852.

Jim Hazlitt is probably the best-known and most-admired of all Finger Lakes grape growers. He has supplied high-quality fruit to regional wineries for a quarter of a century and is considered a founding father of the Seneca Lake appellation. When he graduated from Cornell in 1960 with a degree in pomology, he briefly flirted with the idea of becoming a helicopter pilot before teaming up with his brother Jerry to run the family farm.

For many years, the Hazlitt brothers made modest livings by supplying the Taylor Wine Company with native varieties for their jug wines. Then, when the price Taylor was willing to pay for grapes dropped below $100 a ton, everything changed. Under financial siege, the two men agreed to split their property, and while Jerry could not resist the temptation to turn the horse barn on his half into a winery, Jim decided to replant the vineyards with higher-value varieties on the other half. He would remain a grower, even in the face of unstable prices.

The year was 1977, and Hermann Wiemer was having success with vinifera grapes on the west side of the lake. These were tough times, so, with few other options, Jim began planting Chardonnay and Riesling vines from Hermann's nursery. At first, he sold them for little more than his native grapes, but, with the emergence of new farm wineries in the region, small buyers began to compete with one another for the best fruit. He planted Pinot Noir in 1985, then added Cabernet Sauvignon and Cabernet Franc in 1990. Today, Jim grows fifteen different varieties of vinifera grapes on sixty of his eighty vineyard acres.

Quality of the grapes is the result of precise geography of the vineyards in relation to the lake, and, in fact, Sawmill Creek is one of the warmest sites in the Finger Lakes. His longer growing season combined with ideal soils provides him the advantages he needs to farm for flavor. But, he cautions, even with the best terroir a good grower must be dedicated to balanced pruning. "The most important job on the farm is pruning," insists Jim. He trims his vines so that he gets the right number of buds to match the pounds of wood weight. Underpruning will allow a vine to produce too much fruit, and, without allowing it to fully ripen, quality will suffer.

While balanced pruning dates back to his school days, according to Jim, other more recent viticultural practices have dramatically changed the way grapes are grown in the region. Trellising, or manipulating, the position of the vines' shoots to allow better interception of sunlight by the leaves is accomplished with divided canopies. Cluster thinning is also used to prevent overproduction and subsequent uneven and slow ripening. "That's why the wine quality in the Finger Lakes keeps getting better," he explains. "It's because we do a better job in the vineyard."

Wineries need grapes, and Jim has long-standing contracts with twenty-two local producers. Winemakers visit his vineyards throughout the summer to sample the readiness of his lot for picking. Swedish Hill has Jim use a Scott Henry trellis system for the Chardonnay grapevines he grows in a coveted lot, and they pay him above-market prices for the trouble. That particular wine appears with a Sawmill Creek Vineyard designation on the label, giving credit where credit is due.

Perhaps it is the agricultural roots of the Hazlitts that are reflected in the generous and giving nature of the fruit grown on this property. Jim lives and works in the vineyards, and he grows grapes to see how well he can grow them. Wines produced from Sawmill Creek grapes are a tribute to his distinguished career.

8830 Upper Lake Road
Lodi, NY 14860
(607) 582-6774

Hours: By appointment

Venture Vineyards

He grew up on the streets of Brooklyn, then became a systems engineer for IBM. But perhaps it was his memories of summers in the Catskills where he tended a garden at his grandmother's side that eventually lured Melvin Nass to a farm on Seneca Lake.

Well into a successful career at Big Blue, Mel began contemplating the idea of life on the land. Along with his wife, Phyllis, he began an engineer's methodical exploration of the possibilities. They started out by volunteering weekend labor on Long Island potato and poultry farms. They milked cows at an upstate dairy, then picked grapes on a Hudson Valley vineyard. By the time they made their way to the Finger Lakes, Mel and Phyllis had found what they were looking for.

A Lodi farmer by the name of Frank Halsey was getting ready to retire, and his thirteen acres of fruit trees and thirteen acres of grapes were up for sale. Mel and Phyllis struck a deal with Frank. In the fall of 1973, they settled on the beautiful lakeside slope perfumed by Concord, Niagara, and Catawba grapes, and, as they embraced a new way to earn a living, they called it "Venture Vineyards."

Native Concords that thrive throughout the Northeast were first cultivated by botanist Ephraim Wales Bull in the village of Concord, Massachusetts, in 1843. The vigorous Concord vine made its way to the Finger Lakes, where it has been a reliable source of wine, juice, jelly, and table grapes ever since.

Mel was particularly fascinated by the Concords in his vineyard, even if they didn't get the respect afforded other varieties. He admired the aromatic clusters of robust, blue-black, slip-skin berries with the musky, refreshing, sweet-tart pulp, and he began peddling baskets of the grapes to farm stands and regional groceries. Unlike many of his neighbors, who were ripping out labrusca vines and replanting with higher-end wine grapes, Mel focused his attention on the table grape market.

Fresh-market grapes are hand-harvested by grasping the cluster by its stem and clipping the stem where it attaches to the cane. Long-cane pruning has helped to grow healthy clusters with bigger berries, and because of his minimal reliance on chemicals, Mel's grapes have little or no spray residue. Careful handling is essential to avoid separation from the cluster as mature, plump grapes are packed into individual containers. As his business grew and distribution widened, Mel developed corrugated, cushioned, one-quart retail containers that were not only market-ready but protected the grapes from damage during shipping.

Good-eating Concords begin to ripen in the Finger Lakes by the second week of September, and the season continues until the first freeze, usually the last week in October. To lengthen the limited season, Venture purchases early ripening, Concord-family grapes from growers in Arkansas, whose harvest begins in mid-August. And, working with Cornell researchers, Mel developed sulfur dioxide pads for each master box of picked grapes in cold storage. The atmosphere preserves the freshness of grapes picked near the end of the season and gives him five or six more weeks of selling, all the way through November.

Grapes with shattered skins, either damaged in the vineyard by hail or torn and dehydrated during harvest, are crushed and pressed at Fulkerson's Winery. The juice is delivered to Beak & Skiff Cidery in Lafayette for flash-pasteurization and bottling into a single-strength, pure Concord grape juice product with an extraordinary full-bodied flavor and deep coloration.

Today, Melvin Nass is the "king of Concords," and his table grape operation based in Lodi is the largest of its kind in the United States. He transports table grapes by tractor-trailer all over the country, even to California. Mel says it's like "shipping coals to Newcastle." The kid from Brooklyn not only pioneered commercial growing, but packaging, marketing, and distribution of the Concord and her sister varieties. The availability of these fresh, delicious grapes during nearly four months of the year is his gift to America.

Wagner Valley Brewery

See Wagner Vineyards (page 86) . . . .

Wickham's Twin Oaks Farm

On this hillside 250 years ago, the Seneca tribe of the Iroquois Confederacy tended huge peach and cherry orchards, testament to this temperate "island" within a cool region. During the American Revolution, Seneca warriors sided with the British, provoking American retaliation in 1779 when Major General John Sullivan led a "scorched earth" expedition northward along the lake. Indian villages were burned, every field laid waste, and even the fruit trees were hacked down.

5557 Route 414
Hector, NY 14841
(607) 546-5511

Hours: Call for schedule

With the Indians driven off their land, white settlers moved in. A young man from Connecticut by the name of William Wickham was the first to permanently locate within these parts, building a cabin on a ridge just outside of Bennettsburg in 1791. Two generations later, the Wickham family moved to a property on the lake where they grew peaches, cherries, and grapes. William III planted two oak trees side by side, marking the site that is now called Twin Oaks Farm.

The years have brought many changes, but some things have remained the same, according to Bill Wickham, of the seventh generation. A lifelong fruit grower like most in his family before him, Bill started Wickham Winery in 1979, a venture that was eventually unsuccessful. Today he tends a few acres of Concords on the old farm, but his pride and joy are the fragrant peaches and flavorful sweet and sour cherries that never see a chain store or a packing shed. Bill's production is so small that he picks his peaches himself, and all of his fruit is sold at the roadside stand.

Nothing is better than a fruit in its own season, perfectly ripened and handled with care by the people who harvest it. Earliest to ripen are the Red Havens, a medium-sized variety with brilliant red skin surface covered with a lot of fuzz. The flavor is sweet with a little "zip" that makes the mouth water. Next is Loring, a freestone peach, which means the flesh comes off the pit easily. It's a larger fruit with a bright red blush over a yellow background and a full, sweet flavor. A late season peach, the round, firm Crest Haven is yellow with deep red skin covering yellow melting flesh that has excellent flavor. "I leave my fruit on the tree much longer than anyone else," says Bill, who cultivates the most luscious peaches you've ever tasted. In summer, you know you're near Twin Oaks Farm without reading the sign because of the peachy perfume in the air.

At the appearance of the first of Bill's fruit, a constant succession of home cooks and restaurant chefs begins to arrive. Deb Moglia of Grist Mill Café buys fresh-picked peaches and cherries for her fat pies and fruit tarts. Scott Signori of Stonecat Café smokes Bill's peaches and serves them with mascarpone. "I love the way the sweet musky earthiness of peaches marries with wine and savory foods," says chef William Cornelius of nearby Petioles.

Bill's most hardy and vigorous sweet cherries are the German varieties, Schmidt and Hedelfingen, producing large fruit size with firm texture and rich cherry flavor. Colors range from deep maroon or mahogany red to black, with bright, glossy, plump-looking surfaces. The bright red Montmorency cherries, with clear, juicy flesh, are the best sour, or "pie," cherries.

Peaches with a blush of red on their cheeks and burgundy red cherries beckon from Bill Wickham's fruit stand, where the boss is usually behind the counter making sure you don't leave your fingerprints in the fruit and talking your ear off about his favorite varieties. His cherries and peaches make the world a better place.

RESTAURANTS

Belhurst Castle
See Belhurst Winery (page 52) . . . .

The Café at Fox Run
See Fox Run Vineyards (page 62) . . . .

Castel Grisch Winery Restaurant
See Castel Grisch Estate Winery (page 59) . . . .

The Cobblestone

The spectacular topography of the Finger Lakes was formed by the action of retreating glaciers during the last Ice Age over 10,000 years ago. That same glacial action left behind cobblestones—rocks smoothed and shaped by the pressure and movement of tons of ice. These "cobbles" were used to build imposing structures throughout the region, and one particular homestead is now a beautifully restored and lovingly appointed restaurant called The Cobblestone.

After serving as New York's Lieutenant Governor during Hugh Carey's administration, where she championed the state's emerging farm wineries, Mary Anne Krupsak joined forces with food service administrator Susan Cohen to purchase an Italian neighborhood restaurant in Geneva called Pasta Only. Although not trained chefs, the two women did a lot of experimenting and focused on seasonal ingredients produced locally and organically. When business outgrew their arty little space, they hired Rochester designer Maurice Chacchia to convert the circa 1830 mansion into a fine dining establishment.

The intimate bar area with exposed cobblestone walls is an ideal spot for relaxed drinks with an order of warm, housemade Garlic Potato Chips. Warm tones accented by natural wood create a splendid setting in a dining room dotted with antiques and collectibles—a birdcage here, a grandfather's clock there. Charming miniature lampshades provide a dim glow on each table, creating a sense of intimacy not quite all the way to dining noir. Cobblestones is satisfying and upscale, yet with a refreshingly unstuffy feel about it, perfect for a romantic dinner for two or a convivial night out with a group of friends.

Chef Rich Tyler's kitchen is supported by his visits to the farmer's markets in Geneva and Ithaca and through symbiotic relationships he has formed with many of the region's growers. His food is modern with a smattering of seasonal and traceable local ingredients. Start with appetizers like Greens and Beans—local organic romaine and white beans

Hamilton Street at
Pre-Emption Road
(Routes 5 and 20)
Geneva, NY 14456
(315) 789-8498

Hours:
Lunch, Tuesday–Sunday,
11:30 a.m.–2:00 p.m.;
Dinner, Tuesday–Sunday,
5:00 p.m.–9:00 p.m.

www.pastaonlyscobble-stone.com

sautéed in extra virgin olive oil and roasted local garlic with a bit of red pepper. Entrées include Lasagna Verde, made with fresh local spinach layered with Lively Run goat cheese and caramelized onions with pomodoro sauce; Long Island Duckling, baked, then broiled and served with a sauce made from local pears; pan-roasted breast of McDonald Farm chicken over fettuccini; and Garlic Shrimp, sautéed with a generous portion of local garlic, shallots, baby greens, and Fox Run Chardonnay.

It's difficult to choose among desserts, but pastry chef Kathy Gottschalk's Triple Apple Pie, baked with Fuji, McIntosh, and Jona Gold varieties from nearby Red Jacket Orchards and served with caramel ice cream, is so good it nearly brings tears to my eyes. On the other hand, if you're seeking the perfect accompaniment to a glass of Swedish Hill port, order the decadent Chocolate Souffle.

The wine list is relatively short but fairly priced, and it cleverly touches all bases, sparkling to late harvest. "We want to make wine an interesting and valuable experience," says Susan, and she backs up her words with Finger Lakes gems like Sheldrake Point Pinot Noir and Prejean Gewürztraminer.

So many components need to come together for a dining experience to be both enjoyable and memorable. The Cobblestone's attention to detail, visually stimulating and well-prepared food, interesting and com-patible wines, and attentive, yet unobtrusive service result in something close to perfection.

Geneva on the Lake

50

1001 Lochland Road
Route 14
Geneva, NY 14456
(315) 789-7190

Hours: Breakfast, daily,
8:00 a.m.–10:00 p.m.;
Dinner, daily,
6:00 p.m.–9:00 p.m.;
Lunch, daily (summer only),
noon–2:00 p.m.

www.genevaonthelake.com

Geneva, like its Old World namesake, is a stately grand dame built on a sparkling lake. It's a city full of landmarks, including Hobart, one of the oldest colleges in New York, the South Street mansion of Charles J. Folger, Secretary of the Treasury under President Chester Arthur, and Geneva on the Lake, the replica of an Italian villa.

In 1914, Byron Nester, who inherited the fortune his father made by processing barley into malt for the brewing industry, modeled a lakeside mansion after the magnificent Lancelotti villa in the hills of Frascati near Rome. The villas of Roman nobility, with their beautiful gardens and fountains, are the chief attraction of Frascati, and the surrounding countryside is noted for its wine. The Finger Lakes replica—fortunately for us—has much in common with the original. The mansion remained home to the Nester family until 1949, when it was purchased by the Capuchin Fathers and used for the next twenty years as a monastery. By the time it was acquired by the Schickel family in 1978, the aristocratic preserve had fallen into disrepair. In an extensive restoration, the Schickels turned the property into a resort hotel, rescued the long-neg-lected formal gardens, and contributed paintings, sculptures, and artifacts collected from around the world. With the passing of Norbert Schickel, the visionary family patriarch, Geneva on the Lake was sold to Alfred and Aminy Audi, owners of the Stickley Furniture Company, while remaining under the guidance of the Schickel family.

What was once the villa's ornate vestibule is now called Lancelotti Dining Room, a courtly setting for exceptional wine country dining. The mood is bright and engaging, especially in summer when doors are thrown open for patio dining. The charming atmosphere extends to culinary offerings, anointed with savory herbs from the garden.

It was the arrival of chef Ziad Wehbe from Le Bec Fin in Philadelphia that laid the groundwork for the resort's emergence as a stopover for serious eaters. He and his crew strive to keep the menu fresh and varied, with seasonal changes orchestrating variety from a network of local growers. On any given night, the menu may feature such stylized dishes as a salad of baby spinach leaves with portobello mushrooms, tossed with warm bacon dressing and garnished with a ravioli filled with Lively Run goat cheese, or a salad of in-season mixed greens combined with heirloom tomatoes from Dressner Farms, in a mustard vinaigrette with fresh basil–crusted mozzarella. Chicken Jacqueline is a boneless breast of McDonald Farm chicken with Red Jacket Orchard apples and toasted almonds, finished with a sauce of Lakewood port and cream.

But do take it easy if you wish to make it to dessert, especially if you want to experience the tableside dramatics of Bananas Foster or Baked Alaska. There's a lighter option of seasonal berries, marinated in Atwater Vineyards Riesling Ice Wine, but the best bet may be cheesecake-of-the-day, washed down with a cup of the signature Café Lancelotti, cappuccino with Kahlua, Courvoisier, and Sambucca.

An extensive wine list features a variety from local vineyards and from around the world. Guests have the opportunity to taste a venerable German Mosel next to a local Riesling, or to compare a bottle of Stag's Leap Napa Valley Cabernet Sauvignon with one from Dr. Konstantin Frank. I enjoy sipping a glass of Frascati before dinner, not because it's a particularly impressive wine, but because of its connection to the ancestry of the villa.

The period atmosphere evokes a gentler time, and it is very easy to get lost in the moment here. Any air of intimidation that might stem from the formal setting is dispelled by the warm hospitality of the staff. Geneva on the Lake is clearly a labor of love for general manager Bill Schickel, a former professor of fine arts, who skillfully presides over both the luxurious accommodations and a wine country temple of gastronomy.

Ginny Lee Café

See Wagner Vineyards (page 86) . . . .

3825 Main Street
Burdett, NY 14818
(607) 546-7770

Hours: Monday–Saturday,
7:00 a.m.–3:00 p.m.
(April through November);
Tuesday–Saturday,
7:00 a.m.–3:00 p.m.
(December through March)

Grist Mill Café

The energy to power the old grist mill in Burdett was once supplied by the creek that empties into Seneca Lake at Hector Falls. Local farmers transported whole grain corn and wheat here for grinding into meal and flour, and, as other buildings were added, the mill complex eventually became the village of Burdett and the nucleus of its community.

Tucked away in an old country store, just above the site of the mill, stands a quaint bakery and eatery called the Grist Mill Café. Credit for this regional treasure goes to Deborah Moglia, a former baker both at Glen Mountain Market in Watkins Glen and Hope's Way in Ithaca and former sous chef at Red Newt Bistro in Hector. She bakes baguettes for nearby restaurants and winery tasting rooms, and offers breakfast, lunch, and a bakery case packed with expertly made cakes, cookies, and fat pies full of local fruits.

Breakfast here is a special pleasure. In a warm atmosphere full of yeasty aromas, plates are piled high with cinnamon buns, muffins, scones, and a sourdough coffee cake to partner up with a damn good cup of joe. Egg sandwiches are served on a just-baked croissants or buttermilk biscuits, and, if the season is right, pancakes are loaded with fresh-picked blueberries from Steve Bond's farm, just up the road a piece. On a sunny morning, bring the newspaper and head for one of the tables on the back porch, where you'll be serenaded by the gurgling waterfall.

"I like to think of myself as a baker, first and foremost," says Deb, who handcrafts some of the loveliest crusty brown loaves of bread in wine country. On baking days she is up at four in the morning to get the dough under way. All the loaves are shaped by hand, mixed in small batches from the highest-quality flours, and pulled from the oven just in time for lunch. Breads come in whole loaves, sliced loaves, and buns, and they are the foundation of Grist Mill's small sandwich menu. Selections include fresh mozzarella with tomato, basil, and roasted garlic spread; a fresh-roasted turkey club; and warm roast beef with lettuce, onion, roasted red peppers, and artichoke purée. The venerable Reuben sandwich is served in a classic corned-beef version, as a grilled Tempeh Reuben, or with sautéed local apples in a uniquely delicious Apple Reuben.

The embarrassment of riches here makes every dessert choice difficult. But if you've got to choose only one dessert, it ought to be the chocolate cake, generously filled with mascarpone and peanut butter, then coated with chocolate ganache.

Without a beverage license of its own, the café does not sell wine, but it permits you to bring a bottle you may have just purchased at one of the nearby wineries, and the owner will be delighted to pull the cork and provide glasses. If it's grab-and-go you have in mind, she will fill your hamper with the makings of a first-rate picnic. Grist Mill is off the main winery route, making it a bit of a secret, but a visit is well worth the detour.

APPLE REUBEN

Makes 2 sandwiches

This unpretentious little bakery and café is a favorite with the locals, and Deb Moglia's smart-looking sandwiches on fresh-baked breads attract a steady crowd at lunchtime. My favorite is the Apple Reuben, a warmingly satisfying construction inspired by the pastrami-stuffed version, only here it is made with sautéed local apples.

To make the dressing, combine all of the ingredients in a blender on high speed and place the dressing in a sealed jar. Chill until ready to use.

To make the Apple Reuben, spread enough Thousand Island Dressing to coat one side of each slice of bread. Top each bread slice with 1 slice of cheese. Heat the olive oil over medium heat in a sauté pan, add the apple slices, and sauté for 2 minutes, stirring constantly. Add the sauerkraut and cook for 1 minute more, just to warm. Remove from the heat and spoon the apple and sauerkraut mixture over 2 of the bread slices. Top with the remaining slice of bread, cheese side down. Brush the outside of the sandwich with the butter, place in a dry skillet, and grill slowly on both sides over medium heat for about 3 minutes per side, or until the cheese melts and the sandwich is browned.

THOUSAND ISLAND DRESSING

1/3 cup mayonnaise

1 tablespoon chile sauce

1 teaspoon chopped green bell pepper

1/2 teaspoon chopped pimiento

1/2 teaspoon chopped chives

APPLE REUBEN

4 slices rye bread

4 slices Swiss cheese

2 tablespoons olive oil

16 to 20 thin slices Empire apple, unpeeled

2/3 cup sauerkraut, drained

2 tablespoons unsalted butter, melted

Henry B's

Folks in Seneca Falls will tell you their hometown was the inspiration for the fictional Bedford Falls in Frank Capra's 1946 movie, *It's a Wonderful Life*. Capra, it seems, visited Seneca Falls just before he made the American holiday classic, and, in what has become a local tradition, the film is screened at Seneca Falls High School every Christmas season. In fictional Bedford Falls, the town's favorite Italian restaurant is Martini's. In real-life Seneca Falls, the local choice is Henry B's.

Businessman and civic cheerleader Bruce Henry Bonafiglia has played an important role in the revitalization of his hometown of Seneca Falls, so it was not surprising when he announced that he would

35

84 Fall Street
Seneca Falls, NY 13148
(315) 568 1600

Hours: Tuesday–Saturday, 4:30 p.m.–10:00 p.m.

www.henrybs.com

turn the old Shannon's clothing store into a downtown restaurant to fill a void in the marketplace. He created Henry B's, a cozy and urbane eatery that not only pays homage to the town's Italian heritage, but provides a social crossroads for loyal patrons who make the place, in Bruce's words, "a local haunt."

Exposed brick walls, pressed tin ceiling, polished oak floor, rustic lighting, and crisp white tablecloths add easy sophistication, and the small bar at the entrance serves well-made cocktails, generous on the alcohol. While Henry B's has earned its "bistro" pedigree, it has overcome the tiredness that often comes with an entrenched formula.

"Henry B," it seems, was Bruce's colorful grandfather whose irreverent spirit and love of the good life inspire robust food in gargantuan portions, along with attitude-free camaraderie. Platters are placed in the center of the table with serving utensils to provide an opportunity for patrons to enjoy the interaction as they are passed around the table. There are no split charges, so if a small group wants to share a heap of crispy, housemade zucchini, potato, and sweet potato chips drizzled with warm gorgonzola cream sauce, it can. "Our intention is to create an atmosphere where customers feel like they are family," Bruce explains.

Executive chef Ron Baldasseroni executes a wide-ranging, pan-Italian menu that is simple, flavorful, and cliché-free. His culinary philosophy is embedded in recipes like mixed baby greens with goat cheese, roasted pine nuts, and kidney beans, tossed in a honey balsamic blend; spaghetti tossed with olive oil, garlic, sun-dried tomatoes, and arugula, then finished with Parmigiano-Reggiano; pan-roasted chicken with a lemon-oregano sauce; and grappa-seared tuna on a bed of seasoned green beans with tomato-basil salsa.

One of the kitchen's prized possessions is a wooden gnocchi board made by Bruce's father, Angelo. Each piece of dough is pressed gently against the board to make ridges that help the "pillows" cook evenly and hold the sauces. You can order the gnocchi (a secret Bonafiglia family recipe) with tomato sauce, basil pesto, or in butter with sautéed prosciutto.

For dessert you might try the Crostata di Mele, a freshly baked apple tart with rum-soaked raisins, black walnuts, and vanilla gelato. No matter how full you are, there's still room for a mercifully modest concoction called "The Smallest Sundae in the World."

Credit Bruce's wife, Lisa, with the inspired belief that every meal deserves a fine bottle of wine, and thank her not only for the extensive Italian selections, but for her skill at finding several Finger Lakes bottles to complement the food. Swedish Hill Riesling, with loads of fruity floral aromas and flavors, could stand in for a Pinot Grigio or Fruili, and Fox Run Pinot Noir compares with the best of the Pinot Nero wines that come out of Italy's mountainous areas.

If you plan to visit Seneca Falls, prepare for a Capra-esque experience. The bridge that crosses the Seneca-Cayuga Canal is just like the fateful bridge in the classic film, and there are a Zuzu's Café and a Bailey's Ice Cream Parlor. But at its heart lies Henry B's, now an established magnet for local foodies.

Petioles

See Logan Ridge Wine Cellars (page 76) . . . .

Pierce's 1894

The land between the city of Elmira and the village of Horseheads was once home to a bicycle factory, a furniture factory, a window glass plant, and a knitting mill. When local industry leaders recognized a need to attract workers to their factories, they decided to create a new village by dividing up 2,000 lots and putting them up for sale at $200 each.

228 Oakwood Avenue
(at West 14th Street)
Elmira Heights, NY 14903
(607) 734-2022

Hours: Tuesday–Sunday,
5:00 p.m.–10:00 p.m.

www.pierces1894.com

Parcels were assigned by lottery drawing, and, as luck would have it, an entrepreneur by the name of Crawford Henry Pierce drew the corner property at the center of the village. Previously in the straw hat business and then partner in a cigar factory, Crawford built a hotel on his lot, an enterprise that grew into a bar, café, bowling alley, and gas station. He became the most prosperous businessman in Elmira Heights.

Four generations later, his great-grandson, Crawford Joseph "Joe" Pierce, owns and operates Pierce's 1894 Restaurant at the same location, a local landmark that has evolved into a bastion of fine dining. While Pierce's went through many changes in the first half of its life, the "grand establishment" as we know it was conceived by Joe's father, Joseph Slocum Pierce. The senior Pierce knew early on that he would be a restaurateur. He graduated from Cornell University's School of Hotel Administration in 1942, then took charge of his family's business. A consummate host and gifted arbiter of taste, he built seven opulently decorated dining rooms on three floors, took the restaurant to culinary heights, and helped Finger Lakes wines gain recognition with a series of New York State Barrel Dinners.

In an earlier time, dining at Pierce's meant sitting up straight in your chair, using the proper fork, and listening to piped-in classical music. Try as he might, Joe hasn't been able to sustain either the formality or the prices that go with it, and, recently, the restaurant has begun to shake off its stuffy image. Background music is now jazzy, the menu smaller and lighter, and even the clubby lounge has been renamed "Dirty Joe's" to attract a younger, martini-sipping crowd. Service these days is less formal and the kitchen staff smaller, but Joe and his family have maintained the restaurant's aura of stability and familiarity with their total commitment and passion.

Pierce's stays faithful to some of the old standbys, including Creole Turtle Soup, Crab Rangoon, Baked Stuffed Potatoes, tableside presentation of

Chateaubriand, and a pastry cart that Joe calls "the most indelible mark of our cuisine." Supporters of the restaurant, and there are legions of them, surrender to confections like Whiskey Torte, Chocolate Mousse, and Fort Knox Pie, and local late-harvest wines are displayed on the cart as "dessert alternatives."

Joe is an advocate for great wines surrounding a great meal, and his efforts are handsomely rewarded by *Wine Spectator* citations. If you think this place is too far from the lakes to be considered a wine country restaurant, think again. The wine inventory is outstanding, with seventy-five selections from the Finger Lakes out of a total of 300 bottles. His wine list is packed with authoritative advice and descriptors, which, in Joe's words, "gives someone enough information to be able to make a buying decision based on what the wine tastes like." His customers often select a wine first, then choose food to match, instead of the other way around. Pierce's places wine at the center of the dining experience.

Without this restaurant's contribution to hospitality, Finger Lakes dining would be immeasurably poorer. Even after all these years, a visit to Pierce's never feels like going to a museum, but rather more like plopping down into a favorite easy chair. The Pierce family legacy is an institution that has aged as gracefully as Katherine Hepburn over the years and survived the fickle, constantly changing tastes of the dining public. This restaurant proves, as the great Kate does on film, that a classic is forever.

48

4432 West Lake Road
(Route 14)
Geneva, NY 14456
(315) 789-2020

Hours: Tuesday–Saturday,
5:00 p.m.–9:00 p.m.

www.portscafe.com

Ports Café

Old timers in the Geneva area will fondly remember the "Red and White" country grocery with an ice cream stand out front. Well, the ice cream stand is still there, but the enterprise has evolved into a thriving restaurant called Ports, a comfortable, casual setting for Finger Lakes food and wine.

The color palette of the dining room provides a perfect canvas for an eclectic mix of contemporary furnishings and antique market finds, including framed enlargements of vintage local postcards. Oversize booths dominate the small space, and a whimsical vineyard trellis over polished wooden tables and chairs reinforces a wine country theme. The room buzzes with village locals and tourists, attended to by friendly, efficient servers.

An open kitchen, alive with confident, high-energy cooking, lends to the festivities. Chef Jeff Stanton keeps things interesting with a small standard menu and a long, everchanging list of daily specials. The result is American food focused on freshness and supported by seasonal local ingredients.

Start with the Winter Night Salad, mixed greens with Empire apples, spiced walnuts, cranraisins, red onions, and crumbled gorgonzola with raspberry vinaigrette, or Bella Greens, a salad with baby lettuces, roasted portobellos, sun-dried tomatoes, goat cheese, and toasted pine nuts tossed in a balsamic vinaigrette. Finger foods include Cornmeal-Dipped Calamari-Shrimp Fry, Black Bean and Steak Quesadillas, and "You Peel 'Em" Shrimp Boil with garlic butter or cocktail sauce. Expect imaginative entrée offerings like Frenched Pork Rib Chops seasoned with sea salt and cracked black pepper, topped with caramelized Empire apples and onions, and finished under the broiler with smoked New York State Cheddar. The menu is vast and offers something for every taste and pocket.

Desserts, prepared by CIA-trained Ellie Lewis, might include Chocolate Espresso Crème Brûlée , Coconut Caramel Cheesecake, or Gingerbread with cinnamon cream cheese frosting, drizzled with warm caramel. If you prefer a portable dessert, the ice cream stand dispenses double-dip cones.

Co-owners Jeff Ritter and David Harvey, both Geneva natives, are influenced by their restaurant's proximity to the wineries on Seneca's western shore. The wine list emphasizes Finger Lakes wines selected for their compatibility to the cooking style of the restaurant. Hosmer Cabernet Franc, Glenora Pinot Blanc, and Dr. Frank Celebre are noteworthy entries, not to mention dessert-friendly ice wines from Lakewood and Hunt Country Vineyards. Beer drinkers will find a couple of Ithaca micro-brews on draught, and teetotalers have the option of Glendale Farm organic grape juice by the glass.

Ports is a Finger Lakes translation of the informal, family-run country bistros of France, a place that combines the flavors and freshness of local cuisine with home-grown style, and a place where you'll feel equally at home in a little black dress or a pair of jeans. It's a brilliant little restaurant full of sweet surprises.

Red Newt Cellars Winery & Bistro

See Red Newt Cellars (page 81) . . . .

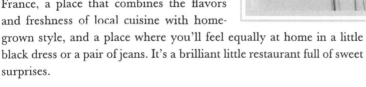

Smokehouse Café

See Standing Stone Vineyards (page 84) . . . .

Stonecat Café
See Bloomer Creek Vineyards (page 57) ....

9013 Route 414
Lodi, NY 14860
(607) 582-7545

Hours: Thursday–Sunday,
5:30 p.m.–9:30 p.m. (April
through October); Friday and
Saturday, 5:30 p.m.–9:30
p.m. (November and
December)

Suzanne

In small-group cookery classes at Brookdale Community College, Suzanne Stack taught her students to create delicious regional dishes using quality local ingredients, to explore local history and culture, and to match indigenous wines. Her Cooking with Suzanne catering company led to membership in the James Beard Foundation, where her talent flourished in the special events kitchen. She was hired to work alongside many of America's best chefs, from Rocco DeSpirito to George Perrier, as part of the DeGustibus culinary program at Macy's Department Store in New York City. At many of these events, she was exposed to the techniques of French classical and nouvelle cuisine, and the more she learned about French country cooking, the more she came to appreciate a chef's relationship with his or her local growers.

Cooking, in her words, is an "all-consuming passion" that inevitably led Suzanne to Seneca Lake and to a venture that she had imagined for many years. In August 2003 she opened the doors to her namesake restaurant in a lovingly restored late Victorian–era farmhouse with a forty-seat dining room. The modest scale was exactly what she wanted— small enough, she says, "so it is *my* hands preparing the food."

Perhaps not being a native of the region has allowed Suzanne to appreciate the abundant bounty with even more zeal than a locally born chef. The property grows walnut, apple, and plum trees—hers for the picking—and herbs used in cooking are harvested from Suzanne's organic garden just a few hours before each meal. Just down the road, Blue Heron Farm provides lettuces and vegetables. Cheeses are from Meadowsweet Farm and Lively Run. Even locally roasted coffee is served with cream from a nearby dairy. The market-driven menu is a gourmet wonder.

Suzanne's inspired creations employ French technique in an arranged marriage with the freshest-possible components harmoniously balanced with fine local wines. The union works best in dishes like Roasted Chicken Breast with Seasonal Vegetables and Riesling Wine Sauce, an extraordinarily subtle flavor composition, or in a liaison of Magret Duck Breast and Potato and Butternut Squash Gratin with Port Wine Sauce.

A compact but thoughtful wine list is deep in neighborhood favorites, including Lamoreaux Landing Chardonnay, Standing Stone Gewürztraminer, and Wagner Cabernet Franc. There are no "left coast" wines and just a few entries from France, Italy, and South Africa. "Ideally," says Suzanne, "wine tastes better by virtue of the food, and food tastes better by virtue of the wine." She caters to moderate drinkers with a dozen wines by the glass.

The dining room is handsomely understated. Soothing, cream-colored walls, adorned with the work of local artists, welcome and stir the appetite, and locally crafted oak furniture provides sophistication and comfort. The charming, pastoral atmosphere includes a fireplace at one end of the room and a view of the lake from the other.

Suzanne, the restaurant, is a stellar example of how regional emphasis can lend authentic flair to the dining experience; Suzanne, the chef, typifies the slow but steady migration of talented culinarians to the Finger Lakes.

POTATO-CRUSTED RED SNAPPER WITH STEWED BUTTERNUT SQUASH

Serves 4

Suzanne Stack regularly updates and modifies her menus to take advantage of the rich, vibrant flavors the time of year offers. The butternut squash for this dish is grown at Blue Heron Farm, just down the road from the 1903 farmhouse she has converted to one of the Finger Lakes' most charming restaurants.

To make the squash, sweat the onion for about 8 minutes over low heat with 1 tablespoon of the butter. Add the garlic and deglaze with the dry Riesling. Reduce the liquid until the pan is dry, about 8 minutes. Add the stock and rosemary and simmer for 10 minutes on medium-low heat. Add the squash and cook for another 10 minutes, or until tender. Swirl in the remaining 2 tablespoons butter, the orange juice, lemon juice, and the parsley. Remove and discard the rosemary sprig and season with salt and pepper to taste. Keep warm over low heat.

To make the fish, place the egg whites and potato flakes in separate bowls. Dip the fish filets in the egg whites and then into the potato flakes. Press to adhere. Cover the filets with plastic wrap and refrigerate for at least 30 minutes, or up to 6 hours in advance.

Preheat the oven to 450°F. Heat 1/4 inch of vegetable oil in a heavy skillet over medium-high heat. When hot, add the fish and brown for about 2 minutes per side. Finish off in the oven for about 6 minutes, until the fish is firm to the touch and opaque.

Place equal portions of the stewed squash in 4 large, shallow soup bowls. Top with a fish filet and sprinkle with parsley and diced tomato.

Note: Use organic potato flakes if available in your area. To speed up the process, the filets can be cooked fully in the sauté pan instead of in the oven, cooking about 4 minutes per side.

STEWED BUTTERNUT SQUASH

- 1 sweet onion, finely diced
- 3 tablespoons unsalted butter
- 1 clove garlic, minced
- 1/2 cup dry Riesling
- 2 cups vegetable stock
- 1 sprig rosemary
- 1 large butternut squash, halved lengthwise, seeded, and cut in 1/4-inch dice
- Juice of 1/2 small orange
- Juice of 1/2 lemon
- 1 tablespoon chopped fresh parsley
- Salt and freshly ground black pepper

- 4 (6-ounce) red snapper filets, boned and skinned
- 2 large egg whites
- 1 cup potato flakes
- Vegetable oil, for frying
- Sea salt and freshly ground black pepper
- Chopped fresh parsley, for garnish
- 1 tomato, peeled, seeded, and diced, for garnish

Veraisons

See Glenora Wine Cellars (page 65) ....

301 N. Franklin Street
Watkins Glen, NY 14891
(607) 535-9797

Hours:
Daily, 11:30 a.m.–10:00 p.m.

Wildflower Café

Watkins Glen is a small town where you can see incredible things—a giant derrick that draws salt from beneath Seneca Lake, Paul Newman driving down Franklin Street in a Porsche, and dinosaurs projected onto the shale cliffs of an ancient gorge. The architecture is a crazy quilt of styles, and, while gaudy fast food chains now clash with colorful Victorian mansions, most neighborhoods still evoke a simpler, less hectic time. The business district has preserved a few historic buildings, like the brick structure that houses Wildflower Café.

At first glance, Wildflower looks more like a tavern than an eatery. A big, red British telephone box is perched on the sidewalk outside, and exposed brick, wooden booths, and a polished oak bar dominate the inside. But here, at the southern tip of Seneca Lake, owner Doug Thayer has established a reliable wine country pub, with good food, smart service, and fair prices.

Doug, who grew up in the Buffalo area, brought a hometown-style gathering place to Watkins Glen in 1990 when he converted a vacant storefront into Wildflower and stamped his personality on it. The original bricks were sandblasted, the tin ceiling was repainted, planks for the bar were milled at a local lumber yard, and furniture was handcrafted by Mennonite carpenters in nearby Dundee. Wildflower got into the local spirit from the ground up.

There are a couple of different ways to enjoy Wildflower Café. You can think of it as a wine bar and brewpub where you can sample from a rotating list of local wines or sip a mug of house-made ale. Locals come to relax, chat with old friends, and occasionally hold a business meeting in one of the booths. The wine list has a modest selection of Finger Lakes' entries, mostly from neighboring wineries, and only an occasional oddity from Long Island. Chris Stamp of Lakewood Vineyards and his family are regulars at Wildflower, and they permit the restaurant to offer an "exclusive pre-release" wine from the winery each vintage year. Leading the beer offerings is Wildflower's Black Walnut Ale, produced under its own label, The Rooster Fish Brewing Company.

You can also come here for a satisfying meal. The small but able kitchen sticks to the basics, and mostly with great success. Doug serves as executive chef, and his rangy menu of sandwiches, soups, salads, honey-crust pizzas, pastas, seafood, and steak is offered for lunch, dinner, or a light bite at odd hours. One of the most memorable dishes is Wildflower Chicken, a skinless, boneless chicken breast lightly coated with panko bread crumbs and sautéed with local mushrooms in Niagara wine (from Lakewood Vineyards). Besides the usual assortment of desserts, Doug makes his own special-recipe vanilla ice cream, and you can turn it into a sundae with raspberry purée or a rich cocoa sauce. Finish up with organic Columbian coffee, fresh-roasted in Ithaca by gimme!, a hometown institution.

Wildflower Café is a cozy outpost and a good place to rest on your way around the lake. When in Watkins Glen, eat where the locals eat.

CAYUGA *LAKE*

(kā-ˈyü-gə)

AT FORTY MILES, CAYUGA LAKE IS THE LONGEST of the Finger Lakes. Fed by stunning waterfalls and deep gorges, it's three miles wide, 435 feet deep, and it holds 2.5 trillion gallons of water. Cyclists are fond of the scenic roads that surround Cayuga Lake, providing the opportunity to conquer a 100-mile loop.

Located at the southern tip of the lake is the intellectual and cultural capital of the Finger Lakes. A local bumper sticker suggests that Ithaca is "Ten square miles surrounded by reality," and most residents like it that way. A small town at heart, politically correct Ithaca is a crazy quilt of academics from Cornell University and Ithaca College, artists, musicians, massage therapists, and progressive entrepreneurs—more often wearing Birkenstocks and driving Volvos than not. It is impossible not to fall in love with this place.

Ithaca is a great restaurant town, attracting talented chefs to the region's fresh produce and abundant variety of local wines. Nationally known Ithaca Farmer's Market is more than a means to connect farmer to consumer; it is a weekly social occasion for locals.

The Cayuga Wine Trail bands together the lake's boutique-size wineries, where it is likely you'll meet owners who still pour their own wines in the tasting rooms. And watch overhead for an occasional hot air balloon, providing an extra measure of wine country ambiance.

Other small gems on Cayuga include delightfully eccentric Trumansburg, site of the annual GrassRoots Festival, and the unspoiled lakeside village of Aurora, home to the women of Wells College since 1868.

Waterloo

Seneca Falls

Cayuga

Auburn

Skaneateles

Canoga

Fayette

Union Springs

Fleming

Owasco

Niles

Romulus

Levanna

Scipioville

Scipio

Owasco Lake

Willard

Aurora

Venice Center

Moravia

Ovid

Poplar Ridge

Cayuga Lake

King Ferry

Genoa

Locke

Lodi

Interlaken

Covert

North Lansing

Caywood

Valois

Trumansburg

Ludlowville

Myers

Hector

Seneca Lake

Jacksonville

Lansing

Etna

Reynoldsville

Mecklenburg

Enfield

ITHACA

Burdett

Watkins Glen

Wineries

1 King Ferry Winery *(KING FERRY)*

2 Six Mile Creek Vineyard *(ITHACA)*

3 Frontenac Point Vineyard *(TRUMANSBURG)*

4 Lucas Vineyards *(INTERLAKEN)*

5 Sheldrake Point Vineyard *(OVID)*

6 Hosmer Winery *(OVID)*

7 Thirsty Owl Wine Company *(OVID)*

8 Cayuga Ridge Estate Winery *(OVID)*

9 Buttonwood Grove Winery *(ROMULUS)*

10 Goose Watch Winery *(ROMULUS)*

11 Knapp Vineyards *(ROMULUS)*

12 Lakeshore Winery *(ROMULUS)*

13 Swedish Hill Vineyard *(ROMULUS)*

14 Montezuma Winery *(SENECA FALLS)*

Farms/Food Producers

15 Finger Lakes Aquaculture *(GROTON)*

16 Baker's Acres *(NORTH LANSING)*

17 Hollenbeck's Cider Mill *(VIRGIL)*

18 Northland Sheep Dairy *(MARATHON)*

19 Fallow Hollow Deer Farm *(CANDOR)*

20 Cornell Orchard *(ITHACA)*

21 Purity Ice Cream Company *(ITHACA)*

22 Ithaca Beer Company *(ITHACA)*

23 Early Bird Farm *(ITHACA)*

24 Stick and Stone Farm *(ITHACA)*

25 Bellwether Hard Cider *(TRUMANSBURG)*

26 Glenhaven Farm *(TRUMANSBURG)*

27 Lively Run Goat Dairy *(INTERLAKEN)*

28 Waid Apiaries *(INTERLAKEN)*

29 McDonald Farm *(ROMULUS)*

Restaurants

30 Aurora Inn *(AURORA)*

31 Moosewood Restaurant *(ITHACA)*

32 Maxie's Supper Club & Oyster Bar *(ITHACA)*

33 Willow *(ITHACA)*

34 Pangea *(ITHACA)*

35 Simply Red Village Bistro *(TRUMANSBURG)*

36 The Restaurant at Knapp Vineyards
(see Knapp Vineyards, ROMULUS)

37 The Café at Sheldrake Point Vineyard
(see Sheldrake Point Vineyard, OVID)

WINERIES

5986 Route 89
Romulus, NY 14541
(607) 869-9760

Hours: Monday–Saturday,
10:00 a.m.–5:30 p.m.;
Sunday, noon–5:30 p.m.

www.buttonwoodgrove.com

Buttonwood Grove Winery

White-bark buttonwood trees thrive in the ravines that border this Cayuga Lake hillside property, native symbols of the region's growing seasons. In winter, after all of the leaves have fallen, one-inch fruit balls remain, swinging from flexible stems that are two to three inches long. In early spring, the balls burst and disgorge seeds that sail on the winds with tiny parachutes, putting on a show for visitors to one of the newest wineries in the region.

Ken Riemer studied horticulture, agronomy, and botany at the University of Tennessee. After graduation, he worked in the pomology department at Cornell's Agricultural Experiment Station in Geneva. In 1975 he opened the Village Greenhouse in Trumansburg, where he has been growing and selling bedding plants ever since.

The disciplines of horticulture and viticulture are, of course, closely related, so it wasn't such a big leap for Ken when he decided to get into the wine game. He worked with growers and winemakers for many years and was fascinated with their "gardens of grapevines." As luck would have it, he owned a piece of property along the Cayuga Wine Trail. In 1997, with a gardener's patience and passion, he began a methodical, seven-year plan to develop a vineyard and winery at the site. "I decided to do something the land deserved," says Ken.

The land, however, was water starved and needed extensive irrigation, so he built a pond and installed two miles of drainage tiles. Then he seeded the vineyard with a cover crop to keep the weeds down. When he was ready to start planting vines, he judiciously selected Cabernet Franc, Cabernet Sauvignon, Riesling, and Chardonnay. Ken located his winemaking facility and tasting room, built from oak, cherry, walnut, and hickory woods culled from the property, on a rise of land above the vineyards, and, by 2004, he was ready to release his first vintage.

You don't have a garden just for yourself, you have it to share, and Buttonwood Grove attracts visitors with sound table wines from good, sound grapes. Although a varietal Cabernet Franc has fairly challenging notes of herbs, peppers, and spices, that same Cab Franc marries with Baco Noir and Marechal Foch to produce a well-conceived blend called Red Bud, its name inspired by a local woodland flower.

The nose offers aromas of ripe strawberries, plums, and a hint of vanilla. There is grip on the palate with chocolate, sour cherry, and blackberry flavors with hints of tobacco, coconut, and smoky oak, and the telltale Cab Franc component adds cassis and fresh herbs to the lingering finish. The wine is powerfully structured and balanced, with each component making its contribution to the character of the blend. I will look forward to tasting the early vintages in a few years, as I suspect a bit of aging will do wonders.

Trillium, a member of the lily family, is the native white flower that gives Ken's proprietary white blend its name. Seyval Blanc and Cayuga White are combined for a smooth, not quite classic, syrupy-sweet dessert wine with apple, pineapple, pear, and citrus characters, and a lovely, long finish.

Both Red Bud and Trillium are the result of strategic blending. Each wine is greater than the sum of its parts, with layered complexity from a palette of flavor components. It is said that a garden gives back more than it receives, and this is particularly obvious in the blended wines from this precocious estate.

Cayuga Ridge Estate Winery

Ovid, New York, was named for the Roman poet and vinophile who wrote: "It warms the blood, adds luster to the eyes; and wine and love have ever been allies." So, Cayuga Ridge Estate in the village of Ovid may have been destined to play a central role in the history of the Cayuga Lake wine region.

6800 Route 89
Ovid, NY 14521
(607) 869-5158

When Tom and Susie Challen purchased the winery from Bob and Mary Plane in 1991, the location was already well-entrenched as one of the Finger Lakes' most important properties. As Plane's Cayuga Vineyard, guided by the noted Cornell chemistry professor and his wife, it was the site of Cayuga Lake's first commercial planting of a fascinating variety, not only genetically designed specifically for this region, but a grape that tells people where they are.

Hours: Friday–Sunday, 11:00 a.m.–5:00 p.m. (April 15 through December 15); 11:00 a.m.–4:30 p.m. (December 16-April 14)

www.cayugaridgewinery.com

Cayuga White, a hybrid cross between Schuyler and Seyval Blanc, named at the Agricultural Experiment Station in 1972, is one of the most productive and disease-resistant varieties grown in the eastern United States. It consistently produces refreshing "sipping wines," often compared to Pinot Grigio.

The mother-block of Cayuga White at Cayuga Estate, blanketing eight acres of the vineyard with vigorous clusters of greenish-gold, translucent grapes, is now entrusted to Mr. Challen. A skilled farmer and winemaker from Canadian wine country, Tom produced experimental wines for T.G. Bright & Company, the largest winemaking operation in Canada, where he had an early opportunity to work with Cayuga White. On a visit to the Finger Lakes in 1989, he fell in love with the region and its wines and resolved to raise his family here.

Undaunted by immigration complications that almost sent him packing, Tom embraced the venerable vines, and, with focus and determination, set about making wines that have surpassed all previous efforts. His off-dry style of Cayuga White unlocks a perfume of apricot, green apples, and lemons. Perfectly balanced with vibrant apple and pear fruit flavors, it drinks clean, crisp, and light-bodied, while the vine age brings with it the benefit of concentration and complexity. Over the years, I've enjoyed vintages of this wine with mild cheeses, fish dishes, barbecued chicken, and even my favorite Chinese take-out.

Soil is the cradle of the vineyard's life. The shale and limestone in lakeside soil are not readily penetrated by roots, so plants struggle in the thin topsoil, producing smaller vines with yields of intensely flavored fruit. Since excellent fruit requires very little manipulation in the wine-making process, varietal characters are easily recognized in the final product. It's an elementary lesson in honest viticulture from Tom Challen: the memory of the ancient soil is transported into the grapes by the vine—no fussy flourishes are needed to improve natural goodness.

The grand old cavernous barn at the heart of picturesque Cayuga Ridge Estate provides a rustic surrounding for tasting not only the historic Cayuga White, but "true to type" Riesling, Chardonnay, Cabernet Franc, and Chancellor.

9501 Route 89
Trumansburg, NY 14886
(607) 387-9619

Hours: Friday and Saturday,
10:00 a.m.–4:00 p.m.,
Sunday, noon–4:00 p.m.
(May through November)

www.frontenacpoint.com

Frontenac Point Vineyard

Be careful not to blink as you drive north on Route 89, a few miles past Taughannock State Park. If you do you might miss a small wooden sign with a coat of arms that directs you to Frontenac Point Vineyard, home to some of the most agreeable and interesting country wines in all of the Finger Lakes.

Three decades ago, Jim Doolittle's desk job at the Department of Ag and Markets in Albany included guiding development of the New York State Farm Winery Bill. That piece of legislation would eventually allow independent grape growers to operate small-scale wineries and sell wines directly from their farms. By the time it became law, Jim was dreaming about his own winery, and he returned to Cornell to study viticulture—ready to get his hands dirty.

The dream came true on New Year's Eve 1977, when he and wife Carol purchased a nineteen-acre apple orchard from Roger King, the remaining piece of a Revolutionary War land grant to the King family. Over the next several years, apple trees were gradually replaced with grapevines on the gentle slope overlooking Cayuga Lake, and Jim adjusted to his newly acquired role as entrepreneur-cum-epicure.

Frontenac Point Vineyard, its name taken from the nearby site of the old Frontenac Hotel, produces 2,000 cases a year, or maybe a little less—on a recent visit I watched a half-dozen deer peck at Chardonnay grapes in the lower vineyard. What's left of the Chardonnay, plus Riesling, Pinot Noir, Seyval Blanc, and Ravat grapes are nurtured in the vineyard personally by Jim, then produced as varietal wines, with his careful attention to every detail in the process.

Although he stubbornly refuses to participate in the cooperative promotional events of his neighboring Cayuga Lake wineries, Jim Doolittle has earned their respect for his winemaking skills, particularly his success with an often-ignored grape variety called Chambourcin.

Bred in France, Chambourcin was at one time widely grown in the Loire Valley. It's still used as a blender in many wines but seldom receives any credit on the label. A hearty French-American hybrid, the grape was a favorite of Jim's mentor at Cornell for its resistance to disease and its ability to produce dark pigment even in cold growing seasons.

Chamboursin and Chamboursin blends now dominate the Frontenac Point portfolio with no fewer than five wines produced from the versatile grape: a varietal Chambourcin, Clos Frontenac (semi-dry rosé from free-run juice), Méthode Champenois (sparkling blanc de noir), Proprietor's Reserve (blend of Chamboursin, Pinot Noir, and Chelois), and Chameleon (blend of Pinot Noir, Chambourcin, Chelois, and Marechal Foch).

While some hybrid flavors, especially among the reds, will challenge a palate accustomed to viniferas, Chambourcin turns out to be an exception. As a varietal, it develops into a tasty, dark, and fresh red wine exhibiting ripe mulberry, elderberry, and cherry flavors, with an underlying gamey note. Jim's most passionate utterances deal with his care in moderating its pronounced tannins, and Chambourcin vinified in this style is nearly perfect with roasted venison or a grilled hamburger. Carol Doolittle has served it with a wild turkey taken on the vineyard.

If you are perplexed by the components in Jim's blends, I fully understand, but please keep an open mind. At the first sip of Proprietor's Reserve, I wondered if the more racy Chambourcin had overwhelmed the graceful Pinot Noir. But as the wine opens up, Pinot characters penetrate the palate to form lingering hints of spicy cinnamon and strawberry, complementing undertones of currant and mint from the Chelois.

Blending calls on experience, memory, and the winemaker's taste buds. For as long as I've known him, Jim Doolittle has enjoyed the challenge that comes with seeking just the right composite of two or more varieties and/or vintages, and creating wines that reach the height of complexity and interest, much like an artist painting with many colors. These are artful wines. And they are earnest wines, as earnest as the man who makes them.

Goose Watch Winery

Chestnuts ripen on trees overlooking Cayuga Lake until they turn brown and drop to the ground, from mid-September to mid-October. Nothing is more fitting on an autumn day than roasting chestnuts and sharing a bottle of local wine with good friends. A bite of chestnut calls for a sip of wine, and the wine in turn calls for more chestnuts.

5480 Route 89
Romulus, NY 14541
(315) 549-2599

Hours:
Daily, 10:00 a.m.–6:00 p.m.

www.goosewatch.com

When Ott Davis put his chestnut farm up for sale in 1996, the Peterson family seized the opportunity to expand the venture they began at Swedish Hill. Set among the rows of chestnut trees, Goose Watch Winery—almost called "Chestnut Ridge"—has built a name for itself as a progressive, albeit slightly capricious, medium-sized winery.

Goose Watch is about exploration and innovation, under the guidance of David Peterson, who has set the winery apart in philosophy from

Swedish Hill. He has challenged his team, headed by winemaker Derek Wilber and quality control technician Tracy Harris, to experiment with a range of wines that include Villard Blanc, a rare hybrid from the south of France; Isabella, a misunderstood and underappreciated grape with a regional history that dates back to the nineteenth century; and Viognier, a classic European varietal, up until now untested in the Finger Lakes.

The French-American hybrid, Villard Blanc, was at one time widely grown in the rocky soils of the Languedoc-Roussillon region of southern France, producing fruity, fragrant wines for everyday drinking. On the Cayuga Lake site its prolific vines produce large golden berries, delicious for eating out of hand. Once vinified at Goose Watch, Villard makes a dry Sauvignon Blanc–like wine with hints of fresh-cut herbs, and, before it goes into the bottle, up to 20 percent Chardonnay is added for body and complexity. A little vanilla sneaks through from the oak, and tangy citrus shows up in a surprisingly long finish.

Isabella is a more educated experiment. First discovered on the Long Island property of Mrs. Isabella Gibbs, her namesake grapes were planted in the Finger Lakes by Father William Bostwick, behind his Anglican church in Hammondsport in 1829. Father Bostwick blended Isabella with Catawba for his communion wine, and, by 1860, commercial winemakers were using an Isabella blend for sparkling wines. Although its skin is extremely dark, the grape doesn't lend itself to big red wines, so Goose Watch crafts Isabella into a salmon-pink, easy-sipping rosé. The aroma is full of spice, orange, and boysenberry; generous candied briary fruit and creamy orange rind fill the mouth; a long, smoky finish is accented with hints of wild strawberry and lime. Rosé of Isabella makes an attractive apéritif, a partner for curries and spicy foods, or a summer afternoon refresher.

The Viognier grape flourishes along steep terraces of a five-acre enclave in Chateau-Grillet, France's second smallest appellation. It produces an exceptional white wine with a flowery bouquet; however, the same grape produces fickle wines with elusive aromatics nearly everywhere else. This relatively sensitive creature, prone to wind and frosts, is seemingly too feeble to survive winters in the Finger Lakes. It's not only difficult to grow and cultivate, but vineyard yields are not encouraging.

Against all odds, Goose Watch Viognier explodes with a spicy, fruity, floral bouquet of apricots, honeysuckle, and orange blossoms. The true-to-variety characters of papaya, mango, and peach, with creamy mouthfeel and crisp, clean finish, is surely enough to overcome the skeptics. Picking the grapes in the cool early morning and gentle handling with minimal crushing help to prevent the loss of those precious flavors and aromas through oxidation. A hint of residual sweetness supports the expression of aromatics, and, even without wood aging, the wine is as full-bodied as an oaky Chardonnay.

Experimentation goes hand in hand with respect for heritage at Goose Watch. The approach here, in David Peterson's words, has to do with "pushing frontiers." His work in the avant-garde of Finger Lakes Cabernet Sauvignon, Lemberger, Merlot, Pinot Gris, Pinot Noir, Melody, and Traminette only adds to the adventure.

Hosmer Winery

6999 Route 89
Ovid, NY 14521
(607) 869-3393

Hours: Monday–Saturday, 10:00 a.m.–5:00 p.m., Sunday, noon–5:00 p.m. (April through December)

www.hosmerwinery.com

Since 1972, the Hosmer family has been farming grapes on a 250-acre tree-clad property near Cayuga Lake. Its first estate wines were produced in 1985, and the rustic tasting room emerged from a refurbished barn in 1990—the same year as the vineyard's first planting of Cabernet Franc.

A red wine most often used as a minor component in Bordeaux blends, Cabernet Franc is a fruitier and less tannic relation to Cabernet Sauvignon. It buds and matures earlier than Cabernet Sauvignon; produces a larger, juicier grape; and needs less heat to ripen fully. It thrives in the French Loire, especially in Chinon, where cooler growing conditions serve to accentuate the grape's herbaceous, grassy aromas. Since Cab Franc is much less susceptible to poor weather, it has found a comfortable fit in the Finger Lakes.

Cameron "Tunker" Hosmer was one of the earliest believers in the wine as a varietal, and his winery boasts some of the best Cab Franc in the region; some say it's one of the finest in America.

His folks sent young Tunker off to Cornell to study pomology, then to Fresno State for an education in winemaking. He returned to the farm stead in 1976 as a grower and, in his words, a "noninterventionist winemaker." He claims that when you look at his winemaking records over the years, wines with the fewest entries usually turned out best. Tunker will tell you the most important part of producing wine takes place in the vineyard, and he insists on letting his grapes "speak" for themselves.

In the process of making fine wines, according to Coach Tunker, "the grower controls the ball." In his sports analogy, if you don't have good grapes to start with, you're playing seven points down. He devises a game plan for the style of the finished wine before he picks a single grape, and, in the case of Cabernet Franc, he believes that vineyard management and ripe fruit are fundamental to success.

With extraordinary dedication to those compact clusters of purple grapes, Tunker produces a vineyard-driven Cab Franc that betrays the wine's true nature. With the ripeness it achieves at his site, fruit flavors of blackberry, blueberry, and raspberry are so overpowering, they need to be softened in French oak barrels for eight to ten months. The smokey oak characters frame a complex palate of pepper, plum, licorice, and dark chocolate, with aromas of fresh tobacco and a spicy, herbal finish.

In a vertical tasting of several vintages, Tunker declares his Cab Franc "wicked consistent," and he believes, from a viticultural standpoint, that it will prove to be a flagship wine for the Finger Lakes, with honest varietal fruit and longevity in the cellar.

Hosmer Farm Winery is dedicated to the respected European concept of making wine only from its own vineyards, where the grapes reflect meticulous tending by Tunker and his crew. His vines receive treatment more reminiscent of gardening than viticulture, and it shows, not only in Cab Franc but in distinctive and complex Chardonnay, Riesling, Pinot Gris, Cayuga, and Pinot Noir, as well.

658 Lake Road
King Ferry, NY 13081
(315) 364-5100

Hours: Monday–Saturday,
10:00 a.m.–5:00 p.m.;
Sunday, noon–5:00 p.m.
Closed in January. Weekends
only during February and
March (call for hours).

www.treleavenwines.com

King Ferry Winery

He was known on Capitol Hill as "the gentlemanly gentleman from Massachusetts." After serving three terms as governor and four terms in the U.S. Senate, Leverett Saltonstall stepped down from public service to become a gentleman farmer. His oldest son, also named Leverett, eschewed politics and instead distinguished himself in agriculture as a professor of agronomy at Cornell, a cattle rancher, and a seed producer on the 700-acre Treleaven Farm, bordering the eastern shore of Cayuga Lake.

One parcel of the original estate remains in the Saltonstall family, and, on a pasture where beef cattle once roamed, twenty-seven acres of wine grapes now flourish. Peter Saltonstall, the senator's grandson, and wife Tacie operate King Ferry Winery on this favored site and produce over a dozen varieties under the Treleaven label, including an exceptional Chardonnay. While it is probably an unlikely source for such a tremendous wine, Peter insists that the site is eminently suitable to the forgiving Chardonnay grapes. Even the dense clay soil, he believes, imparts Burgundian-like mineral notes to the character.

Peter, who was raised on the farm, planted a two-acre Chardonnay vineyard in 1983, and his early success inspired additional plantings in following years. He and Tacie had never been to Macon or Beaune, but they admired the region's wines and intended them as models for their own Chardonnays. So off they went to France. They visited venerable vineyards throughout Burgundy, spent time in the cellars of ancient estates, and observed the winemaking firsthand. They learned old-school techniques of gentle agitation called *batonnage* to develop aromatics, lees aging to enhance body and mouthfeel, and the blending of lots from different barrels for complexity and richness. Taking another page from the French who govern yields by law, Peter and Tacie learned to pay close attention to crop load.

King Ferry's grapes are grown at moderate yields, then harvested in late October after a long maturation and "hang time" in order to reach optimal aroma, flavor, and color. Hand-picking takes place in the early morning hours before the fall sun has had a chance to warm the vineyard, and the crew sorts through the clusters of each vine, selecting only what is evenly ripened and disease free. After destemming, gentle pressing, and settling, the juice is fermented in French and Hungarian oak barrels. Following yeast fermentation, secondary malolactic bacterial fermentation adds flavor complexity and softens the wine's acidity.

Combating unpredictable weather requires careful canopy management, and Peter has an effective system in place. He employs a vertical shoot positioning trellis system with multiple catch wires to provide the most wide open canopy possible. The open canopy allows for maximum air circulation to dry the fruit and foliage when it's wet from dew or rain. The result is healthy fruit with plenty of character.

Treleaven Chardonnay is crisp, with ripe lemony, citrus, and herbal flavors, and smoky, toasty notes in a sophisticated style. The vineyard annually culls up to one-third of its best production for the Chardonnay Reserve, an opulent, fuller-tasting wine with aromas of lemon, honeysuckle, and spice. On the palate it exhibits notes of peach, mango, and orange, amplified by Melba toast with a touch of smoke. Its subtle buttery element reminds me of a brassy California Chardonnay, and, sure enough, the 2000 vintage captured a gold medal at California's Riverside International Wine Competition.

The Saltonstalls have a proud heritage of talent, commitment, and ambition. These influences, it seems, have combined in a family winemaking endeavor to produce wines made in the classical cool climate tradition to complement rather than overpower food flavors. Among them are Chardonnays of truly great stature and distinction.

Knapp Vineyards/
The Restaurant at Knapp Vineyards

In the feeble dawn of winegrowing in the region, Doug Knapp operated one of the region's few mechanical harvesters. As he traveled around the Finger Lakes, harvesting grapes for other growers, he became convinced that the best grapes were the ones growing on his own sixty-five-acre property. By 1982 he summoned the ambition to fill out bonding forms and produce commercial wine.

2770 County Road 128 (Ernsberger Road) Romulus, NY 14541 (800) 869-9271

Winery Hours:
Monday through Saturday, 10:00 a.m.–5:30 p.m., Sunday, 11:00 a.m.– 5:30 p.m. (April through December)
Restaurant Hours: Lunch, daily, 11:00 a.m.–4:00 p.m.; Dinner, Thursday–Sunday, 5:00 p.m.–8:00 p.m. (April through December)

www.knappwine.com

Doug figured out how to make a uniquely rich style of Chardonnay in the 1980s, nailed powerful but refined Cabernet Sauvignon and Cabernet Franc in the 1990s, and continued to experiment with and improve his many other wines through 2000, when the winery was sold to Glenora Wine Cellars. The new owners are on a path to maintain and enhance the magic and charm of this wonderful place.

Knapp's flirtation with Sangiovese, a rare varietal in the Finger Lakes, has been a challenge. Early vintages were shy on varietal character, concentration, and complexity, but while the wine may never reach the level of great Tuscan Brunello, more recent bottles display tart red cherry aromas, satisfying spicy raspberry and cherry notes, and floral nuances of violets and herbs. "For more consistency in our Sangiovese, we've learned to use innovative farming practices, Italian yeasts for fermentation, and new oak aging," explains winemaker Steve diFrancesco.

In 1995 Knapp became the first winery on the East Coast to operate an alembic pot still for the production of grappa and brandy. The grappa is hand-distilled from fermented seedless grape varieties, including Lakemont, Reliance, and Vanessa. A single run through the still produces a high-proof fiery spirit with a refined concentration of flavor, a gentle perfume of the grapes, and a delightful, almost sweet, aftertaste. For brandy, Catawba and DeChaunac wines are distilled twice, then aged separately for at least two years in toasted wood barrels so they develop the characteristic brown color. Finally, the varieties are blended to create a brandy of fruity delicacy and finesse—perfect for after dinner at the winery's restaurant.

One of the Finger Lakes' most engaging chefs is Eric Pierce of The Restaurant at Knapp Vineyards, a lovely space with a patio overlooking its own vineyards. He offers an ever-changing menu of countrified Northern Mediterranean cuisine, influenced by the style of the house wines, with liberal use of local bounty, including seasonal produce, cheeses from nearby artisans, and herbs from the restaurant's own garden. Eric trained under Arthur Kelly at Glenora Wine Cellars' Veraisons restaurant and graduated with honors.

The chef demonstrates the breadth and depth of his balancing act with a menu that complements Knapp's food-friendly wine portfolio. He believes that cooking with wine adds "density and complexity" to many of his dishes, and he proves it with a spicy tomato sauce laced with Merlot in Clams Alla Deavola and a splash of port in Ruby Black Bean Soup. Prism, a Bordeaux-style blend produced at the winery, is reduced or simmered slowly over heat for a sauce that adds elegance to a filet mignon. For perfect compatibility with the dish, Eric suggests serving the same wine that has been cooking in the pot.

Anyone who loves Meritage blends will revel in Knapp Prism. Cabernet Sauvignon forms the backbone of this wine, at 66 percent, complemented by Cabernet Franc (26 percent), and Merlot (8 percent). A deep ruby opaque color greets you, followed by some oak and herbs. Stylish, with lovely fruit and modest complexity on the palate, its components meld in a wine that is supple in texture, soft of tannin, and long on the palate.

Although many chefs use "cooking wines," Eric warns, "Don't cook with a wine you wouldn't drink. Reduction brings out the worst in an inferior wine." He recognizes that he has the luxury of cooking at a winery restaurant, but insists that it is not a waste to use a fabulous wine for a sauce: "The quality will ultimately ring true in the final dish."

Desserts offer inspired and unconventional combinations, such as Rum and Molasses Baked Apple Pie stuffed with raisins, Peach Crème Brûlée made with perfectly ripe peaches, and Strawberry Supreme, a "sundae" of vanilla ice cream and local strawberries, drizzled with grappa, topped with whipped cream, and garnished with toasted coconut and chocolate lace.

The completeness of the wine country experience is what makes Knapp Vineyards special. The dizzying array of wines, stunning food, and idyllic surroundings produces something greater than the sum of its parts.

Lakeshore Winery

Two precious acres of hand-tended grapevines surround Lakeshore Winery's rustic barn, situated on a historic farmstead that dates back to 1825. Chatty, informal wine tastings take place near the warmth of a working stone fireplace, where you're invited to pull up a rocking chair, relax, and perform sensory evaluations while sampling morsels of compatible foods. It's like going to someone's home to learn about wine.

5132 Route 89
Romulus, NY 14541
(315) 549-7075

Hours: Monday–Saturday, 10:30 a.m.–5:00 p.m., Sunday, noon–5:00 p.m. (April through December); Weekends only, noon–5:00 p.m. (January through March)

www.lakeshorewinery.com

Owned and operated by John and Annie Bachman, who purchased the property in 1994 from the winery's founders, Bill and Doris Brown, Lakeshore offers a spectacular view of the lake and a dock for visitors who arrive by boat. The way John tells the story, he was thinking about retirement even as he made the transition from technical director for Cadbury-Schwepps to gentleman winegrower at Lakeshore. Unlike many of their neighbors, the Bachmans' enterprise represents an alternative lifestyle choice, one they intend to keep on a small, personal scale.

Of all the transplants of European varieties to the Finger Lakes, Cabernet Sauvignon may be the greatest challenge. It essentially requires a longer growing season than is generally found in all but the most favored locations in our region. John's painstaking canopy and irrigation management in the vineyard is supported by the site's longer growing season and rich alluvial soil, as he coaxes expression from the noble grape. Since 1978, Lakeshore has delivered Cabernets with exceptional cool climate characteristics.

Average harvests furnish just one and a half tons of fruit from the single acre of Cabernet vines, and although this is an extremely low yield, wines produced from this level have intense, complicated flavors. Recent vintages show vanilla and perfumed aromas, Burgundian dusty, fruity, blackberry, and spicy notes, with an herbal-vegetal component and firm tannins moderated by toasty American oak. Lakeshore Cabernets are delicious and satisfying, with rustic personality.

In mid-November, Lakeshore releases a "nouveau" wine that provides not only the first taste of the vintage, but a good excuse for the annual weekend-long party at the farm. Inspired by the celebratory tradition of French Beaujolais Nouveaux, whole grape clusters are fermented, bottled, and offered as a reward for the labors of harvest. A French-hybrid varietal, Marechal Foch, provides Lakeshore Nouveau some bright and lively fruit flavors, but, barely six weeks out of the vineyard, it's no more than a simple quaff, best enjoyed when served slightly chilled.

Aunt Clara and Uncle Charlie, I should explain, are not relatives of the Bachmans, nor are they folks you should expect to meet in the tasting room. Rather, these are whimsical names attached to two versions of Catawba, made into compulsory picnic wines with grapes purchased from a nearby farm. John and Annie put their hearts, skill, and wit into every bottle, and Lakeshore has become a favorite stop for both locals and visitors because it's as fun and unpretentious as its wines.

3862 County Road 150
Interlaken, NY 14847
(607) 532-4825

Hours: Monday–Saturday,
10:30 a.m.–5:00 p.m.,
Sunday, noon–5:00 p.m.
(January through April);
Monday–Saturday,
10:30 a.m.–5:30 p.m.,
Sunday, noon–5:30 p.m.
(May through December)

www.lucasvineyards.com

Lucas Vineyards

Family is number one in every aspect of this unlikely wine-producing endeavor. Ruth and Bill Lucas uprooted their family in 1975, moved out of the Bronx, and resettled upstate in order to grow grapes on a patch of land overlooking Cayuga Lake. For Bill it was a stark contrast to his job as a tugboat captain in New York Harbor, but he was married to a remarkable partner. Ruth's enthusiasm and optimism set an example for her family, as she mastered the economic and agricultural basics of the winegrowing business. Even the Lucas daughters, Ruthie and Stephanie, worked the land from an early age, tying vines, picking grapes, and driving the tractor.

At first the family supplied grapes to a number of Finger Lakes wineries, including Taylor and Glenora. Then, with the 1980 harvest, the Lucases seized the opportunity to make their own wines. Starting with production of just 400 cases of Cayuga and DeChaunac, they carefully expanded the fledgling operation with the help of consulting winemaker Dave Bagley of Poplar Ridge Vineyard. The string of accolades and competition-winning medals that followed attests to the hard work and determination of the entire clan.

Today the vineyard is a balanced mix of hybrid and vinifera grapes, featuring "museum vines" in the original nursery block. Its star performer is Cayuga, historically at the heart of the Lucas white wine program. Besides making a Germanic-style still wine, this early harvested grape is crafted into the delightful Extra Dry Sparkling Wine. Clean and refreshing on the palate with bright fruit and lively bubbles, it displays flavor notes of lime and green apples and just a hint of sweetness at the finish. This regional progeny pays homage to the pioneering vision of Ruth Lucas, a sparkling wine enthusiast who uses the traditional, labor-intensive French Champagne production method with nontraditional Cayuga grapes.

Lucas women are involved in every aspect of the venture. For them, being part of a winemaking family is both a way of life and a way to make a living. Ruthie functions as business manager, in charge of wine sales and distribution. Stephanie manages the winery hospitality/retail center with a particular focus on public relations, visitor programs, and special events. Ruth, now sole owner of the family estate, spends most of her time dealing with vineyard and winemaking concerns.

She suggests that women may be better winemakers since they are more nurturing of their wines. She compares turning grapes into wine with bringing up children—babies when first picked, sometimes troublesome teenagers during fermentation, more mature in oak barrels, then all grown up in the bottle, ready to send out into the world.

The gracious tasting room at Lucas Vineyards offers fifteen different wines, including Chardonnay, Gewürztraminer, Riesling, Cabernet Franc, and Pinot Noir, as well as French-American hybrid varietals and the "Tug Boat" series, everyday blends tied to family roots.

Montezuma Winery

The extensive marshes at the north end of Cayuga Lake were left behind ten thousand years ago in the last retreat of the melting glaciers. With a mixture of nutrient-rich waters, lush and diverse vegetation, and rich invertebrate and insect life, the wetlands provide a resting, nesting, and feeding habitat for waterfowl and other migratory birds on their journeys to and from northeastern Canada.

2981 Route 20 East
Seneca Falls, NY 13148
(315) 568-8190

Hours:
Daily, 10:00 a.m.–6:00 p.m.

www.montezumawinery.com

"Montezuma" was the name that New York City physician Peter Clark gave his marshland estate in the early 1800s, inspired by his trip to Mexico City and the site of the Aztec Emperor's palace. Eventually, the marsh, the local town and village, and the wildlife refuge, established in 1938, all adopted the name.

In 2001 George Martin and his family expanded the honey farm they operated in Sterling, near Lake Ontario, with a winery and meadery at the edge of the wildlife refuge that offers mead and melomel produced from their 500 beehives, as well as wines made from local orchard-grown fruit.

Historical recipes are combined with modern technologies to create mead in three different styles, each pale golden in color, each from the blend of clover and alfalfa honeys foraged by the bees from local dairy farms. After the honey is blended with spring water, it is filtered and then fermented with the same process as a grape wine. The "ultrafiltration" process, developed by Bob Kime at Cornell's Agricultural Experiment Station, removes high–molecular weight proteins from the honey, speeding up the fermentation and aging process to a matter of weeks. Wine yeasts, fermenting at cooler temperatures, enhance fruity characters and result in a more winelike mead.

Montezuma meads range from a dry, crisp honey wine with a floral fragrance, to semisweet, a more traditional style with notes of beeswax, to sweet, a rich, creamy wine with fruity characters that suggest Niagara grapes—differing styles that depend on residual sweetness retained from the honey.

Melomel is the name given to a blend of fruit wine with mead. Montezuma Raspberry Melomel blends semisweet mead with wine produced from local Red Jacket Orchards vine-ripened raspberries. It's a fruit-forward drink, with rich aromatics of raspberry and blackberry, slight tartness on the palate, and creamy, integrated honey characters in the finish. King George's Pyment blends dry mead with Marechel Foch, a red grape wine, for a drink with complex notes of raspberry, black cherry, plum, and honey.

The Martins translate the pure fragrant essence of apples, strawberries, blueberries, raspberries, cranberries, peaches, plums, and even rhubarb into prizewinning, stand-alone fruit wines. Local farms and orchards supply the ingredients used to make light and balanced "country sippers" that provide a taste of fruit at the peak of the season all year around.

7448 County Road 153
Ovid, NY 14521
(607) 532-9401

Winery Hours:
Daily, 11:00 a.m.–5:30 p.m.
(May through October); Daily,
noon–5:00 p.m. (November
through April)
Restaurant Hours: Call for
schedule

www.sheldrakepoint.com

Sheldrake Point Vineyard/ The Café at Sheldrake Point Vineyard

In the late 1800s, a sidewheel steamboat called the *Frontenac* shuttled wealthy vacationers to the Cayuga Lake Hotel, perched on a sweeping stretch of lakefront called Sheldrake. The majestic hotel accommodated guests in high style for over thirty years before succumbing to fire in 1909.

The prominent point at Sheldrake-on-Cayuga is not natural topography, but rather a construction of gravelly loam "fill" carted in by horses during the early nineteenth century, to create bedding for a hamlet of summer cottages and gracious lakefront estates. Over the years, Sheldrake has provided summer homes for such notables as George Westinghouse and Rod Serling.

The Point's agricultural legacy includes a 160-acre orchard and dairy farm, operated from 1850 until the mid-1980s. That property, resting at the water's edge, is now the site of a youthful vineyard of Chardonnay, Riesling, Gewürztraminer, Pinot Gris, Pinot Noir, Gamay, Merlot, Cabernet Franc, and Cabernet Sauvignon grapes, the ambitious effort of winegrower Bob Madill. With the support of partners and investors, he established Sheldrake Point Vineyard in 1997, determined to take full advantage of what he calls the "Sheldrake Effect."

Although the average depth of Cayuga Lake is 179 feet, just off the beach at Sheldrake it plunges to 435 feet. Since deep water heats and cools more slowly, it delays both the onset of warm temperatures in spring and the first frost in fall. Cold air masses are warmed significantly as they cross the lake, and clouds formed by the exchange of heat and moisture moderate surrounding temperatures. Sheldrake Point's microclimate lengthens the growing season to 170 days, more than two weeks longer than many other areas in the Finger Lakes. In addition, the east-facing slope warms up faster in the morning hours than west-facing slopes, and deep gorges on both sides of the vineyard promote effective air drainage, inhibiting both frost and disease.

Bob Madill's passion for this site is rewarded by the prolific vineyard and its remarkable wines, especially the Pinot Noirs. In the very short time since the winery's founding, he has explored the idea of allowing Pinot Noir, in his words, to become a "voice from the vineyard," a distinct personality.

One of the oldest of grape varieties, Pinot Noir is among the most sensitive to terroir, an expression of each individual vineyard. The Sheldrake Point imprimatur is strawberry and tea leaf aromas, with the richness of ripe cherry, smoke, and spice, wrapped in a warm core of toasty oak. At the finish, even more varietal characters penetrate the palate to form lovely, lingering hints of cinnamon.

In the adjacent Café, chef Jack Carrington takes the enterprise a step further in its effort to define the essence of this place. His modernized version of American food depends on seasonal, local ingredients for the subtle style that makes it a natural companion to Sheldrake Point wines. The food and wine are intended not only to complement each other, but also to inspire one another.

Since farming is the first step in cooking, the chef's prowl for local ingredients starts in his own garden, just yards away from the kitchen. Setting the groundwork for his menu, Jack personally selects the lettuces, fruits, vegetables, and herbs for each growing season, then supplements his needs at nearby farms.

Dishes are developed around flavors—isolating them, maximizing them, and combining them. A pan-seared and oven-roasted lamb chop drizzled with rosemary-thyme sauce ramps up the earthy flavors of the Pinot Noir. The same wine with grilled breast of duck and a winter pear-green peppercorn sauce acts almost like another ingredient in the sauce, never overpowering the other textures or flavors. Both dishes harmonize perfectly with the wine.

Amid landscaped gardens and sloping lawns, with a close-up view of Cayuga Lake, the interplay of wine and food is emblematic of the Sheldrake Point experience, a showcase for some of the best the region has to behold and savor.

Six Mile Creek Vineyard

In the mistaken belief that wine grapes could not survive on their property, Roger and Nancy Battistella nearly decided to grow blueberries instead. Although nestled on the southwest slope of a lovely valley near the headwaters of Ithaca's Six Mile Creek, the site is a frost pocket, too far from the winter-moderating protection of Cayuga Lake.

Cool temperatures during the growing season would affect flowering of the vines, predicted Cornell Cooperative Extension, and cold weather at harvest would retard ripening of the grapes, resulting in thin, tart wines. But, in 1982, the Battistellas ignored conventional wisdom and bravely planted six acres of white French-hybrid and vinifera grapes on their patch of land. The extra care they took to assure the health of the vines helped the young plants to withstand temperature extremes, and, by 1987,

1551 Slaterville Road
(Route 79)
Ithaca, NY 14850
(607) 272-9463

Hours:
Daily, 11:00 a.m.–5:30 p.m.

www.sixmilecreek.com

they had produced grapes that confounded the experts. In a happy consequence, the vineyard's lower yield of fruit resulted in greater concentration of varietal characters in the wines.

Six Mile Creek Vineyard overlooks the wooded, stone-walled creek gorge near Businessman's Lunch Falls, now capped with Van Natta's Dam to create a reservoir for Ithaca's drinking water. A pre–Civil War cemetery borders one end of the historic grounds; an old stagecoach stop marks the other. Winemaking takes place in a restored Dutch-Colonial barn, moved in its entirety to the new foundation.

The vineyard's flagship wine, appropriately called Ithaca White, is a near-dry, proprietary blend that clearly reflects where it comes from. The Cayuga-Chardonnay combination proves successful—the former for pear, peach, and honeysuckle notes, the latter for complexity and finesse. Cayuga's relatively simple fruity flavors make it a natural candidate as a blending base, and a dollop of Chardonnay adds nuances that are hard to isolate apart from the total bouquet and taste.

Dr. Battistella, a senior professor of Health Policy and Management at Cornell University, denies that he administers rigorous academic discipline to his agricultural practices. He describes two types of winemakers. One is technically oriented and works strictly by the book; the other is less disciplined and sometimes flies by the seat of the pants. While grape growing and winemaking feed his creative drive and his intellectual curiosity, Battistella places himself somewhere in between the two.

He explains that his greatest challenge has been to find grape varieties that can be grown within the limitations imposed by the climate, especially on a site with contradictory attributes. His commitment to hard work and long-term planning is reflected in the steadily increasing quality of Six Mile Creek wines over the past decade. He has achieved much of what he set out to do.

4565 Route 414
Romulus, NY 14541
(315) 549-8326

Hours:
Daily, 9:00 a.m.–6:00 p.m.

www.swedishhill.com

Swedish Hill Vineyard

Swedish culture is rich in traditions. One of the most revered customs is mixing "glogg," a concoction of mulled wine with dried fruit and spices, served during Christmas season. It is usually made by the man of the house and stewed very slowly on his wife's kitchen stove.

David Peterson remembers stories about his ancestors in Sweden, especially about a great-grandfather who made his own wine for the holiday glogg. Family folklore serves as inspiration for the seasonal drink produced at Swedish Hill, a spicy and aromatic Concord-based wine blended with cardamon, cinnamon, and cloves and bottled for wintertime visitors to the winery. Add raisins, cherries, orange slices, and slivered almonds, then heat and enjoy!

The old country was very much on their minds when David's parents, Dick and Cindy Peterson, named their farm "Swedish Hill" in 1969 and began growing and selling grapes to area wineries. In 1986, with a weakening market for local grapes, the Petersons decided to produce a small quantity of their own wines from Aurora, Catawba, Vignoles, and Chardonnay—and a farm winery was born.

David, who holds a Ph.D. in viticulture, taught at Southwest Missouri State University, then worked in research at Cornell before assuming management of winemaking at Swedish Hill in 1996. His academic foundation places him among the new breed of high-tech winemakers, but his progressive approach is tempered with a strong respect for regional tradition. Striking the right balance between indigenous grape varieties and their noble European counterparts has proved to be a winning strategy.

As the winery operation began to expand, the Petersons concluded that they ought to purchase grapes from established growers rather than take on financial investors. Today, Swedish Hill enjoys mutually dependable relationships with twenty-nine different growers whose contracts are bargained and settled, as they have been since the early days—with handshakes. David maintains that these agreements are based on the most specific quality standards and production practices in the region and that his growers value the long-term commitments and fair prices paid. Only 20 percent of Swedish Hill's wines are produced from estate-grown grapes, so, he suggests, his growers have become, in a sense, "investors."

The rustic tasting room, where two-thirds of wine sales originate, is a bit like a country general store, very atmospheric, homey, and friendly. I learned, to my great surprise, that Swedish Hill's Svenska series of labrusca-based products are the winery's best sellers, outdistancing many of the more glamorous wines.

The flavor profile of these wines is unashamedly driven toward characters of the native varieties, with a white wine blend of Delaware, Golden Muscat, and Diamond; a red blend of Concord, Delaware, and Rougeon; and a blush wine derived from Catawba and Isabella.

On the other end of the spectrum, Swedish Hill's bullwork with "hot pressing" has helped establish the Finger Lakes as a legitimate and promising region for Cabernet Franc. In cool, damp years, underripe grapes have a tendency to develop herbaceous odors during fermentation. Thermal treatment at 135 degrees reduces "grass" and "green pepper" flavors and adds complexity along with a balanced, round mouthfeel. Swedish Hill Cabernet Franc has a deep and intense garnet color. The nose, absent unpleasant vegetal characteristics, is dominated by aromas of almonds and chocolate, and the palate is full and round, with flavors of coffee, cassis, and blackberry.

The vitality of the Swedish Hill enterprise must be credited to its depth and range of wines, supported by state-of-the-art equipment and technical expertise. The prodigious portfolio of dry whites, sweet whites, dry reds, fortified reds, sparkling wines, and brandy consistently earns top honors and gold medals in state and national wine competitions.

6799 Elm Beach Road
Ovid, NY 14521
(607) 869-5805

Hours:
Daily, 11:00 a.m.–5:30 p.m.

www.thirstyowl.com

Thirsty Owl Wine Company

The Rieslings of Thirsty Owl are bottled history. When Jonathan Cupp purchased a parcel of the former Plane family estate in 2001, he inherited the oldest Riesling vines on Cayuga Lake. Dr. Robert Plane, an educator and viticulturalist, planted noble Rieslings on this site in 1972, and, after three decades, each drop of wine reflects the character of its grapevine's struggle to survive.

Older vines have roots that find more abundant water and extract higher levels of mineral nutrients from the soil. The root systems, which have labored over the years to reach down as deep as eight to ten feet into the granite-laced soil, pick up flavors of the earth unobtainable from younger counterparts. Although climatic extremes are tempered by the property's close proximity to the lake, its mature vines have come to terms with the unpredictability of seasons in the Finger Lakes.

While Jon is engaged in diplomatic chores at the estate, the winemaking is assigned to Nancy Newland, former owner of New Land Vineyard on Seneca Lake, and Shawn Kime, who manages the vineyards as well.

"A lot has been asked of these vines and these soils over the last thirty years," says Nancy, "and they keep coming through." While diminished yields are expected from older plantings, the vines here show excellent health and vigor. It's a sign of maturity that the vines seem to be producing more balanced grapes, with less disparity between the sugars and acids.

Riesling may be the loveliest of all white wine grapes in the world, if only because of its ability to transmit the unique characteristics of the vineyard in which it's grown. Nancy takes full advantage of the well-developed fruit, carefully managing the distinctions between her two versions of the varietal. The lively, citrusy nose of Dry Riesling is a preview to lots of lime, fruit syrup, and a touch of fresh herbs on the palate. Spice and minerals add to the peach and apple flavors in the lengthy finish. In a semi-dry version, the wine reveals a delicate floral nose of tangerine and quince followed by sweet tropical fruit flavors and green apple and pineapple on the finish.

Thirsty Owl Pinot Noir displays well-integrated flavors of dark cherry fruit, toasted almonds, dried herb, tomato, white pepper, and a long finish with a little heat. The same Pinot Noir moderates aggressive tannins and cedar of Chancellor in a blend called "Lot 99," named for Revolutionary War Sergeant Florence Marony's original land-grant designation.

One of the oddest things about Thirsty Owl is the winery's name. Jon explains that it was inspired by the tale of his father's sighting of a huge horned owl in the family's backyard. He suspects that the elder Cupp's wine consumption may have been responsible for exaggerating the bird's proportions, so, when it came to selecting a name, Jon couldn't resist making an owl the symbol of his winery.

FARMS/FOOD PRODUCERS

Baker's Acres

16

Cornell Chicken can be found most any Saturday or Sunday throughout the summer, sizzling on a barbecue somewhere around the Finger Lakes, the centerpiece of a fundraiser for a volunteer fire department, church group, or service club. One-half chicken per person is usually served with boiled potato and coleslaw, a soft dinner roll, and a pat of butter.

The formula for delicious Cornell Chicken was devised in the mid-1940s by Dr. Robert Baker, a food scientist at Cornell University, during his quest for the ultimate marinade to flavor, moisturize, and tenderize chicken. For his efforts, Dr. Baker has become a local legend. His prized recipe inspired the All-American backyard barbecue that became part of our culture in the 1950s, and millions of plump chickens have been slathered with the savory sauce ever since.

Dr. Baker continued Poultry Extension research while teaching courses in Poultry and Egg Product Technology at the university for four more

1104 Auburn Road
(Route 34)
North Lansing, NY 13073
(607) 533-4653

Hours: Tours Wednesdays,
1:00 p.m.–2:00 p.m.;
self-guided tour, daily,
9:00 a.m.–5:00 p.m.

www.bakersacres.net

decades. Along the way, he was singlehandedly responsible for development of the chicken hot dog, chicken nuggets, and thirty other chicken products, besides the classic Cornell Chicken marinade.

Every year since 1949, the Baker family has barbecued Cornell Chicken at the annual New York State Fair in Syracuse, a showcase for the best of what New York agriculture has to offer. There, under a sheltered outdoor pavilion with picnic tables, they've been known to serve as many as 2,500 chicken dinners in a single day, and, in 2002, the "Chicken Coop" proudly served Cornell Chicken to special fairgoers, former President Clinton, Senator Hillary Rodham Clinton, and daughter Chelsea.

Baker's Acres was undertaken as a modest family pursuit when Dr. Baker first contemplated retirement from teaching in 1980. Today, the estate is one of the largest perennial growers in the Finger Lakes, as well as an herb farm that supplies restaurant and home gardens throughout the region. Inspired by Mrs. Baker's interest in horticulture, display gardens include shade and sun perennial beds, a rock garden with a lily pond, a bog garden, an English rose garden, tree and shrub berms, and an everlasting flower garden. Plus, there are 600 apple trees and two acres of asparagus, providing both retail sales and home-grown ingredients for

Yield: 3 cups

1 egg

1 cup vegetable oil

2 cups cider vinegar

3 tablespoons salt

1 tablespoon poultry seasoning

½ teaspoon freshly ground black pepper

Note: Adjust the quantity of the salt or eliminate altogether to meet individual health needs and taste preferences. Leftover sauce can be stored in a glass jar and refrigerated for several weeks. Because this sauce contains raw egg, it should only be used as a basting sauce for meats during cooking.

CORNELL BARBECUE SAUCE

The delicious sauce has its roots at Cornell University, where legendary Professor Robert Baker developed this recipe for the Poultry Science Department. First, split young dressed chickens and marinate in the barbecue blend, then grill at a low temperature (about 350°F). Finger Lakes classicists contend that this is the only way to fix barbecue. Local volunteer fire departments support themselves with fundraisers featuring succulent "Cornell Barbecue Chicken."

In a bowl, beat the egg, and then add the oil and beat again. Add the remaining ingredients and stir.

When using the sauce for basting meat, brush on the meat every few minutes during cooking.

the farmstead tea room. Dainty lunches are appointed with edible flowers from the greenhouse, and a favorite dessert is apple pie served with farm-fresh cider.

If you visit Baker's Acres on any Sunday from mid-April to early July, you'll be treated to a time-honored feast of genuine Cornell Chicken, cooked by Dr. Baker himself—now well into his eighties but still active on the farm. With his background as an educator, he'll happily share everything he knows about the art of barbecue. You'll learn to turn frequently and baste the chicken to prevent burning and drying, to mist hot spots or flare-ups in the fire with a small amount of water, and to check doneness by twisting the drumstick to see if it will turn easily in the joint socket. The only thing you won't learn is how to say no to second helpings.

Bellwether Hard Cider

25

Sweet apple cider is, literally, apple juice, the product of squeezing fresh apples. True cider, or "hard cider," is the result of fermenting fresh apple juice, and the long-forgotten craft is experiencing a renaissance in the apple-rich Finger Lakes.

9070 Route 89
Trumansburg, NY 14886
(607) 272-4337

A passion for cider has existed for centuries. Apple trees for cider production were among the first fruits planted in the British colonies, and practically every home in Early America set aside a barrel of cider for the wintertime. Hard cider continued as the country's most popular alcoholic drink until Prohibition, but, with the return of legal drinking, America had acquired an appetite for beer. Cider making virtually became a lost art.

Hours: Monday–Saturday, 10:00 a.m.–5:30 p.m., Sunday, noon–5:30 p.m. (April through December); Saturday, 10:00 a.m.–5:00 p.m., Sunday, noon–5:00 p.m. (January through March)

In the fall of 1996, Bill and Cheryl Barton began by blending fresh-pressed local apples and then slowly fermenting the juice over the winter. By the following year they were in the hard cider business.

www.cidery.com

Bill describes what he calls a "tortured path" to what is now a formidable enterprise on a gentle slope of land above Cayuga Lake. With previous career turns in geophysics, resource economics, and software development, he has finally settled in to the dream job he has imagined since grad school days at Cornell.

The well-chosen site enjoys many of the same attributes as nearby grape-growing farms, and its longer growing season means higher acid and tannin levels in the fruit. Malic acid gives cider its sharpness; bitter characters derive from the tannins. Late harvested apples give cider its "bite."

While patiently waiting for their own three acres of cider-apple seedlings to mature at Bellwether, the Bartons purchase Liberty apples from the Geneva Experiment Station, Northern Spy and table varieties from Red Jacket Farms, and European cider varieties such as Brown Snout, Chisel Jersey, Dabinette, Doux Tardif, Harry Master's Jersey, and Hereford Redstreak from Professor Ian Merwin's Black Diamond Farm. A wide choice of locally grown apples gives the cider makers a lot to work with, and the results are exceptional varietals and blends, produced in the styles of northwestern France, western England, and Colonial America.

Four to seven of the table fruit varieties, including Empire, Gala, and Fuji, are combined in Bellwether Original Hard Cider, pale gold in color, medium-bodied, lightly sparkling and dry, with gentle apple aroma; Liberty Spy Hard Cider has mellow, refreshing flavors from the blend of honeyed Liberty and Northern Spy apples; Cherry Street Hard Cider is a unique mixture of tart cherries and apples, with a slightly cloying sweetness.

Lord Scudamore Dry Sparkling Hard Cider, the Dom Perignon of ciders, is made from tart Northern Spy apples using the labor-intensive Champagne method. Secondary fermentation in the bottle produces a finely carbonated brut, nutty and tangy, with a distinctive tannin profile and abundant apple flavor.

Bellwether's Heritage Hard Cider is an artisanal triumph. The blend of up to twenty-five varieties of bittersweets and bittersharps produces a full-bodied drink of rich complexity in a food-friendly style that could rival a fine Riesling.

Bill suggests drinking his ciders at the same temperature as white wine, about fifty-five degrees, and insists that hard cider's acidity and lower alcohol make it an even better match with food than many wines. As I sipped from a chilled glass of the heritage blend, accompanied by a wedge of local Cheddar cheese, I was grateful to the Bartons for the renewal of a craft that is so much a part of both the Finger Lakes and America.

709 Dryden Road
Ithaca, NY 14850
(607) 255-4542

Hours: Tuesday–Friday,
8:00 a.m.–5:30 p.m.;
Saturday, 8:00 a.m.–
4:30 p.m.

www.hort.cornell.edu/
department/facilities/orchards

Cornell Orchard

Forty-five stately and productive Cortland apple trees proudly reign at the center of a rolling stretch of land, just as they have since the 1920s. They are surrounded by sixty acres of apple, cherry, peach, and pear trees, along with grapevines and berry plants that are part of the working orchard, a short walking distance from the main campus of Cornell University. In addition to the large storage facility and laboratory, a salesroom offers local folks and visitors some of the world's most delicious, interesting, and useful fruit.

For most of the past century, Cornell Orchard has been the primary research and teaching facility for the Horticulture Department in the New York State College of Agriculture and Life Sciences at the university. Throughout its history, the experimental orchard has contributed to refinements in technology and dramatic improvements in the quality of fruit, supporting the American apple industry. The discovery that apples could remain fresh and crispy for a year if given low oxygen, high carbon dioxide, and cool temperatures was made right here. By using a strategy known as integrated pest management, Cornell scientists proved that apples can be grown using lower amounts of pesticide.

Rick Reisinger has managed the primary orchard and another ninety-acre orchard along Cayuga Lake since 1988. Under his careful and well-considered guidance, students have an opportunity to experience the challenges of fruit growing. Pomology students study trees, vines, and berry plants; entomology students look for insects among the strawberry and fruit trees; pathologists search for disease symptoms in the apples; ecology students study the interrelationships among the soil, living organisms, and crops.

There is activity in an apple orchard all year around. In winter, while the trees are dormant, pruning begins. Limbs are sawed off and clipped to allow maximum sunlight into the growing structures. Buds start to swell in spring, and, with the opening of the "King" blossom, bee colonies are brought to the orchard for cross-pollination. Pest control, mowing, and shaping practices continue throughout the summer, while, in dry years, irrigation is critical to fruit size and firmness. In the fall, as the fruit ripens, apple varieties are picked by hand to prevent bruising. With the harvest complete, it's time to prepare again for winter.

There seem to be as many apples as there are tastes, with some fifty different varieties grown by Cornell. Up to half of the apples are considered heirlooms, that is, good old farm apples that date back a century or more. The crisp, juicy Spitzenberg, with brilliant orange-red skin and rich, yellowish flesh, was Thomas Jefferson's favorite apple, and green-skinned Newtown Pippins were grown at Mount Vernon by George Washington. Regional heirlooms include Tompkins King, a large, solid red fruit, and Chenango Strawberry, an apple with the faint flavor of strawberries. The thick skins of Russet varieties make them the best "winter keepers," while many other heirlooms, too bitter for anything but cider, are called "spitters," for obvious reasons.

In a typical year Rick expects to bag two-thirds of his apples for retail sales and press one-third of the harvest into cider. Cortland, Empire, and Jonagold are favored by the locals, along with Spigold, a Golden Delicious–Northern Spy cross from the Geneva Experiment Station. Its yellow flesh is fine-grained, crisp, and cracking, yet it melts in the mouth, producing both the juiciness of Spy and the sweetness of Golden Delicious.

What doesn't go into bags goes into the cider bin. Using a rack-and-cloth press, a mix of up to twelve varieties of sweet and tart apples is pressed into cider, put into tank trucks, and delivered to the Cornell Dairy Plant for pasteurization. The process involves heating the cider to 160 degrees for a few seconds to kill any bacteria that might be there and then immediately re-cooling to prevent a cooked taste. Refreshing cider is offered for sale by the gallon jug or in ten-ounce containers at Cornell dining units.

The progressive teaching orchards and extensive field trials, supported by the research team at Cornell University, provide a rare local bounty of gourmet apples—hand-pampered, grown to perfect ripeness, and well-educated.

Early Bird Farm

806 Elmira Road (Route 13)
Ithaca, NY 14850
(607) 272-1056

Farm Stand Hours:
10:00 a.m.–7:00 p.m.
(mid-July to mid-September)

Bright green husks of sweet corn are harvested each morning just before ten o'clock, trucked across the farm to the roadside stand, loaded into a bin, and sold to customers who have been faithful to this Ithaca institution since 1955. Local corn season lasts only two months, but every year, throughout the precious weeks, we enjoy the sweetest, juiciest, most flavorful corn you've ever put in your mouth. Sweet corn at Early Bird Farm is probably the most anticipated and most revered vegetable grown in our region.

Professor Raymond Sheldrake moved from Georgia in the early 1950s to teach vegetable crops and greenhouse horticulture at Cornell. He purchased a house and farm in Inlet Valley and raised both a family and the best sweet corn around. As a young boy, his son Greg towed the wagon for pickers and, by age ten, operated the farm stand with the help of his brother, George.

"Summer sweet corn has nearly three times more sugar at peak harvest than it did back in those days," explains Greg, whose sugar-enhanced hybrids now include Custer, his sweetest variety, one that he compares to "the inside of an éclair." Other varieties grown on the farm are Welcome TSW (tablesweet), Tuxedo, Merlin, and the bi-color Seneca Dancer, an exceptional, full-season corn with extraordinary quality and true corn flavor.

A yield of 1,000 dozen ears per acre is considered a good growing season, with one and sometimes two ears per stalk planted eight inches apart. The farm's stony soil—mostly glacier gravel—provides good drainage and heats up quickly in the sun. Varied height along the acres of corn rows indicates as many as seven staggered plantings of the varieties that mature in fifty-five to ninety-two days. According to Greg the trick is to have premium corn to sell steadily from the first pick to the first frost. Cold nights make the corn sweeter, so the best eating takes place during late summer and early fall.

Sweet corn is ready for harvest when the ears reach full size for the variety, husks are tight, and silks are dried. It has a fresh corn smell, and if you dare prick a kernel, it will spurt milky juice.

Greg harvests the tender varieties by hand, removing each ear from the plant with a cane knife. He grabs the tip with his lead hand, makes the cut with his back hand, then tosses the ear into the barrel strapped to a leather harness he wears around his waist. He pulls the barrel down the row he's working until it's half full, then turns around, and by the time he's worked back to the truck, he's got a full load. Once he's filled five barrels, he delivers the corn to the stand.

To enjoy the best flavor of sweet corn, it must be eaten as soon as possible after it's picked, because the precious sugars that give corn its seductive sweetness begin converting to starches as soon as it's off the stalk. I'm very lucky. I live just a mile or so from Early Bird, so my wife sets the water to boil while I drive down the hill to fetch half a dozen ears (sometimes they add an extra ear when you buy six).

For perfectly cooked corn, you've got to fill the pot with enough water to cover the corn, bring it to a full boil, drop in the corn, bring it back to a boil, and then turn off the heat—you're done. Leave the corn in the water until you're ready to eat it. It will taste good the next day even if you leave it in the water overnight, but when you take it out of the water, the kernels will start to shrivel and dry out, so eat it or shuck it and add the corn kernels to another dish right away.

And how do you eat fresh corn? "Use lots of butter," insists Greg. "First you smear the butter on the hot corn, then you salt it. When the butter is put on first, the salt sticks to it." Butter and salt are perfect partners; a twist or two of fresh ground pepper is optional.

By the time most corn on the cob ends up in a pile on the grocer's shelf, it might be as long as a week since harvest. At Early Bird Farm as many as 100 dozen ears of sweet corn are sold daily during the growing season, none more than a couple of hours off the stalk. For the past half century, the farm has provided picnics, clambakes, barbecues, and summer suppers with fresh, golden-yellow nuggets of pleasure.

Fallow Hollow Deer Farm

The town of Candor was a long, broad belt of land that extended from the mouth of the Owego River to the head of Cayuga Lake when it was first established in 1794. Ridges were covered with massive pines, and many of the small streams were put to work sawing the trees to build houses. Among the early settlers was Enoch Williams, whose property in Candor's Catatonk Valley is now Fallow Hollow Farm, operated by his direct descendant, Martha Williams Goodsell, and her husband, Brian.

125 Williams Road
Candor, NY 13743
(607) 659-4635

Hours: By appointment

www.fallowhollow.com

Where Onondaga Indians once hunted white tail deer for meat to eat, skin to wear, and antlers for tools, the Goodsells now raise free-running European fallow deer to supply upscale restaurants and specialty markets.

Fallow Hollow represents a benchmark for farmed venison. Without question, its rolling foothills and woody pastures are ideally suited to raising fallow deer. The animals roam freely on 425 acres of breathtaking landscape, previously the Williams family dairy farm, surrounded by eight and a half miles of eight-foot-high fencing. With a herd of 2,200 deer, it has grown to become the largest venison farm in New York State.

The fallow deer graze on meadow grass and wild herbs, forage on bushes and foliage, and drink pure water. To supplement their diet in winter, they are fed natural corn, roasted soybeans, and sun-dried hay. The result is succulent game that takes on flavors from its surroundings. Martha describes the taste as slightly sweet, mildly gamey, with herbal notes, but without the "wild" characteristics of their woodland cousins.

European fallow deer are half the size of other deer species grown commercially for venison. A whole carcass weighs only fifty-five to seventy-five pounds. Consistent with the proportion of the animal, the texture of its meat is finer, and sizes of the cuts are well suited to plate presentation.

In the shocking practice of conventional farming, deer are loaded onto a trailer, taken to a slaughterhouse, and run through an apparatus where they are killed and processed. If an animal is stressed at slaughter, its muscles will tense up, causing lactic acid to be swept away by the blood before the animal has died. This leaves insufficient lactic acid to tenderize the meat, rendering it both tough and lacking in flavor.

The field-harvesting technique at Fallow Hollow is quite different. The grounds are quietly searched for ready-to-harvest deer, usually at eighteen to twenty months old, and each animal is taken with a single shot to the head from long range. Carcasses are skinned and eviscerated within an hour of harvest, chilled, and then dry-aged over seven days for maximum tenderness and intensity of flavor.

Never mind the slow-cooking methods recommended for ordinary venison. Fallow Hollow venison is exceptionally tender and moist, especially when cooked quickly over high heat to rare or medium-rare doneness. The award-winning dining room at Mirbeau Inn and Spa in Skaneateles features a Roasted Fallow Hollow Venison Chop with Sautéed Bulgur Wheat, Roasted Squash, and Berry Gastrique; New York City's Hudson River Club creates a Pepper-Cured Prosciutto with Fallow Hollow venison; Fallow Hollow is the venison of choice for dinners at the prestigious James Beard House.

The timeless vision of this historic family farm is carefully preserved. The Goodsells live in the farmstead's gracious country house, surrounded by the herds of gentle fallow deer. While production agriculture lies at the center of their lives, they place a high priority on family values, humane treatment of the animals, and progressive land stewardship. Fallow Hollow is the very essence of family farming.

HUNTER STYLE CHILI

Hunters say that venison makes the best chili. If you don't have a hunter in the family, farm-raised venison is another option. The controlled diet of farm-raised venison results in a rich, meaty flavor that is only mildly gamey. At Fallow Hollow, Martha Goodsell recommends this recipe for her tougher cuts of farm-raised venison.

Brown the venison in a heavy skillet over medium-high heat. Remove the meat and transfer to a Crock-Pot, stock pot, or Dutch oven.

In the same heavy skillet, add the oil, onions, peppers, carrots, and garlic. Cook over medium heat until tender and the vegetables begin to brown. Add the cooked vegetables and the remaining ingredients to the pot and stir to combine. Cover and simmer for 4 hours over low heat. Serve hot in bowls with bread for dipping.

Serves 8

3 pounds ground venison

1 tablespoon vegetable oil

3 large yellow onions, coarsely chopped

3 large green bell peppers, seeded, deribbed, and coarsely chopped

3 large carrots, shredded (1 1/2 cups)

3 cloves garlic, crushed

3 teaspoons beef bouillon

3 tablespoons chili powder

3 teaspoons ground cumin

3 teaspoons dried oregano

1/2 teaspoon red cayenne pepper

1 teaspoon hot sauce

2 (28-ounce) cans tomato sauce

1 (28-ounce) can kidney beans, drained

Finger Lakes Aquaculture

Legend says tilapia was the fish used to feed the multitudes in the miracle of loaves and fishes. Aristotle gave it its name, and the pharaohs raised it in ponds. Now, the tropical fish has found a home in the Finger Lakes. A professor at Cornell University developed crucial technology for a large-scale, indoor aquaculture operation, and a former Cornell Ag School student made the project a reality.

As sales of fish began to outpace the ocean's capacity to put seafood on the table, Dr. Michael Timmons, who focused his research on poultry production for fifteen years, turned his attention to fish farming. At Cornell, Dr. Timmons has become professor of agricultural and biological engineering and co-director of the Cornell Aquaculture Program in the College of Agriculture and Life Sciences. His progress with an intensive water-recirculation system attracted a former student, Paul Sellew, whose family is prominent in the East Coast wholesale seafood market. Finger Lakes Aquaculture is the result of their collaboration, and the $5 million farm on a Groton hilltop harvested its first fish crop in 2000. It is already one of the largest tilapia growers in North America.

A tilapia farm is unlike anything I've ever seen. The process begins with the selection and mating of mature tilapia. Once the eggs are laid and fertilized, they are collected and taken to a hatchery designed to

15

502 East Cortland Road
Groton, NY 13073
(607) 898-7684

Hours: By appointment

www.Indoorfish.com

replicate their natural environment. The eggs hatch after seven days, and as they begin to swim, they are moved to special ponds, where they grow into fingerlings. When the fingerlings are about four inches long, they are cultivated through a series of carefully controlled circular tanks, maintaining a precise eighty-five degrees to simulate the warm waters of the Nile River. This state-of-the-art fish-farming operation produces half a million fish annually from its 50,000-square-foot facility.

Researchers at Cornell have developed a uniquely formulated soybean-based "gourmet diet," fed every hour on the half-hour, around the clock, dropped automatically to the water's surface. The fish thrive on the enriched vegetarian diet and high feeding rate and grow from fingerling to market size in eight months. At slightly more than one pound, the fish are moved to a purging tank, where they are starved for three days to clear their digestive tracts. Once purged, they're loaded into insulated aquarium trucks bound for Boston, New York City, and other urban centers, where they are distributed live to grocery stores, fish markets, and restaurants.

Tilapia's semi-firm texture and mild, sweet flavor have been compared to perch. It also resembles sole or red snapper and can be substituted for either fish in many recipes. Paul insists it is the most versatile seafood on the market—steamed or poached, grilled, barbecued, baked, or broiled.

TILAPIA ETIENNE

Serves 4

2 tomatoes, diced (1 1/2 cups)

4 shallots, coarsely chopped (1 cup)

1/2 cup dry white wine

1/2 teaspoon curry powder

Sea salt and freshly ground white pepper

4 (6-ounce) tilapia fillets

4 tablespoons unsalted butter

Chopped fresh parsley or chives, for garnish

Note: This dish is a minor twist on the classic Duglére presentation, differing in the addition of curry and herbs. Vidalia onions may be substituted for the shallots. The chef suggests an H.J. Wiemer Dry Riesling for the white wine in the dish, as well as for a nice wine pairing.

Famous dishes have historically taken their names from the chefs who invented them—Sole Dugléré, for example, was named after French chef Adolphe Dugléré. As a consultant to Finger Lakes Aquaculture, distinguished local chef Etienne Merle, who once ran well-loved Ithaca restaurants L'Auberge du Cochon Rouge and Valentine Café, created a recipe for Dugléré-style tilapia. The addition of curry and herbs gives the dish Etienne's unmistakable touch.

Preheat the oven to 350°F.

Place the tomatoes, shallots, wine, and curry powder in a bowl and add salt and pepper to taste. Stir to combine and then transfer the mixture to an ovenproof platter. Place the tilapia fillets on top and sprinkle salt and pepper over the fish. Cover the platter with aluminum foil and bake for 12 to 15 minutes, or until the fillets are opaque and flake easily when prodded with a fork.

Remove the fillets to a serving platter, cover, and set aside. Stir the butter into the cooking liquid to slightly thicken the sauce, and pour the sauce over the fillets. Garnish with the fresh herbs and serve.

Glenhaven Farm

Blueberries are indigenous to the Finger Lakes, where Native Americans once revered the fruit as a gift from the Great Spirit. Wild blueberries were eaten fresh in summer or dried, then ground into a paste for juice, syrup, tea, medicine, and dye in winter.

The climate and soil of this region provide perfect conditions for blueberry plants to thrive, and cultivated blueberries are newly valued here for niche farming. Local growers have tamed the wild native blueberry and developed prolific "high bush" varieties, standing up to six feet tall, which deliver lots of plump, fresh fruit to the kitchen table.

After graduating from the Ag School at Cornell, John Tamburello, along with his wife, Andrea Beesing, purchased a ten-room Trumansburg farmhouse and fifty acres of land, intent on developing a commercial blueberry operation on the property's scenic landscape, no more than a few miles from Cayuga Lake. The house was built in the mid-1800s by William Jeffers, who was known as one of the best practical farmers in the area, so both history and the fertile, gravelly loam soil of Glenhaven Farm were on their side.

John and Andrea planted one acre of blueberries in 1979, then added more plants each year for the following three seasons, ending up with about eleven acres in total. In growing blueberries one must be willing to practice patience, since the plants don't begin producing fruit until their third season, nor do they become fully productive for another six years. John and Andrea's first substantial crop of berries was transported to the Ithaca Farmer's Market and sold for $2 a pint. In 1986, the Glenhaven crop was sizeable enough to invite "u-pick" customers, and the farm began to enjoy the prospect of profitability.

Few types of berries are so easy to pick. You just use your thumb and forefinger and roll the berries off. Ripe berries will nearly leap into your container, and the underripe will stay on the bush. It's best to place the fruit directly into one-pint market boxes, which are set in a shallow metal holder and worn on a strap around the picker's neck in the field. This reduces the amount of handling the berries will be exposed to—the more you handle them, the more you damage them. Since blueberries don't require peeling, stemming, coring, or pitting, they are ready to eat right off the bush.

Making blueberry wine allows the couple to use excess fruit produced on the farm. They believe that high-quality fruit wines are equally as worthy as those made from the grape and that blueberry wine has its place complementing food. At Glenhaven Farm, John and Andrea produce three styles of wine from their beloved blueberries. Two varieties, Blue Crop and Elliot, are picked by hand in August, combined, lightly crushed, fermented, oaked, then bottled. Wine is ready for sale by the following summer.

26

6121 Sirrine Road
Trumansburg, NY 14886
(607) 387-9031

Hours: Monday–Friday,
8:00 a.m.–8:00 p.m.;
Saturday–Sunday,
8:00 a.m.–5:00 p.m. (first
week in July to first week in
September)

www.glenhavenfarm.com

Although I do not usually drink fruit wines, I found the dry blueberry wine to be pleasantly reminiscent of a Beaujolais—it could easily be mistaken for a rich, young red wine made from grapes. The medium-bodied style offers hints of herb, cherry, and plum flavors, a bit softer and smoother than grape wines due to the lower level of tannin. Served at cool room temperature, this wine is certain to match well with a wide range of grilled dishes. It won over this wine lover's heart.

Glenhaven produces raspberry, blackberry, cherry, and peach wines, as well as Pinot Noir and Cabernet Franc from locally purchased fruit. John has a skill for making wines that reflect the personality of each, but the blueberry is where he makes his mark. He is passionate about the crop, the land that grows it, and the way of life it provides.

17

1265 East State Road
(Route 392)
Virgil, NY 13045
(607) 835-6455

Hours:

Daily, 9:00 a.m.–8:00 p.m.
(September through
December);
Wednesday–Sunday,
9:00 a.m.–6:00 p.m.
(January and February)

Hollenbeck's Cider Mill

Virgil is a quiet farming community in the hilly Cortland County countryside that comes alive each autumn, as the rural craft of apple cider–making begins at Hollenbeck's, just as it has ever since 1933. Thousands make the pilgrimage to purchase just-pressed cider in what has become an annual Finger Lakes tradition.

The main attraction at Hollenbeck's is, of course, the room where people view the continuous process that begins as bushels of apples roll down a long wooden chute into a stainless steel bin. Apples are brushed and washed as they are carried by conveyor to the grinder, then shoveled by hand onto an ancient, century-old Boomer and Boschert wooden press, where juice is extracted. The fresh juice is passed through a screen and then pumped past an ultraviolet light to kill bacteria before it flows into the bulk tank. A gravity-fed hose attached to the tank is used to fill gallon jugs with the golden liquid. Visitors watch the cider being made, then line up to take some home.

Under the supervision of cider maker Bruce Hollenbeck, whose father, "Doc" Hollenbeck, built the mill during the Depression, a dozen apple varieties are added to the mix, some for color, some for flavor. Medium in size and vigor, native Cortland apples are perfumed and slightly acid. The fine-grained flesh is juicy, tender, and white. Cortlands are good for cider making because they don't brown after grinding. Distinctive tangy and tart characters are added from Ida Reds; tannins from Northern Spys and Crispins give the cider extra body, sweetness, and overall oomph.

The exact formula for Hollenbeck's apple cider is apparently a guarded family secret, but Bruce did share some privileged information. An heirloom variety called Greening makes the best apple pies, and the glorious, flaky, baked-on-premises pies at Hollenbeck's prove it.

It is said that the first Greening seedling was found in 1700 outside a tavern at Green's End in Newport, Rhode Island, and the apple went on to be propagated widely throughout the Northeast. This apple was a favorite of Benjamin Franklin for its thin, tender skin covering a crisp, rich, juicy flesh.

At Hollenbeck's, a noisy, mechanical four-cup peeler cores and peels the green skin, then, in one motion, slices each apple into sixteen pieces to make life easy for the bakers. The sweet-tart flavor of Greenings intensifies when heated, so they're just dandy in fresh-out-of-the-oven apple pies.

If you're going to enjoy cider and pie, it might as well be in a place like Virgil. Fall weekends at Hollenbeck's Cider Mill capture a small town America that we thought existed once upon a time and were pretty sure was long gone.

Ithaca Beer Company

606 Elmira Road
Ithaca, NY 14850
(607) 273-0766

Hours:
Tuesday through Saturday,
11:00 a.m.–6:00 p.m.

www.ithacabeer.com

Support your local brewery. That's what we do in Ithaca—we know a good thing when we drink it. Well-established as part of local culture, the Ithaca Beer Company cranks out provocative mainstays like Pale Ale and distinctively crafted brews like Nut Brown Ale, and, in the process, has built a loyal fan base that extends throughout the Finger Lakes.

If it's true that every man would like to own his own brewery, then Dan Mitchell is living the fantasy. Working his way through Cornell behind the bar at a local saloon, Dan became intrigued by the national craft-brewing movement and began to dream of a commercial brewing venture. After graduation he decided to make beer a career.

His brewery's twenty-five-barrel system is under the cooperative command of Jeff Conuel and Jeff O'Neil. Mr. Conuel earned his chops at the Mountain Valley Brew Pub in Suffern, New York, where he put into practice his beer-making studies at Chicago's Seibel Institute, America's oldest brewing school. Mr. O'Neil crafted beers for Gordon Biersch in Palo Alto, California, then at the Jupiter Microbrewery in Berkeley, a place locals there call "beer church." Watching these two at work, it becomes clear that brewing beer is an effort that requires excellent smelling, listening, tasting skills—and imagination.

At Ithaca Beer Company, the brewing team not only pushes the envelope with an unfiltered, unfined Double IPA, but they use farm-fresh regional hops to do it. In the first collaboration of its kind since Prohibition, Cascade, Mt. Hood, and Willamette hops, grown in New York State (on Pedersen Farms in Seneca Castle), are utilized by a commercial brewery.

Besides supporting the revival of Finger Lakes hop farming, this project mimics the extremes of eighteenth-century British brews made with extra doses of hops to inhibit spoilage during transport to colonial India. The result is a stronger, hoppier addition to the permanent collection, adding seven and a half pounds of hops per barrel, compared with three pounds per barrel in traditional India Pale Ale. Pedersen Farm hops are especially flavorful due to the minimal processing and short time from field to brew kettle, and their fragrant oils are extracted by boiling and straining the juices. Taking a sip of the finished beer is like sticking your nose in a bucket of hop cones fresh off the vine.

The hoppy aroma provides a pungent, earthy, herbal backdrop. Its mouthfeel is crisp and thick, but not syrupy, and the burly, toasty malt backbone balances complex flavors of caramel, pine, and grapefruit rind bitterness. The hops caress the palate, sustain a citrusy, robust finish, and linger in the aftertaste. (The slightly cloudy appearance is due to the large portion of hop protein left in the beer.) Self-proclaimed "hops freak" Jeff O'Neil suggests that Double IPA is best enjoyed with "spicy food, blaring reggae, and cherished old friends."

Ithaca Beer Company has evolved from a tiny microbrewery to a regional institution. The team works diligently to keep a broad array of styles in the market, including Apricot Wheat, Nut Brown, Amber Ale, Pale Ale, Stout, and sultry concoctions of Ginger Beer and Root Beer. Each one is full-flavored, yet highly drinkable.

Seeing beer as equal to, if not superior to, wine, Dan Mitchell designs his products to complement food. Because of this effort, you can walk into any café or fine restaurant in the Finger Lakes and be pretty sure of finding an Ithaca beer on tap.

Lively Run Goat Dairy

27

8978 County Road 142
Interlaken, NY 14847
(607) 532-4647

Hours: Daily, except
Thursdays and Sundays,
11:00 a.m.–3:00 p.m.

www.livelyrun.com

Originally, the village of Interlaken was called Farmerville. But when town fathers applied for a post office name, "Farmerville" had already been given to a post office in Cattaraugus County, so the village became known as Farmer, New York. Folklore has it that the wealthy Westinghouse family, owners of a summer home on Cayuga Lake, didn't think well of having their friends come by train to a place called Farmer, so they urged the community to take a more dignified name. A local schoolteacher who had spent her vacation in Europe and visited Interlaken, Switzerland, suggested "Interlaken," since the village was between Cayuga and Seneca Lakes.

You can change a name, but you can't change the nature of a place. Of the 175 families who make their home here, most are still farmers who cherish their rural heritage, nurturing the land and animals.

Lively Run Goat Dairy had its roots as a family farm, then as a farmstead cheese dairy operated by Dick and Beth Feldman. Named for the stream that crosses the original property, Lively Run was purchased by Steve and Suzanne Messmer, who have preserved tradition and produced artisan cheeses since 1995.

A visit to the goat farm leaves nothing to the imagination. A herd of 120 floppy-eared, Roman-nosed Nubians, rabbit-eared Alpines, and selected crossbreeds provides whole milk for cheese production. Nubian milk is high in protein and butterfat, while the Alpines give high-volume, high-quality milk. They combine for a better yield and more complex flavor.

High-quality goat cheese begins with well-fed animals. Lively Run's goats are fed a controlled diet consisting of corn supplied from a neighboring farm, homegrown alfalfa, and custom-mixed grains. Since nearly all of the milk is from the Messmers' herd, the distinctive cheeses clearly reflect this place, just as a wine reflects its vineyard, the source of its grapes.

Nannies are fed twice a day and yield about seven or eight pounds of milk that within one or two days is turned into cheese by culturing the milk, separating curds from whey, placing the curds in molds, and allowing the cheese to take shape.

Lively Run is best known for a creamy, farm-fresh chèvre, excellent when served warm in a salad or as the topping on a pizza, where the satisfying flavor explodes on the palate. Other versions of the chèvre cheeses come rubbed with fine herbs. My favorite of the dairy's herbed cheeses is the luxurious Provence-style combination of summer savory, fennel, thyme, rosemary, and lavender.

Steve and Suzanne have developed several longer-ripening cheeses, including a crumbly feta and a mellow gouda. But do not leave this place without tasting the Cayuga Blue. It's a distinctive, carefully aged version of blue cheese, produced, of course, from 100 percent goat's milk instead of traditional sheep's milk, and bathed in roqueforti penicillin from France, resulting in mold, or "bloom," on the cheese. If compared to most commercial blue cheeses, Cayuga Blue is toasty and warm to the taste, rather than pungent, and the Messmers prefer the flavor intensity of winter milk as its base. Since the animals drink less water in colder weather, they produce less, but richer, milk.

Plump Finger Lakes goat cheese is an obvious passion and key ingredient in our region's cuisine and beyond. Lively Run products are ubiquitous on the menus of local restaurants and sought after by New York City showplaces such as Daniel and Artisanal Fromagerie. Visitors to the farm may not only purchase cheeses at the farmhouse door, but also get to meet the inquisitive, playful goats on their home turf.

CAYUGA BLUE CHAMPIGNONS

Serves 4 as an appetizer

12 large champignon mushrooms or large button mushrooms

1 small yellow onion, chopped

2 strips bacon, chopped

1 large clove garlic, chopped

2 tablespoons unsalted butter

4 ounces Lively Run Cayuga Blue cheese, crumbled

Salt and freshly ground black pepper

In The All American Wine & Cheese Book, *food writer Laura Werlin named Lively Run's fresh goat cheese as one of the two best chèvres in the country. A concentrated burst of blue cheese flavor adds zest to an appetizer created by Steve and Suzanne Messmer of Lively Run.*

Preheat the oven to 400°F.

Remove the stems from the mushrooms and reserve. Scoop out the central portion of the gills from the mushroom caps and chop the reserved mushroom stems into small pieces. Sauté the stems, onion, bacon, and garlic in a skillet with the butter over high heat until the onion is browned, about 5 minutes. Remove from the skillet, place in a bowl with the Cayuga Blue cheese and salt and pepper to taste, and mix thoroughly with a wooden spoon. Place 1 teaspoon of this filling into each mushroom cap.

Place the mushrooms on a baking sheet and bake in the oven 20 to 30 minutes, being careful not to burn the dish. Serve hot.

29

5374 Route 414
Romulus, NY 14541
(607) 869-9928

Hours: By appointment

www.pasturepride.com

McDonald Farm

Nearly three-quarters of the American population lived on farms in the 1800s, but economic necessity gradually attracted young men and women away to mills, cities, and nonagricultural pursuits. That trend continued well into the twentieth century, until a back-to-the-farm, down-to-earth movement emerged, providing sustainable, chemical-free agriculture and an alternative way of life.

There is something endearingly old-fashioned about the McDonald Farm, a family-run venture in the vanguard of this movement. Peter McDonald earned a degree in agricultural science, but worked as a video producer, then operated an excavation company and performed as a musician before settling down to life on the farm. In Peter is the soul of a poet, and it's this soul that finds so much joy in life on the farm he owns with wife, Shannon, and their nine children.

A carpet of thick grasses covers much of the 220-acre property, providing ideal pasture for up to 8,000 Cornish Rock chickens during each season. The stately, dignified, and industrious creatures are allowed the liberty to feed on fresh, nourishing grubs and medicinal herbs and scratch into the fertile soil for worms and insects. As they graze, they spread their manure, providing a fertilizer mix of nitrogen, phosphorus, and potassium, which helps the grass grow faster than they can eat it.

Peter believes that a pastured approach to farming promotes a connection to the earth and the seasons. His chickens are raised in harmony with natural seasonal patterns, and fresh poultry is available from May through November.

The birds arrive on the farm each week as day-old chicks from a nearby hatchery. After three weeks in the warm brooder house, they move to hoop houses set on the pasture, and, as in nature, the birds are allowed the dignity of breathing fresh air and foraging for greens. They have room to chase bugs, preen, and sprawl outside in the sunshine. In other words, they enjoy a lifestyle that Peter calls "a fullness of their ability."

When the birds are eight to ten weeks old, they are caught in the early hours of the morning to avoid stress and panic. They travel only a short distance to an abattoir on the farm, and, after a "kosher kill," they hang overnight at thirty-eight degrees while naturally occurring enzymes begin to tenderize the meat. By the following day they are ready for delivery to regional shops and restaurants or for sale at the Ithaca Farmer's Market.

Scott Signori of Stonecat Café in Hector is one of the many chefs who recognizes the remarkable difference between these pasture-fed birds and conventionally raised animals. He brines the birds overnight to tenderize their firm texture, then grills each half under a hot fire brick to seal in the juicy, tasty flesh. "They are full-flavored, like game," says Scott. "Old-timers tell me this is what chickens used to taste like."

Peter explains that his is the only business or pursuit that is defined by what it is not: no growth hormones or antibiotics, no herbicides or pesticides, no confinement, no beak or toe clipping. With compassion for the animals and respect for the fertile land, Peter defends the superior quality of his pasture-raised poultry to the last feather.

Northland Sheep Dairy

18

3501 Hoxie Gorge Road
Marathon, NY 13803
(607) 849-3328

Hours: By appointment

Karl North is a writer, social anthropologist, and accomplished farmer who makes the case—as if one needed to be made—for sustainable agriculture. He is passionate in his championing of holistic farming methods, and he's set his own standards well above the bar required for organic certification.

To study the traditions of old-world farming, in the late 1960s Karl and his wife, Jane, moved from upstate New York to a village in the French Pyrenees. In 1980 they returned home to establish Northland Sheep Dairy on a hilltop in Freetown, just north of Marathon, and production of sheep's milk cheese began eight years later. In addition to selling the farm's artisan cheeses to restaurants and local markets, they produce lamb, yarns, sheepskins, and hand-knit clothing from a flock of fifty-five crossbred dairy sheep on the property.

Model farms by their very name suggest excellence and integrity. Frankly, some of what they practice at Northland does seem a bit extreme, but there's usually a good reason for what Karl and Jane do, be it scientifically or holistically based. Or both. Northland's antitechnological approach to farming seeks to balance economic, ecological, and social issues while remaining independent from the wholesale agricultural marketplace.

Since nutritional quality, taste, and aroma of cheeses are so dependent on what the animals eat, the farm's abundant grasses and clovers are overseeded with trefoil and chicory. The "pasture salad," as Jane calls it, enhances their natural diet and results in products that are unique to

Northland. Because the sheep are pastured outdoors most of the year, their manure fertilizes the pastureland without need for human labor. Haflinger draft horses replace the farm tractor for much of the mowing, raking, and seeding. This is nothing short of a miracle to many experts who visit his farm frequently.

Sheep's milk is creamy and luscious—too rich for drinking, but ideally suited for cheese making. With her original French recipes, Jane turns small batches of fresh, raw, organic milk into a variety of cheeses, then ages them in a humid, cool environment to develop flavor and texture.

Tome Bergere, or "Shepherd's Wheel," is zesty and exuberant, while its consistency is firm and somewhat dry. It is fashioned after manchego, a longtime family favorite from Spain's La Mancha region. Fragrant Bergere Bleu is a rich, blue-veined, dessert cheese in the Roquefort tradition, creamy and soft, with a complex tangy-sweet flavor. Folie Bergere is firm, with a buttery, slightly nutty character and overtones of the sheep's milk. Italian-style Bergerino is aged a full twenty-four months, during which time it develops flavors characteristic of Pecorino Romano—salty, with a fruity tang that becomes steadily more robust. Another version of this cheese is called Pepperino, inspired by the Sicilian tradition of adding black peppercorns to Romano.

There's no doubt that the rustic cheeses produced at Northland are quite special. Besides supplying the local faithful through the Ithaca Farmer's Market and Greenstar Co-op, the cheeses are flown to chefs at such notable restaurants as New York's Grammercy Tavern, Seattle's Dahlia Lounge, and Commander's Palace in New Orleans.

Smallness of scale, sustainable farmstead management, and respect for tradition are guiding principles of these two gentle shepherds, Karl and Jane North, and their remarkable enterprise. The Norths are fired by a passionate belief in retreat from technology and the return to basic methods dating back hundreds of years. The slow and careful cheese-making techniques they practice at Northland create products with superior tastes, nearly forgotten in an age of industrial farming.

Purity Ice Cream Company

21

When the large red-and-white striped canopy over the patio of Purity Ice Cream goes up, it signals the official end of winter in Ithaca. Get ready to stand in line for your favorite treat. For nearly seventy years this local pleasure palace has been serving freshly made ice creams by the cone, by the cup, or hand-packed to take home.

Ithaca's long-running love affair with the cool comfort of hometown ice cream began in 1936, when Leo Guentert opened a shop on First Street. It was apparently the right venture at the right time. Ice cream was not simply considered a chilly treat during the thirties but was recommended by physicians and nutritionists for its food value and digestibility. Purity Ice Cream was an immediate and unqualified success.

Guentert had emigrated from Germany to study dairy science at Cornell University, then worked for the Nestle' Company in nearby Syracuse before returning to Ithaca to set out on his own. He wanted the business name to stand for something, so he called it "Purity" to reflect the strict hygienic standards he learned at Cornell.

Chocolate ice cream was his personal favorite, and he labored to make it better than anything else on the market. There was no secret, really. Guentert simply melted a block of high-quality European chocolate in a large double boiler, then added it to the cream mixture. His original recipe for small-batch chocolate ice cream produces a wonderfully rich and velvety version, a far cry from the generic, oversweet flavor of the mass-produced factory stuff sold in supermarkets.

Vanilla, the ultimate test of a good ice cream, is sublime in its freshness and creaminess. Purity's version begins with fragrant Madagascar Bourbon Vanilla Bean Extract, producing a dense, complex layering of flavors, satisfyingly clean and cool on the palate. This is ice cream as good as can be found anywhere—there's simply no question about it.

Our region, as it turns out, is prolific dairy country, and Purity has always depended on high-quality, locally produced milk as the basis for its products. In the old days, the folks at Fall Creek Farm in nearby Freeville milked their small herd by six o'clock in the morning, processed it the same day, then delivered it to the Purity facility cold and fresh the following morning. When the dairy's two dozen Holsteins could no longer keep up with increasing demand, Purity turned to a cooperative of other small local dairies for a dependable supply of high-grade milk.

A good partnership is icing on the ice cream cake. After Leo Guentert retired, his family continued operating the business until a suitable buyer appeared. In 1998 the husband and wife team of Bruce and Heather Lane purchased the Purity Ice Cream Company—lock, stock, and barrel— while agreeing to continue production in small batches and remain faithful to the time-honored recipes. Together they have provided a talented force that maintains tradition yet has expanded distribution.

700 Cascadilla Street
Ithaca, NY 14850
(607) 272-1545

Hours: Sunday–Thursday, 11:00 a.m.–9:00 p.m.; Friday and Saturday, 11:00 a.m.–11:00 p.m.

www.purityicecream.com

Purity's market now reaches to Norwich in the east, Binghamton in the south, and the fringes of Syracuse and Rochester to the north. It has grown to serve Finger Lakes groceries with pint and half-gallon containers, as well as regional restaurants and scoop shops with three-gallon bulk containers.

Today, Purity is known as a sweet-tooth fix for Ithaca natives, as a magnet for the college kids, and in general, for the indisputably largest single scoop ever to teeter on a cone. The whirlwind of wholesome, natural flavors includes coffee made with locally roasted coffee, strawberry with real crushed berries, and a bittersweet that is the stuff of local legend. I would be remiss in my duty if I didn't mention a flavor fancifully named "Finger Lakes Tourist." It's a base of chocolate ice cream loaded with chunks of dark chocolate and whole hazelnuts, and well worth a long waiting line—another reason Purity remains first in the hearts and stomachs of Central New Yorkers.

1605 Trumansburg Road
Ithaca, NY 14850
(607) 564-7701

Hours: By appointment

Stick and Stone Farm

Small farms have been able to develop niche markets similar to those of artisanal farms in Europe. Thanks to Stick and Stone Farm, the tables of local restaurants are distinguished by some splendid vegetables.

Since 1973, Charles and Susan Planck of Wheatland Farms have been growing vegetables and small fruits on about thirty-five acres of a sixty-five-acre property in Loudon County, Virginia. Mostly college-age seasonal workers are hired to work in the fields, and they sell the farm's produce directly at as many as fourteen markets in the region. During summer vacations from Oberlin College, a young biology student by the name of Chaw Chang worked at Wheatland, where his interest gradually moved to plant science and sustainable agriculture. After graduation in 1995, he went to work for Blue Heron Farm in Lodi, where he had the opportunity to observe a more diversified operation, marketing at both retail and wholesale.

With two other alums of Wheatland, he began planting a range of crops on five hilly acres in Newfield, just outside of Ithaca, and they called their venture Stick and Stone Farm. By 2001, they had run out of space, and, as his partners left to pursue other interests, Chaw purchased forty acres of Monroe Babcock's poultry farm in Ithaca and relocated to the more favorable site near Cayuga Lake. He started working the soil that once supplied grains of wheat to feed Babcock's Leghorn hens, and, in 2003, delivered his first harvest to the Ithaca Farmer's Market.

There are joys and sorrows in selling local vegetables at the Farmer's Market. While it provides a social atmosphere for local farmers, food producers, artisans, and the community, and while it is an important showcase for Chaw's produce, it takes a lot of time away from his farming. At first, he peddled to a few restaurants from market leftovers, but as production expanded and he had more to sell, he started knocking on more restaurant doors.

The owner of Maxie's Supper Club showed him the way restaurant business is done. "Chick told me that he couldn't just buy stuff off the back of my truck," says Chaw, "so I went out and bought a fax machine and a cell phone." Once he began sending out fact sheets, listing types and varieties, availabilities and prices, orders started coming in. "I found I could sell much more in much less time," he explains.

Chaw has changed what he grows to concentrate on specialty items that restaurants can't get from traditional distributors. He uses sequential plantings to make sure clients have a steady supply throughout the season. He makes sure buyers know what's up and coming so they can plan ahead, and he can move his crops as soon as they're harvested.

Today he has seven acres reserved for a steady market of restaurant clients. In all, he sells to a dozen local restaurants, including smaller establishments that "just love great ingredients." There's a big demand for standard vegetables like romaine lettuce and tomato varieties, as well as for the more exotic items like Deer Tongue lettuce, a summer lettuce originally grown by the Cayuga Indians. Chaw delivers his field-ripened produce the same day it's picked. Although many restaurants shop among suppliers hoping to get the lowest price, chefs working for high-end restaurants are willing to pay top dollar for this level of freshness.

Chaw values his solid relationships with the chefs, as well as the opportunity to receive immediate feedback on his products. Chefs, in turn, value the high-quality goods along with the opportunity to support local producers.

Stick and Stone Farm recently partnered with Remembrance Farm in Danby, specialty growers of salad mixes, developed cooperative marketing for additional products from a single offering sheet, and expanded delivery routes to include the nearby wine trails. As an entrepreneurial farmer, Chaw Chang provides an important link to our local restaurants from the "belly of the Finger Lakes."

28

8661 Powell Road
Interlaken, NY 14847
(607) 532-4391

Hours: By appointment

Waid Apiaries

Dr. Richard Taylor was an internationally renowned ethicist and bee-keeper who lived his retired years in Trumansburg, New York. A tenured professor at Columbia University, he authored over a dozen books in philosophy, but the honeybees he first kept on a balcony outside his apartment overlooking New York's Central Park were his true passion.

When Dr. Taylor moved upstate, he grew a long beard and began to dispense useful advice for amateur and professional beekeepers. His series

of self-published works, including *The How-to-Do-It Book of Beekeeping*, was first printed by a small shop in nearby Interlaken, owned by a gentleman named Duane Waid. As the two men became friends, Waid was increasingly fascinated by Taylor's unabashed enthusiasm for his bees, and, in 1976, Waid acquired his own colony of bees. Attracted by the romantic history of the craft and inspired by Dr. Taylor's joy in the bee yard, Waid eventually sold his printing business and took up beekeeping as a profession.

Now in his mid-seventies, Duane Waid has been an artisan honey producer for over a quarter century, with a reputation for making honeys that reflect the terroir of berry fields, apple orchards, and wide meadows of wildflowers between Cayuga and Seneca Lakes. Varietal monofloral honeys are comparable to varietal wines, only the honeys are harder to find. To obtain true varietals, Waid gathers honey that's derived from the nectar of strictly local flora that blooms when nothing else does.

The season's first honey comes from the early spring blossoms of apple trees. Waid carries his hives on a flatbed truck to the orchards of local growers, who rent his honeybees for pollination, then brings them home with the nectar they've collected. The bees convert the apple blossom nectar into a viscous, gently fruity honey with herbal and floral notes.

Each honey precisely reflects not only the flavor, color, and aroma of each floral source, but the characteristics of each year's growing season. Bright yellow locust honey typically draws mild woody, grassy flavors from the large, fragrant blossoms of black locust trees; basswood honey is suggestive of mint and green fruit with a pleasant bitterness on the finish; honey from the alfalfa pasture has a subtle, soothing flavor and intoxicating honeysuckle aroma; delicate white flowers of hard-to-find buckwheat grain yield an unmistakable mahogany-colored honey with a silky texture and nutty, robust characters reminiscent of molasses.

If several, perhaps dozens, of different flowers are in bloom at the same time, you end up with blended honey, explains Waid, whether you like it or not. Brandy-colored wildflower honey, gathered in midsummer, is so labeled because it is difficult to determine the specific nectars in it. Late in the season, goldenrod and wild aster predominate in his personal favorite, the coppery-colored, intensely perfumed "fall flower honey," with a viscous texture and very sweet, almost apricot flavor.

Unlike large-scale producers, who fine and filter their honey so that it is brilliantly clear and heat it above 140 degrees to prevent crystallization, Waid's honeys are processed under low temperature and strained through fine-weave cloth to retain pollen and healthful enzymes. Without damaging high temperatures, these honeys may naturally crystallize in the jar, but they easily reliquify with gentle heating.

Duane Waid is a naturalist and businessman who performs his craftsmanship with the bees and makes a comfortable living from it. He keeps about 100 colonies of bees and produces between 10,000 and 15,000 pounds of honey each year. Besides finding their way onto local tables and into dishes prepared by our region's chefs, Waid supplies Meadowsweet Farm with honey to sweeten yogurts and Wagner Brewery with honey to sweeten the honey ales.

At home, these extraordinary honeys can be used as sweeteners in coffee or tea, in marinades for game, married to a plate of cheeses, or decadently spooned over ice creams. But the best way to fully enjoy each varietal honey is from a small silver spoon, dipped into the jar. Once you've tasted the golden ambrosia, it's like discovering a fine local wine. You can never go back to the generic brands.

RESTAURANTS

Aurora Inn

30

The village of Aurora, on the east side of Cayuga Lake, is home to Wells College, one of the oldest chartered women's liberal arts colleges in the United States, established in 1868 by Henry Wells. Wells made his fortune in the partnerships of Wells Fargo and American Express, and he saw to it that his stagecoaches stopped at the Aurora House, a local respite for weary travelers, built by Colonel E. B. Morgan, native of Aurora and co-founder of The New York Times. Throughout its colorful history, the three-story Federal-style hotel has entertained such notable guests as Robert Frost and Norman Mailer.

391 Main Street
Aurora, NY 13026
(315) 364-8888

Hours: Breakfast, Lunch, Dinner (call for hours)

www.aurora-inn.com

A multimillion-dollar face-lift of this community anchor, now called the Aurora Inn, was completed in 2003, providing ten chic guestrooms overlooking the lake. In a style some townfolks have compared to a Beverly Hills boutique, today's inn is a bit luxurious by local standards, and some of the makeover seems a bit excessive. Neighbors are still gossiping about the day that three forty-foot pine trees were unearthed and replanted in order to improve the view for guests from the patio dining area. But this is where any romantic will want to eat, facing the manicured lawn that runs down to the water's edge. In summer it's an idyllic scene right off the pages of a Jane Austen novel. During the other three seasons, floor-to-ceiling glass doors open into a nineteenth-century-inspired dining room, illuminated with armillary chandeliers and brass wall sconces and warmed up with a working fireplace. Tables are decked out in crisp white linens and crystal, but you may be tempted to curl up in one of the snug wooden booths near the corner bar.

The Aurora Inn's kitchen has a history of reverence for local ingredients. A maverick French chef by the name of Henry-Paul Benveniste made a practice of prowling area farms and farmer's markets while overseeing the kitchen during the 1990s. Happily, the new team has adhered to same philosophy.

Executive Chef Greg Rhoad brings nearly two decades of culinary experience to the inn. He spent seven years in Skaneateles as chef at Rosalie's Cucina, where he worked under the tutelage of hospitality legend Phil Romano, developing instincts for populist food. He also worked at the critically acclaimed Inn at Little Washington and credits a stint at Spike and Charlie's in Baltimore with nurturing his love of wine.

At the Aurora Inn, Greg is adept at finding regional ingredients for his uncomplicated yet sophisticated cooking. Traditional Pot Roast is slow-cooked in its own broth with roasted vegetables; "MacKenzie-Childs" Chicken, homage to the town's renown maker of whimsical tableware and home furnishings, is a honey-garlic-seared breast with creamy goat cheese, wild mushrooms, and a piece of country bread toasted in the pan; a Maple-Grilled Pork Chop is served with braised red cabbage, apples, and onions. I am particularly fond of Greg's moist and delicious Meat Loaf with mashed potatoes. It's a humble entrée, very American, and right at home here at the inn. Desserts include a classic ice cream sundae with a choice of rich, housemade caramel or chocolate sauces.

The wine list is commendable for including an eclectic mix of red and white varieties that are likely to match up with the chef's food. Interesting Finger Lakes entries include Standing Stone Gewürztraminer, Dr. Konstantin Frank Rkatsiteli, and Treleaven Reserve Chardonnay from nearby King Ferry Winery.

This may be as close as it gets to a flawless dining experience. The Aurora Inn seduces with its setting and impresses with its cuisine. Regulars have created something of a social club here, but one that welcomes newcomers. Service is expert, yet warm and friendly—waiters wear tags with their names and hometowns. Personal touches and attention to details add up to a complete and remarkable Finger Lakes classic.

37

The Café at Sheldrake Point Vineyard

See Sheldrake Point Vineyard (page 132) . . . .

Maxie's Supper Club & Oyster Bar

The three most frequently displayed bumper stickers in Ithaca are "Ithaca is Gorges," "Bush Must Go," and "Maxie's Supper Club." That's enough to tell you about the local landscape, prevailing politics, and where to eat.

In a city with no shortage of restaurants, Maxie's takes the cake. The best thing about being in Ithaca these days is that there are so many good places to eat, and this loveable, offbeat café turns out some of the finest food in town. Few restaurateurs combine talent and hard work quite like the compulsive and conscientious couple Chick and Dewi Evans, who converted the old, creaky Farmers and Shippers Hotel into Maxie's.

Armed with a diploma from the Cornell Hotel School, Chick went to work for Lettuce Entertain You Enterprises in Chicago, where he met Dewi, an assistant manager of the Four Seasons Hotel. Together they took off for Santa Fe, where they found jobs at Café Escalera and Coyote Café. It was then on to Boulder, Colorado, and more practice, this time at Zolo and Jax Fish Bar.

By 1999 the two were back in Ithaca with a concept called Maxie's, honed from their experiences and inspired by their creative chemistry. Chick and Dewi's gifts to the city include fresh fish, raw oysters, jazzy food, late hours, live music—all in a place that hums with a kind of manic good cheer.

Maxie's has been crammed with locals since opening day, but only lately have there been enough seats to satisfy demand, since a new dining room has been added to the tight corner space. And it was just in time, now that the slow-smoked barbecue pork ribs have become the buzz around town. Match them with the Local Bounty Salad of arugula and shaved red onions (Stick and Stone Farm) with maple vinaigrette (W. & E. Allen Farm), double-smoked bacon (Seneca Smoke House), and feta cheese (Lively Run Goat Dairy).

It's quite an achievement to prepare inventive fish dishes without overpowering them. Grilled Arctic Char with chipotle tarragon aïoli, red pepper–cornbread pudding, and sautéed local organic greens has a delightful mix of flavors, but also finesse.

Maxie's brand of New Orleans cuisine stays true to the culinary art form, cooking roux for the Mighty-Mighty Gumbo to a dark brown, for a rich, deep, nutty flavor. Plump shrimp are sautéed in a spicy, creamy tasso sauce and served over yellow grits; Cajun Bloody Mary Sauce wakes up Cornmeal-Fried Oysters; Bananas Foster is spiked with rum and bourbon.

Dewi not only takes credit for the fantastically friendly and consistently efficient service at Maxie's, energized by her experience at the service-obsessed Four Seasons, but for refining and restocking the cellar with a rainbow of worldwide appellations and local wines. Esoteric Finger Lakes selections include Lakewood Semi-Dry Riesling, Fulkerson Merlot, and Dr. Frank Rkatsiteli. She also takes the time and effort to

635 West State Street
Ithaca, NY 14850
(607) 272-4136

Hours:
Daily, 4:00 p.m.–1:00 a.m.

www.maxies.com

educate the waitstaff in the subtleties and complexities of her choices. Everyone on the staff is a walking wine encyclopedia.

The success of this remarkable enterprise hangs in a balance between the fancy and the schmancy. It's a masterly planned equilibrium in which community, palate, and ambiance combine to establish what has already become an Ithaca institution. Maxie's Supper Club defines what a local restaurant is supposed to be and has developed a cult following in the process.

SPITZENBERG APPLE CAKE

Yield: 2 round 9 by 2-inch cakes

1/4 pound unsalted butter plus 1/2 pound unsalted butter, melted

2/3 cup water

2 1/2 cups sugar

3 teaspoons ground cinnamon

2 1/2 pounds Spitzenberg heirloom apples, peeled, cored, and thinly sliced

2 cups all-purpose flour

2 teaspoons baking powder

1/2 teaspoon salt

4 eggs plus 6 egg yolks

4 tablespoons Calvados

4 teaspoons pure vanilla extract

Consider the Spitzenberg. The heirloom variety ripens in mid-October, when Chick Evans buys every one of these local beauties he can get his hands on. Black Diamond Farm supplies the Spitzenbergs, and Chick turns them into a delicious apple cake, spiked with apple brandy. If you can't find Spitzenbergs, substitute Ida Red, Cortland, or Granny Smith apples.

Butter two 9 by 2-inch cake pans and coat with sugar (tap out excess). Preheat the oven to 350°F.

Melt the 1/4 pound butter in a large sauté pan over medium-high heat. Stir in the water, 1 1/2 cups of the sugar, and 1 1/2 teaspoons of the cinnamon and bring to a boil, stirring occasionally.

Add the apples and cook until just tender, about 4 minutes. Remove the apples from the pan using a slotted spoon and arrange in a circular pattern in the prepared cake pans. Continue boiling the liquid until it is thick and syrupy, and then pour over the apples.

Sift together the remaining cinnamon, flour, baking powder, and salt into a medium bowl. Place the egg yolks and whole eggs in a mixing bowl, add the remaining 1 cup sugar, and using a handheld mixer, whisk until pale. Add the Calvados and vanilla and blend well. Gradually add the dry ingredients to the bowl and, using a rubber spatula, fold in the 1/2 pound melted butter.

Pour the batter evenly over the apples in the cake pans. Bake for about 45 minutes, or until a skewer inserted in the center of the cakes comes out clean.

Remove the cakes from the oven and cool in the pans for 5 minutes. Loosen the sides of the cakes with a sharp knife and invert each onto a cake round. Continue cooling on rack.

Moosewood Restaurant

The cultural and culinary phenomenon known as Moosewood probably could not have happened just anywhere. It might only have happened in an enlightened, "centrally isolated" place that welcomes alternative lifestyles, a community that nurtures originality and craft. It was a network of shared values that first made this idealistic enterprise possible, and adherence to those same values has been responsible for its longevity. Although I've probably eaten at Moosewood a hundred times over the years, whenever I enter, I know I'm in the presence of greatness.

Back in the era of Richard Nixon and Earth Shoes, seven friends opened Moosewood Restaurant in the basement of the old Ithaca High School, unaware that they were on their way to making culinary history. They simply intended to serve the kind of food they themselves wanted to eat and explore a common passion for creative, flavor-driven cooking. They never consciously thought about serving "health food," yet the process of making traditional dishes vegetarian also made them healthy.

It was a range of influences, including Frances Moore Lappe's *Diet for a Small Planet*, that helped give birth to a vibrant, original meatless cuisine. The Moosewood Seven laid the foundation for a new way of eating, and it was accomplished within the structure of a worker-owned collective.

When founding members left the group, others showed up to take their places. David Hirsch abandoned his job in a New York City architectural firm and landed on a commune just outside Ithaca in 1975. One day he showed up at the restaurant with a big bag of garden-grown basil, and he was offered a couple of dinners in trade. Before long, David went to work in the kitchen, seduced by the creativity and camaraderie of the Moosewood family. With hair and beard a bit grayer now, he has remained actively involved in running and managing the restaurant for nearly three decades.

David believes that the restaurant's collective ownership is part of the uniqueness of Moosewood and the source of its sustained energy. All of the current owners, now numbering twenty, are involved in varying degrees with the daily operation of the restaurant and its extended projects. They each earn Moosewood "shares" based on years of membership and hours of service. All major decisions affecting the restaurant are put to votes among the members, true to the collective spirit.

According to David, a succession of ten influential cookbooks refutes the old adage that too many cooks spoil the broth. The writing process mines the group's creativity and fosters continued innovation in the kitchen. With each volume, the restaurant and its many owners make healthy, vegetarian eating more accessible, and millions of readers have made at least one of the Moosewood cookbooks an important part of their lives.

31

215 North Cayuga Street
(DeWitt Building)
Ithaca, NY 14850
(607) 273-9610

Hours: Lunch,
Monday–Saturday,
11:30 a.m.–2:00 p.m.;
Dinner, Sunday–Thursday,
5:30 p.m.–8:30 p.m.;
Friday and Saturday,
6:00 p.m.–9:00 p.m.

*www.moosewood
restaurant.com*

Since its earliest days, the Moosewood mission has been supported by relationships with local, small-scale farms and a dedication to pursuit of high-quality organic produce. Organic foods taste better, insists David, because they're unadulterated and picked at the height of their growing season. Finger Lakes Organics (FLO), a cooperative of small growers, is a dependable supplier, as is Chaw Chang's Stick and Stone Farm. Savory multigrain breads are delivered fresh daily from nearby Ithaca Bakery.

While not exactly signature items, some dishes do seem to appear in the menu rotation more often than others. Potage Jacqueline, a dreamy sweet potato soup, is one, Tomato-Garlic Soup, another. The lively blend of nearby culinary influences in Moussaka Stuffed Eggplant and Pumpkin Mushroom Lasagna ensures their frequent appearances on the blackboard menu. It is one of life's guilty little pleasures to indulge in Moosewood's decadent fudge brownie, topped with Dennis Casio's ice cream flavor of the day, handmade exclusively for the restaurant.

Management of the bar is assigned to Neil Minnis, who tastes and selects wines for a list that favors small independent producers from around the Finger Lakes. Diners can always depend on a food-friendly Hermann J. Wiemer Riesling among the selections, as well as at least one of Richard Figiel's organic wines from Silver Thread Vineyard.

So, what else can you say about a small-town restaurant that *Bon Appétit* listed among the most influential restaurants of the past century, alongside Four Seasons, Spago, and McDonald's? Moosewood has certainly aged well over its thirty-plus years and, in fact, now enjoys the grown-up serenity you would expect of a legendary restaurant. After all this time, you can still enjoy honest and functional food, food that satisfies and sustains, food that perfumes the table, is visually intriguing and always delicious.

34

120 Third Street (at Madison)
Ithaca, NY 14850
(607) 273-8515

Hours:
Daily (except Tuesday),
from 5:30 p.m. Closing
times vary. Reservations
are recommended.

www.pangearestaurant.com

Pangea

The continents of Earth are slowly shifting. About 250 million years ago, the land masses were clustered together in one supercontinent called "Pangea." Projecting 250 million years into the future, the continents are expected to position themselves once again into a single land mass. At that time, the Atlantic Ocean will be just a distant memory, and Earth's inhabitants will be able to walk from North America to Africa.

Ithaca's Pangea is a restaurant with inspiration from all parts of the globe, morphed into a kind of multiethnic culinary internationalism. Co-owners Paul Andrews and Nina Hien call it "precontinental" cuisine (with a poke at the idea of continental cuisine), and together they prove that a big idea can fit into a small restaurant.

Paul's early work in restaurant kitchens was characterized with a passion to learn. He sharpened his knives and his culinary skills with Master

Chef Todd English in his hometown of Boston before heading to the heartland. In Columbia, Missouri, he opened a bistro at Les Bourgeois Winery, acquiring a taste for native wines and networking with local hog, dairy, and vegetable farmers. After refining his techniques in Portland, Maine, and New York City, Paul headed to Ithaca with Nina at his side.

At Pangea, Paul's menu offers small, medium, and large plates of artfully presented and nuanced dishes, accommodating appetite, budget, and the temptation to share. Paul obviously enjoys preparing extraordinary food, and he does it with the help of a wood-burning oven that, he says, "helps to satisfy some primordial urge."

Although he takes advantage of the local bounty, there is an intermingling of ingredients and multiple influences from the outside world, with Japanese mizuna and shiso greens, Peruvian quinoa, African millet, and Vietnamese tamarind as favorite components. Noteworthy main dishes have included Balsamic-Glazed Flank Steak with ginger-scented millet and chile oil; Monk Fish braised with almonds, large-grain couscous, and coconut milk; and Grilled Salmon with smoked black beans, roasted beets, and harissa.

Pangea's visual environment is in sync with the imaginative food. A sexy, dimly lit dining area called the Wine Den offers an alternative menu featuring cheese fondue, pressed sandwiches, and thin-crust pizzas. In the summertime, a choice of menus is available for dining under the stars in the Ginkgo Garden, an ivy-enclosed private courtyard.

Nina draws from her own multicultural background as she rounds up a rotating selection of interesting and affordable wines as idiosyncratic as the food. The list always includes a few wines she calls "jewels of the Finger Lakes," and recent jewels have included Hermann J. Wiemer Dry Riesling, Hosmer Cabernet Franc, and McGregor Rkatsiteli-Sereksiya. For her part, she defends her own inclinations and provides wines to match Paul's food.

I've lost count of the number of restaurants that have occupied this space at the corner of Third and Madison Streets. It's without a doubt the most unlikely dining location in town and is nearly impossible to find without good directions. But if you don't mind heading off the beaten path, you are in store for an adventure in unfamiliar tastes and sensations, a terrific gathering place that satisfies a wide range of moods.

The Restaurant at Knapp Vineyards

See Knapp Vineyards (page 127) . . . .

BLUE POTATO AND DUCK CONFIT HASH

Serves 4

2 duck legs

2 sprigs thyme

2 cloves garlic, halved

3 cups plus 3 tablespoons olive oil

1 pound blue potatoes, unpeeled and cut in ¼-inch dice

3 shallots, diced

½ cup diced sweet red peppers

Salt and freshly ground black pepper

Our region's most important restaurant chefs cultivate relationships with local growers and express their creativity through daily special menus. Paul Andrews's confit method leaves the duck meltingly tender and moist, while locally grown blue potatoes add a subtle, nutty flavor to the hash.

In a stock pot over extremely low heat, cook the duck legs with the thyme and garlic in 3 cups of the olive oil, or enough to cover the duck legs, for 3 hours.

Remove the duck legs from the pot and set aside to cool for 2 hours. Peel the skin off the duck legs and then pull the meat off the bone. Discard the bones and skin. The duck meat can be prepared up to 24 hours in advance and refrigerated until ready to use.

To make the potato hash, heat a pan with the remaining 3 tablespoons olive oil on medium heat. Add the potatoes, shallots, and red peppers and sauté until cooked through, stirring occasionally with a wooden spoon, for about 20 minutes. Cook for an additional 5 minutes on low heat. Season to taste with salt and pepper.

35

53 Main Street
Trumansburg, NY 14886
(607) 387-5313

Hours: Monday,
5:00 p.m.–10:00 p.m.;
Thursday–Saturday,
5:00 p.m.–10:00 p.m.;
Sunday,
5:00 p.m.–9:00 p.m.

www.simplyredbistro.com

Simply Red Village Bistro

For his services in the Revolutionary War, Abner Treman received 600 acres of land, now in part occupied by the village of Trumansburg. It was once known as Shin Hollow because, legend says, folks bumped their shins on tree stumps as they made their way home from the local tavern. The village was later re-named for the Treman family, but was misspelled "Trumansburg" by the postmaster (perhaps after visiting the same tavern), and so it has remained.

Today's Trumansburg is still basically a one-road town, an old-fashioned Main Street with shops, professional offices, distinctive homes of unique architectural designs, and a homey restaurant that the entire community seems to have taken to heart.

Simply Red Village Bistro is named for the chef-owner's red hair, usually tied into pigtails and worn under a baseball cap. Samantha Izzo hails from the beachside city of Durban, South Africa, in a region known for its mix of ethnic influences. As a young girl, her Welsh-Dutch mother introduced her to cookbooks along with storybooks, and her childhood was seasoned with the flavors of many cultures. (The first apron her mother bought for precocious four-year-old Samantha is proudly displayed behind the restaurant counter.)

Samantha came to the United States in 1987, finished school, and landed a management job with the Cheesecake Factory. She honed kitchen skills at Boston's Six Burner Café, where she created all menu items and daily specials, then continued her culinary journey with a position at the Brownstone Bistro in Buffalo.

In Trumansburg, Samantha successfully pulled off what most chefs only fantasize about. She opened her own restaurant, and she is busy being her own woman in the kitchen. She sets out to cover all bases—pasta, seafood, chicken, and steak—and creatively combines colors, textures, and flavors. She draws from her deep-rooted education in home cookery, her professional training in classic techniques, and her curiosity for international influences, and then nurtures everything she's learned with respect for the finest, freshest local ingredients.

The innovative and frequently changing menu allows Samantha to use seasonally available products from such regular suppliers as Hoffmire Farms, Wixson's Honey, Ithaca Bakery, Backbone Hill Farm, and W. & E. Allen. Winter and fall menus feature heartier meals, while spring and summer menus are lighter, offering entrées like Overstuffed Green Pepper with rice and fresh herbs served over a roasted eggplant and tomato ratatouille. Regional ingredients are what make her best dishes work. "Killer Shrimp" in the shell are sautéed in Ithaca Nut Brown Ale, and a French-inspired onion soup is loaded with cloves of roasted regional garlic, onions, and fresh herbs.

The locals love it. By six o'clock each evening the dining room is filled with the chatter of happy eaters. Simply Red seems to thrive on Trumanburg's curious mix of artists, farmers, musicians, professors, construction workers, yoga instructors, and seasonal second-home owners. There's just enough leftover atmosphere from the former diner that occupied this space to put everyone at ease.

Workers from nearby wineries are also part of the faithful regulars—young winemakers in their flannel shirts and hiking boots, often accompanied by newly released vintages for Samantha to try. In particular, she favors white wines from Lamoreaux Landing and red wines from Sheldrake Point, and a few bottles of her native South African wines are also on the well-balanced list.

Samantha Izzo's personal approach to preparation and presentation makes every meal at Simply Red a truly distinctive and, I might add, always delicious dining experience. She has brought a passion for food, love of wine, and gentle nature to both her menu and the village of Trumansburg.

KILLER SHRIMP

Serves 4

CAJUN BUTTER

5 tablespoons dried oregano

5 tablespoons dried basil

5 tablespoons dried thyme

5 tablespoons cayenne pepper

5 tablespoons salt

5 tablespoons freshly ground black pepper

10 cloves garlic, thinly sliced

¼ cup Worcestershire sauce

1 pound unsalted butter, cut into cubes, at room temperature

SHRIMP

6 jumbo (13 to 15 count) shrimp, deveined, shell on, with tails

8 tablespoons Cajun Butter

2 cups dark ale

2 cups clam juice

1 baguette, sliced

Note: The extra Cajun butter can be reserved in a sealed container for future use. The butter goes well with grilled fish or steak.

Follow these rules, as set forth by Chef Samantha Izzo, when you order a bowl of her shrimp, and you'll understand how they achieved "killer" status. You want to make sure to sop up all of the spicy broth without missing a drop. Make sure to wash your hands well before eating, as they will be your only utensils. Have extra napkins on hand, although licking your fingers is proper etiquette. For the dark ale, Samantha uses Ithaca Nut Brown ale. The bread is used for sopping up the delicious, spicy sauce.

To make the butter, place the herbs, salt, pepper, garlic, and Worcestershire sauce in a bowl and whisk by hand until the ingredients are well incorporated.

Transfer the mixture to a food processor and add one-quarter of the butter cubes. Process on high speed, slowly adding the remaining butter cubes one at a time until you can no longer see white pieces of butter.

To make the shrimp, use a paring knife to make a slit up the back of each shell to faciliate easy peeling and to let the flavor in. Heat a skillet over medium-high heat. Place 8 tablespoons of the Cajun Butter in the hot skillet and allow to melt, being careful not to burn it. Toss in the shrimp and cook for 1 or 2 minutes. When they start to turn pink, turn them over and cook for another 1 or 2 minutes, being careful not to overcook. When almost fully cooked through, cover the shrimp with the ale and clam juice and reduce the heat to medium-low. Bring to a low simmer and cook for 15 minutes. Divide into bowls and serve with the baguette.

33

202 East Falls Street
Ithaca, NY 14850
(607) 272-0656

Hours: Tuesday–Saturday,
5:00 p.m.–10:00 p.m.

www.willowithaca.com

Willow

The majority of Ithaca's many waterfalls can be found in the three creek beds that bisect the city on their way to Cayuga Lake. Closest to the lake is Ithaca Falls, the 150-foot-high crown jewel towering over the quiet, residential Fall Creek neighborhood.

Just a few blocks from downtown, Fall Creek has its own Buddhist monastery, a small theater that shows independent and foreign films, and a popular neighborhood restaurant called Willow. Neighbors, mostly young families and grad students, have found they can go out the front door, walk a few blocks, and enjoy a truly wonderful meal. For the rest of us in the foodiest city in the Finger Lakes, Willow is only a slightly more ambitious dining destination.

Sean O'Brien studied the culinary arts at Johnson and Wales, and Amy Walker studied ballet at SUNY Purchase. After graduation, the two native Ithacans set out along the same path. Sean cooked at Washington D.C.'s Oval Room, while Amy danced with the Washington Ballet. When Amy joined the Connecticut Ballet, Sean landed a job at the Black Bass Grille, not far away. Then, in 2001, when a restaurant space opened up in their hometown, they joined forces to open Willow.

The style-conscious room reeks of refinement, with artistic appointments and genteel music. Service is attentive and knowledgeable, and Amy greets her guests at the front with sweet conviviality. Her pleasure shows with each customer who enters the door, and she tiptoes through the restaurant, seeing to everyone's comfort and enjoyment. Inspired by her professional dancing, Amy regards the restaurant's activity as a nightly performance.

Although menus change with the season, it's with his daily specials that Sean's kitchen takes advantage of fresh, vibrant flavors from the home-grown, in-season ingredients he encounters at the Ithaca Farmer's Market. His weekly shopping sack might be filled with organic vegetables from Sacred Seed Farm Commune, fruit from Little Tree Orchards, or Carl Whittaker's locally harvested mushrooms.

Sean is a wizard with ingredients, as evidenced by such surprises as Goat Cheese–Crusted Diver Scallops with strawberries two-ways, frisée and roasted garlic vinaigrette, or Vanilla Apple Compote–Stuffed Quail glazed with apple cider and served with wild rice and salsify. Pesto-Marinated Half Chicken comes with tobacco onions, cauliflower gratin, and pan jus. Every dish reveals awe-inspiring attention to flavor combinations and detail.

Excellent homemade desserts on the autumn menu include a heavenly Butternut Crème Brûlée, Champagne Rhubarb Sorbet, and a roasted local Gala apple with figs, dates, almonds, and cinnamon anglaise.

Besides such local darlings as Treleaven Chardonnay and Hermann J. Wiemer Dry Riesling, I was pleased to find Sheldrake Point Gamay on the wine list. This fruit-filled, easy-drinking wine is compatible with Sean's style of cooking, even with dishes more often accompanied by a white wine.

Like one of our fine local wines, regional cooking has had to mature to reach its current delectable stature. Places like Willow, run by young, talented, dedicated professionals, prove that Finger Lakes cuisine has come of age.

SKANE-ATELES
LAKE

(ˌska-nē-ˈat-ləs)

SIXTEEN MILES LONG, A MILE ACROSS at its widest point, and 350 feet deep (holding 425 billion gallons of water), Skaneateles is probably the most tranquil of the Finger Lakes. It is surrounded by farms for growing corn, soybeans, and cabbage, and with temperatures a bit too chilly for growing wine grapes, you'll find just a few newly planted acres of vines on the lake's west shore.

Skaneateles, the charming and somewhat eccentric village nestled at the north end of the lake, welcomes visitors with annual events such as "Dickens's Old-Fashioned Christmas," featuring costumed locals acting out scenes from Dickens's *A Christmas Carol* during the holidays.

Architecture of the area's homes is mostly Greek Revival and Victorian, including seasonal "cottages" along the lake. Antique shops and boutiques flourish in the business district—malls and fast-food outlets are outlawed. The culinary arts flourish in several very good restaurants, and Skaneateles is home to Mirbeau, an extravagant spa where pampering has been elevated to a high art form.

In sharp contrast is the rustic village of Moravia on the southern end of the lake, rich in agricultural bounty, but lacking in tourist attractions. One exception is "Fillmore Days," celebrating the birthday of Moravia's favorite son, Millard Fillmore, the thirteenth president of the United States, with a bathtub race down Main Street.

Jordan

173   Warners

31   695

Weedsport   31C   590   81

Elbridge   5   **Camillus**   5

34   Fairmount   173   **SYRACUSE**

321   Onondaga

Sennett   174   175   173

5   Marcellus

38   **6 8**   174

5   **SKANEATELES**   Onondaga

Auburn   20   **9 10**

34   Marietta   South Onondaga

38A   80   20

41A   **Otisco Lake**   Amber   Cardiff

41   Boredino   Otisco   11A   11

Owasco

Wycoff   **Owasco Lake**   **Skaneateles Lake**   81

Niles   Vesper

Scipio   38   New Hope   80

34   **3**

2

Venice Center   38A

41A

Moravia   Scott   Preble

Genoa   41   281

90   Locke   **1**   **7**

4   Little York   81   11

Montville   13

North   90

Lansing   Summer   Homer

34   Hill   281

Groton   222   **Cortland**

38   215

34B   13   Polkville   11

Farms/Food Producers

1 Cobblestone Valley Farm *(PREBLE)*

2 Tierra Farm *(NEW HOPE)*

3 Harvest Home Organics *(MORAVIA)*

4 Grisamore Farms *(LOCKE)*

5 New Hope Mills *(AUBURN)*

6 Elderberry Pond Farm *(SENNETT)*

 Restaurants

7 Kettle Lakes *(TULLY)*

8 The Restaurant at Elderberry Pond
(see Elderberry Pond Farm, SENNETT)

9 Rosalie's Cucina *(SKANEATELES)*

10 Mirbeau Inn and Spa *(SKANEATELES)*

FARMS/FOOD PRODUCERS

2023 Preble Road
Preble, NY 13141
(607) 749-4032

Hours: By appointment

www.cobblestonevalley.com

Cobblestone Valley Farm

Named for Commodore Edward Preble, a gallant hero of the Barbary Wars in North Africa, the village of Preble is situated in a fertile valley with a long agricultural history. The first Holstein cows in Cortland County were introduced by Millard Nye, a noted Preble farmer, and the first cabbage seeds were planted here by Perry Haynes in 1885. By 1890, the Knapp family had settled alongside the Tioughnioga River, and, as operator of Cobblestone Valley Farm, Paul Knapp represents the fourth generation on the farm. He, his wife, Maureen, and their family live in the farmhouse that his great-grandfather built.

Some of the most important inhabitants of Cobblestone Valley are the eighty Holstein cows who graze rotationally on eighty acres of organically grown orchard grass and white clover to produce milk sold commercially to Organic Valley, a cooperative that accounts for 30 percent of organic sales nationwide. Although he was raised on conventional agriculture, Paul explains that the organic niche offers a viable way to help keep rural communities and small farmers economically and socially healthy.

Since 1999, the Knapps have sold milk produced without antibiotics or growth hormones in the herd, and have not used pesticides or herbicides in the fields. Paul concedes that this style of dairying is much more work-intensive, but with consistently increasing demand and higher prices paid for their milk, the new farm management system will keep them in business long-term, and he hopes to have the fifth generation become even more involved.

Unlike large corporate farms, small family farms need to have more than one source of income. Besides the certified organic dairy herd, the Knapps maintain old-fashioned farm diversity by raising pasture-fed poultry and beef and growing strawberries.

From June to October, they raise 1,000 chickens, a Cornish crossbreed, processed on the farm, with a portion grown for the restaurant trade. Additionally, 100 turkeys are raised for Thanksgiving, and six to eight bull calves are sold in halves, quarters, or in retail cuts, processed and aged for two weeks locally at a small USDA processing facility. Paul contends that meat from grass-fed cattle has less than half the fat of grain-fed beef.

The ten-acre "pick-your-own" strawberry fields have also made it through the organic transition, producing exceptionally high-quality fruit. Varieties include Early Glow, producing a moderate to small fruit from one of the sweetest varieties, and peaking during the first part of June. As the season progresses, Honeoye produces large, firm, bright red berries, followed by late-harvest Jewel, plump, red, and bursting with flavor. "We have some really great soils for strawberries," says Paul, "with good drainage and good perculation—you can't do too much wrong with it."

Cobblestone Valley Farm has been able to develop grassroots community support as well as a local market for its products. "Where farmers use resources more sustainably and where land is more productive, people have more dignity," says Paul. "For all the things we do, we are more in touch with the people, the consumers. You lose that when you're just producing a commodity."

The Finger Lakes are, for the most part, a landscape where glaciers have carved out hills and valleys that have limited the size of many farms in the region. Our small farms are beginning to develop niche markets similar to those of artisanal farms in Europe, and the enterprise at Cobblestone Farm is an economically viable, ecologically sound, and socially responsible model for the future.

Elderberry Pond Farm/ The Restaurant at Elderberry Pond

Every year, Merby Lego, a registered dietician, and her husband, Lou, an electrical engineer, planted a garden together and shared the harvest. As their gardens got bigger with each passing year, it occurred to them that perhaps they ought to be growing on a farm scale. So, they abandoned jobs in the city and purchased an old dairy farm in the sleepy town of Sennett. That was twenty-five years ago, and today Elderberry Pond Farm grows a variety of vegetables, small fruits, herbs, and flowers at one of the most diverse agricultural and culinary enterprises in the Finger Lakes.

3978 Center Street Road
Sennett, NY 13021
(315) 252-3977

Store Hours:
Thursday–Saturday,
10:00 a.m.–5:30 p.m.
Restaurant Hours: Lunch,
11:30 a.m.–2:00 p.m.;
Dinner, 5:00 p.m.–8:00 p.m.
(March through December)

www.elderberrypond.com

"We have a passion for growing things," Lou says about his unusually extensive range of crops. Get him started on the apple, and he'll expound on more than one hundred varieties in the orchard, many of which are obscure antique varieties, including Caville Blanc D'Hiver, a ribbed, pale-green French dessert apple with splashes of red and more vitamin C than an orange, and Ashmead's Kernel, a small, dark English apple that needs to store for six months before it's ready to eat. "It's got a rich, strong flavor, almost like brandy," he explains.

Merby and Lou talk obsessively about the sweet, smooth, spicy, rich aromatic flavor of Seckel pears and the supple skins and juicy pulp of Japanese plums. Their gardens are lush with radicchio, arugula, rhubarb, fava beans, and asparagus—purple and green—as well as beets, Swiss chard, snap peas, turnips, rapini, hardneck garlics, and all sorts of delicate baby lettuces. Part of the grove is devoted to less mainstream fruits, including gooseberries, kiwi, apricots, quince, pawpaws, plus seedless grape varieties, including Canadice, Interlaken, and Mars, and, of course, there are elderberries.

Young Christopher Lego inherited his mother's love of cooking, while he cleared brush, planted trees, and picked fruit with his father, who taught him reverence for ingredients. After high school he was off to study restaurant management at Paul Smith's College, but his heart was in the back of the house. He worked in a couple of local kitchens, and then, in 1990, he enrolled at the Culinary Institute of America, where, as part of the program, he served an externship at the City Grille in Atlanta—peeling vegetables, learning chopping and carving skills, and cooking on the line.

Back in the Finger Lakes, Christopher's first important position was at The Restaurant at Knapp Winery, where he developed a model of simple cooking with vegetables and herbs from the kitchen gardens and furthered his appreciation of regional wines. After five seasons at Knapp, he took a job at the Springside Inn in Auburn, as he began planning for what had long been a family dream. In August of 2004, the Legos opened The Restaurant at Elderberry Pond, a project Chris's father describes as the pinnacle of the family's labors on the farm.

A narrow driveway leads to the secluded restaurant-on-a-farm, ensconced in a structure that perfectly fits the discrete charm of the enter-

prise. Stained-glass double doors open into a rustic and uncluttered dining room with oak floors and oriental rugs, hardwood wainscoting, rough-hewn beams, and wood-planked fireplace, set off nicely by Mission-style chairs and starched, white linen tablecloths. "We call it 'farmhouse chic,'" laughs Chris.

As executive chef, he uses the farm's organic garden as his palette. "Growing and harvesting the fruits and vegetables you prepare make you respect them more, and you handle them with so much more care," says Chris. "It gives me enormous pleasure to cook with these vibrant ingredients." Clearly, this is the job he was born to do.

He turns the principles of restauranting upside down, sending the waitstaff out to pick each meal's salad greens leaf by leaf, including Black-Seeded Simpson, Outrageous, and Lola Rossa, just before opening time. It inspires special pride every time the salad plate is delivered to a table. Earthy-flavored potatoes, freshly dug each morning by the chef, include big, round Purple Vikings, or Russian Banana and Rose Finn Apple fingerling varieties that, according to Chris, "don't need sauces or a lot of spices—they just need to be perfectly cooked so you can taste the potato itself."

A salad niçoise is composed of grilled tuna with Nickel Haricot Vert, bright green stringless beans, Sun Gold, sweetest of the cherry tomatoes, sweet bell peppers called Sir Galahads, and potato of the day. Chioggia beets, an Italian heirloom variety with alternating concentric rings of scarlet red and white inside and a slightly peppery taste, are drizzled with raspberry-mint vinaigrette for a salad of local goat cheese and toasted walnuts. Bruschetta is topped with brie and just-harvested, roasted Roumanian Red garlic. "Garlic is best right out of the ground," explains Chris.

A luncheon burger is ground from Black Angus beef raised on Spring Brook Farm in Weedsport, New York, and topped with a slice of vine-ripened Brandywine tomato, the esteemed late nineteenth-century heirloom, along with blue cheese and the fresh-picked greens. Vegetable Lasagna includes petite Patty Pans, Benning's Green Tint, and Zephyr summer squash, Costa Romanesque green-striped zucchini, and Bright Light Swiss Chard with stalks that hold their rainbow of colors in cooking. When one vegetable is gone, something else is in season. There is a natural rhythm to this kind of cooking.

Chris imbues dishes with the essences of herbs, creating a perfect balance of delicate flavors that embellish yet somehow never overpower. Rosemary mayonnaise accompanies the Free-Range Chicken Sandwich, and thyme, mixed with lemon and garlic, perks up Shrimp Scampi. He deploys a cilantro and lime butter as a counterpoint to Grilled Swordfish. Perhaps inspired by Simon and Garfunkel, the Organic Free-Range Chicken is dry-rubbed with parsley, sage, rosemary, and thyme. Dishes are never fussy; instead, they are quite subtle and harmonious.

Lovingly baked Heirloom Apple Pie, filled with numerous varieties throughout the season, makes a grand finale at Elderberry Pond. Duchess of Oldenburg is the earliest culinary apple, followed by Wolf River in mid-season, then Smoke House, a variety favored in Pennsylvania Dutch cooking. "Like cider, mixing apple varieties makes the pies more interesting," insists Merby. And, speaking of cider, by late September, the cider room is turning out traditional-style antique-apple blends of Cox Orange Pippin, Golden Russet, and Winesap.

Changing the way people think about eating is no small thing, but it seems that Chris Lego is on a mission. "I want to provide an experience you can't get anywhere else," says the chef.

He has handpicked an eclectic range of wines, intended to favor like minded growers who employ sustainable farming practices. Finger Lakes bottles include Dr. Frank Semi-Dry Riesling, Hermann J. Wiemer Dry Riesling, and Standing Stone Chardonnay.

The Elderberry Pond enterprise can be viewed as a kind of metaphor for the Finger Lakes wine country itself. While many regional restaurants make the special effort to connect with local farms in order to serve the freshest and tastiest food available, the Legos have completely erased the line from grower to chef. It turns the act of eating into an unforgettable experience.

Goose Street at Cowan Road
Locke, NY 13092
(315) 497-1347

U-Pick Hours: May through
December—strawberries,
sweet cherries, raspberries,
blueberries, currants, apples,
winter squash, pumpkins

www.grisamorefarms.com

Grisamore Farms

Each June, as many as 400 pickers a day come to Grisamore Farms to fill buckets with the sweetest, reddest strawberries in the land. Things haven't changed much since the Grisamores began welcoming u-pickers to the strawberry fields. The juicy berries are still bursting off the bushes with the flavor and aroma only vine-ripened local berries can acquire.

Dairy-based enterprises were the mainstays of Locke throughout most of its history, and in 1927 Maurice Grisamore quit his conductor's job with the New York Central Railroad, uprooted his family from Chicago, and set out to milk cows on his newly purchased farm. In 1939, an acquaintance by the name of Glenn Rexwinkle showed up with 300 strawberry plants from his family's large Michigan farm, where they sold berries by the railroad boxcar. Maurice made a special trip to Michigan to learn everything he could about growing strawberries commercially, and Glen helped out with the following year's crop. The first $36 worth of strawberries sold to the Stevens and Hicks grocery store in Locke was comparable to a month's wages in those days, and the Grisamores decided to keep planting. By 1941, they had an acre of berries, enough to sell to Atwater's grocery store in Ithaca, as well as to passersby from the front porch of the house.

In 1952, with the biggest crop of plump beauties to date and no way to get it all harvested, they advertised "pick-your-own" strawberries, besides offering fruit already picked for wholesale and retail. Picking in the ripe strawberry fields at Grisamore Farms became an annual early summer tradition for many families in the region, and, for many, it just wouldn't be summer without just-picked fruit on a big helping of strawberry shortcake.

Thirty acres of strawberries, or nearly 2 million individual plants, grow on raised beds, and, while it's true that strawberries can grow almost anywhere, they thrive in the warm, sunny days and cool nights here, not to mention plenty of irrigation from the pond. Each of the farm's three varieties has been chosen for its peculiarities, which include ripening time, resistance to disease, shelf life, color, size, and taste. Early Glow, deep red in color with firm texture, is a favorite at the farm for both earliness and sweet flavor. Northeaster is a vigorous mid-season variety with a strong flavor and aroma. It produces large berries that hold their size throughout the season. Everyone loves Jewel. It has great flavor, high yields, and produces big, beautiful berries with good internal color until late in the season.

We're so lucky to have the chance to pick ourselves what most folks can only buy in a supermarket. You can stand in one spot and fill up a quart. Select only berries that are a deep, glossy red all the way to the tip; pinkish or white-tipped ones aren't fully ripe and won't be as sweet. Fill your bucket loosely or the berries on the bottom will bruise from the weight of the ones above them, since berries are fragile. Pick early or late in the day; strawberries keep better when it's cool. Bring along an insulated cooler to give the little babies a safe ride home.

In 1972, heavy rains flooded the farm, and the Grisamores watched their strawberry crop float away. Without income from strawberries, they planted broccoli, cauliflower, cabbage, and twenty-five acres of blueberry bushes. In 1975 they planted an apple orchard, and three years later, both sweet and sour cherries. Now, besides prized strawberries, there are many more delicious reasons to visit Grisamore Farms.

STRAWBERRIES WITH BALSAMIC VINEGAR AND BLACK PEPPER

It is hard to imagine how the flavor of fresh-picked Jewel strawberries could possibly be improved. But with traditional balsamic vinegar, the gorgeous, sweet-tart, syrupy vinegar made from local grapes in Modena, Italy, it is ridiculously easy to make the strawberry taste burst out in an incredible way. If you can, use Jewel strawberries.

Halve the strawberries if the strawberries are large, and quarter them if they are very large. They should be in bite-size pieces. Put the berries in a mixing bowl and sprinkle with brown sugar. Toss and set aside for 30 minutes.

Sprinkle the balsamic vinegar and pepper on the berries and toss again. Serve at room temperature for the fullest flavor.

Serves 4

1 quart Jewel strawberries, washed and hulled

4 tablespoons brown sugar

2 teaspoons balsamic vinegar

1/8 teaspoon freshly ground black pepper

Note: The amount of sugar may be adjusted, depending on the sweetness of the berries.

Harvest Home Organics

Moravia, New York, is an agricultural community whose favorite sons include Millard Fillmore, the thirteenth president of the United States, born five miles east of the village, and oil magnate John D. Rockefeller, whose boyhood home is five miles north. Just off what is now Rockefeller Road, descendants of the Duryea family farm a picturesque hilltop property, and, with a deeply held commitment to sustainable agriculture, they call the venture Harvest Home Organics.

Rose Ryan is a woman of the earth, a caretaker of the family spread, and a joyous garlic farmer. She has dedicated herself to a labor-intensive organic regimen for the fifty or so different crops she cultivates for market, yet there seems to be a particular love and care that she reserves for her garlic. She has propagated years of magnificent harvests from a bucket of seeds originally planted by Gene Schepker, a garlic-growing legend around this part of the Finger Lakes.

3

4574 Duryea Street
Moravia, NY 13118
(315) 497-0351

Hours: By appointment

"Garlic should be big, plump, and firm," says Rose. "If you think about the sensuous curve of the bulb, about eating it raw and tasting the 'bite,' garlic is very sexy." She cultivates a Rocambole variety called German Red and Northern White, a Porcelain variety, both winter-hardy with a circle of four to eight large cloves around a central woody stalk, yet each with a distinct aroma, flavor, growing time, and harvest time.

She'll tell you her favorite is the German Red, light brown cloves with a faint purple at the base, strong, hot, and spicy in flavor. Since this is a late-maturing variety, it's in the ground longer, taking more time to develop true garlic characters. "Some years it's extremely bold," she explains. "The flavor hangs around in your mouth for hours."

The Northern White is vigorous in flavor with bulb wrappers that tend to be very thick, luxuriant, and parchment-like, tightly covering their few, but large, cloves. These cloves are easy to peel, with skins that won't cling to your fingers, cutting board, or knives like the papery skins of other varieties. Northern White garlic is extremely popular with restaurant chefs because it's so user friendly.

Just before planting in October, choice, disease-free bulbs are separated into cloves, with care not to damage the root plate at the base. Cloves are planted by hand in raised beds with voluminous amounts of compost and mulched with straw for protection against the winter. As Rose explains, it's important to "know thy grower." What we know about her is that she grows her garlic in fifty-yard rows, five feet on center, four inches deep, six inches apart, and without the use of chemical pesticides or herbicides.

In spring, when the garlic flower stalk, known as a scape, bursts upward, she plucks it off to focus the plant's energy on bulb development. Mildly pungent but full of garlic flavor, these tender garlic greens are a short-lived delicacy that can be steamed lightly and eaten like asparagus or made into a pesto. The garlic is ready for harvest around the end of July, when just under half of the leaves have died and turned brown.

After these "truffles of the Finger Lakes" are dug up, they are moved into the barn, where the bulbs and roots are cleaned up, then spread in a drying room for a couple of weeks to cure before going to market. Rose makes the most of garlic's ornamental nature, as she combines part of the harvest with dried larkspur, thyme, and heirloom grains into braided works of art to decorate a few lucky kitchens. But nothing is quite like eating the season's local garlic, from the sense-filling bite of a crushed, raw clove to the smoky, mellow taste of a roasted bulb.

Slow-roasted garlic loses most of its heat and turns nutty and sweet, with a pleasant, mild-garlic flavor. Squeeze it from its skin and spread it on French bread; it turns ordinary mashed potatoes into an intensely rich and satisfying dish. Or, as I learned from Rose Ryan, it's a Finger Lakes farm tradition to smear roasted garlic all over a steaming ear of sweet corn. There's no choice then but to surrender to the garlic goddess.

New Hope Mills

The historic grist mill at New Hope began supplying the Finger Lakes with whole-grain flours in 1823, when Judge Charles Kellogg discovered a unique location along Bear Swamp Creek, just before it empties into Skaneateles Lake. He built the flour mill below a twenty-eight-foot water-fall with a dam above that would store water each night to turn the millstones on the following day. Kellogg was succeeded in this venture by Horace Rounds in 1851, then nearly a century later by the Weed family.

Grains were gravity fed from the hopper through a hole in the center of the huge, slow-turning, granite and burr stones. The rotation of the top stone worked the grain from the center to the outside edge of the mill. As grains journeyed from the center, they were ground finer and finer, and space between the slow-rotating stones was precisely adjusted to produce the consistency of flour.

The New Hope Mills tradition still survives, although most of the select wheat, corn, and rye grain is now milled in newfangled facilities, no longer depending on an inefficient water stream and an antiquated facility. A portion of the grains is delivered from regional farms to the high-speed roller operation at Log City Milling in King Ferry, and buckwheat flour is processed by Birkett Mills in Penn Yan. With proprietary formulas, New Hope has been able to outsource production of the flours for its mixes, yet maintain its legendary high quality. "We use facilities as local as possible that can grind to our specs," says Dale Weed, president of New Hope Mills. "Flours in our products retain the entire whole grain kernel, keeping all the nutrients nature intended."

Pancake mixes, the company's signature products, are made up of flour, leavening, and seasoning. Highest-grade unbleached and unenriched flours, free of chemical additives, are blended with baking powder and salt or sugar, according to closely held formulas, bequeathed from generation to generation. New Hope Mills was one of the very first commercial producers of pancake mixes, and, today, the product line includes mixes for buttermilk pancakes, blueberry pancakes, apple cinnamon pancakes, oat bran muffins and pancakes, buckwheat pancakes, whole wheat pancakes, Belgian waffles, and corn muffins.

From the factory store in Auburn, the company sells its pancake mixes, as well as syrups, spreads, spices, and baking supplies. New Hope Mills pancakes have been essential to country breakfasts in our region for generations, and a steaming plate of flapjacks swimming in local maple syrup reminds me of the honest values of a simpler time.

181 York Street
Auburn, NY 13021
(315) 252-2676

Hours: Monday–Friday, 9:00 a.m.–4:00 p.m.; Saturday, 10:00 a.m.–2:00 p.m.

www.newhopemills.com

6407 Glen Haven Road
New Hope, NY 13152
(315) 496-3287

Hours: By appointment

Tierra Farm

Skaneateles Lake is one of the cleanest lakes in the world and also one of the most beautiful. It is surrounded by some of the richest agricultural land in the state, home to a small but prolific community of passionate farmers intent on creating new culinary traditions. Tierra Farm is one of the lake's most influential growers of seasonal produce.

Owner Gunther Fishgold started his ecological training at a young age. His parents were full-fledged back-to-the-landers who joined an agricultural commune at a time when small-scale organic farming was seen as a somewhat utopian and uneconomic pastime. After obtaining a master's degree in public policy, Gunther became a lobbyist in Washington, D.C., promoting legislation to address health and environmental issues.

The way he explains it, organic farming isn't about turning back the clock at all; it's about moving forward. In 1993, Gunther pursued his personal vision of sustainable, entrepreneurial micro-farming with the purchase a twenty-five-acre piece of gentle countryside he called Tierra Farm. Not only were the growing conditions ideal, but the site provided a central base for servicing both Syracuse and Ithaca markets.

The area is favored by unpolluted air and a high-alkaline, well-drained, chestnut brown soil that grows anything from tomatoes and potatoes to apples and pears. He maximizes output with hand tilling as much as possible, combined with biointensive, labor-efficient methods. Health and vigor of the soil are maintained through the use of composted crop residue and vegetable waste. Close seeding spacing is used to protect the soil microorganisms, reduce water loss, and maximize yields. Companion planting facilitates the optimal use of nutrients, light, and water, encourages beneficial insects, and creates a vibrant mini ecosystem within the farm. Abundant buckwheat crowds out other weeds, provides protection against pests in the other crops, and improves aeration of the soil.

Gunther raises a diversity of superb vegetable and fruit crops, and the farm adheres to certified organic standards. He recognized early on that organic foods would play an expanding role in food service, and he has steadily grown his business over the years by providing his dedicated restaurant clients with niche crops and value-added heirloom varieties. He reads *Food and Wine* magazine to learn what progressive chefs are demanding, and he works at producing early and late crops of salads and other vegetables to extend their seasons.

"If you're good at wholesale, you can be very efficient," says Gunther. "You know you can sell everything you grow, and you don't have to pick it until it's ordered." I asked chef Edward Moro of Mirbeau why he is so loyal to Tierra Farm. "Flavor," he says. "Their produce is picked when it's perfectly ripe, and delivered to me the same day."

Over the years, the business has evolved, reflecting the owner's personality and changing interests. These days, while Gunther is busy developing an organic nuts and dried fruit business, he still finds twenty-five hours a week to spend in the field, and he always finds time to talk about the culinary-agricultural nexus he has established at Tierra Farm.

RESTAURANTS

Kettle Lakes

The restaurant called Kettle Lakes is as much about place as it is about fine food. A kettle is a depression formed when a block of stranded, buried glacier ice gradually melted. Many of the small, deep lakes in our region are "kettle lakes."

As an aspiring chef, Brian Shore read *Escoffier* the way some of us read novels. He learned that the legendary chef disdained elaborate garnishes, emphasized the use of seasonal ingredients, and advocated lighter sauces. Escoffier's approach to his craft was an inspiration throughout Brian's culinary training, and he has stayed true those principles throughout his career.

The young man from East Syracuse took Food Service Management classes at Onondaga Community College while working as sous chef at the University Sheraton. He moved from one kitchen to another, always advancing his knowledge and skill. He served as chef at the Brewster Inn in Cazenovia, then spent three years as the creative force at Fayetteville's Arad Evans Inn before venturing out on his own.

As executive chef and owner of Kettle Lakes, Brian describes his cuisine as "seasonal new American, influenced by the country's melting pot of cultures," and he takes an ingredient-based approach to food. His style is polished but not pretentious, original yet not over the top.

Dinner at Kettle Lakes begins with amuse-bouche, a small token offered to patrons without charge. A canapé of chicken liver pâté, a ramekin of asparagus soup with mint, or even a "happy spoon" of vegetable mousse might be at the whim of the chef, whose sense of craftsmanship informs every byway of the menu.

The menu is a masterful blend of elements of the old world with the new, and one that also reflects his seasonal approach to food. In summer, I've enjoyed an Heirloom Tomato Tart with tasso ham, basil, and local chèvre baked in a light pastry shell; Butterhead Salad with local Bibb lettuce, ratatouille vinaigrette, sharp Cheddar, and crisp fried onions; and Applewood Cold-Smoked Wild Salmon, oven roasted and glazed with local maple syrup and soy, served over a salad of toasted orzo, fresh melon, and prosciutto, with tarragon.

Brian, it seems, is obsessive about produce at its peak, and about ensuring the shortest distance from farm to plate. When he realized that a number of regional growers were driving their goods right past his location off Route 81 on the way to the Ithaca Farmer's Market, he made arrangements for regular deliveries of their just-picked vegetables, herbs, and

Best Western Marshall Manor
Route 80 and Route 11
(Exit 14 off I-81)
Tully, NY 13159
(315) 696-6627

Hours: Tuesday–Thursday,
5:30 p.m.–9:00 p.m.;
Friday and Saturday,
5:30 p.m.–10:00 p.m.;
Sunday, 4:00 p.m.–7:00 p.m.

www.kettlelakes.com

micro-greens. He uses tender baby lettuces, dressed with citrus vinaigrette, as both vegetable and creative garnish. "Flavors of the greens are so vibrant," says Brian. "You wouldn't think something that young would have so much flavor."

This is a chef who is brave and bold with single, stand-alone flavors. He considers fennel a vastly underrated flavor, especially with seafood, and you'll detect a hint of fennel along with sea salt and cracked pepper in the crusty, fresh-baked bread served with dinner.

Leave it to Brian to come up with mignardises, another pleasant surprise from the kitchen, this one designed to accompany coffee and after-dinner drinks. At Kettle Lakes, his pastry chef, Kathleen Barney, offers a plate of cookies with white chocolate chips, pecans, coconut, and vanilla, slightly gooey and still warm from the oven. It provides splendid closure to the dining experience.

Kettle Lakes has a warm, yacht-club feel, vaulted oak ceiling with slow-turning fans and framed black and white photographs of old Tully. An oak bar divides the main dining room from the "bistro," which features a separate menu offering smaller portions and smaller prices. This option was originally a downscale concession to guests in the adjacent hotel. Tapas-style plates include a B.L.T. Salad with smoked bacon, half head of lettuce, ripe tomato, and aïoli; Fresh Corn Risotto with chervil salad; and Cavatelli Macaroni and Fontina Cheese with cream and oven-dried tomatoes.

Torrey Grant's wine program focuses on small producers with artisan wine-producing styles. Although the cellar is stocked with Rieslings from Heron Hill and Hermann J. Wiemer, Chardonnays from Dr. Frank and Standing Stone, and Hosmer Cabernet Franc, I will be more impressed when the wine list better reflects the kitchen's regional pride.

Chef Brian Shore credits his successful career in part to the strong work ethic he developed at an early age. With a talent for infusing regional ingredients into sophisticated cuisine, he has established a high standard for Finger Lakes cooking and a destination for culinary pleasure.

851 West Genesee Street
Skaneateles, NY 13152
(315) 685-5006

Hours: Breakfast, Lunch, and Dinner, daily

www.mirbeau.com

Mirbeau Inn and Spa

Near his home in Giverny, France, Claude Monet rechanneled a tiny creek to supply a pond for growing aquatic plants. Then he erected a footbridge modeled after a Japanese print and covered it with blue and white wisteria. The exotic water garden with its meditative water lilies became the subject of many of the most beloved paintings by the great French Impressionist.

On a dozen wooded acres just outside the village of Skaneateles, Gary Dower and Linda Dal Pos have reproduced a serene French country estate called Mirbeau Inn and Spa, with pale yellow guest cottages, enclosed gardens, and lily ponds straight out of a Monet canvas. The partners have combined the warm hospitality of a country inn, a full range of spa facilities, and a restaurant kitchen under the direction of a distinguished chef.

Edward Moro has an unwavering devotion to the culinary arts. A native of Hershey, Pennsylvania, his early training at the Stouch Tavern in nearby Womelsdorf led to a European-style apprentice program at the Hotel Hershey. There, young Edward spent his first three years in the pastry shop, learning to train both hands and eyes before stepping into the kitchen. Once immersed in the environment of the high-volume kitchen, he was able to keep up the fast pace, yet still pay close attention to detail. After honing his skills for two more years, he joined the award-winning culinary team of the Little Nell Hotel in Aspen, Colorado.

But it was his starring roles at Napa Valley's Brix and Pinot Blanc, then at Portland's Avalon, that pushed his talents into the limelight. Having been exposed to the bounty of West Coast growers, he places a high priority on the farm-to-table connection. At the acceptance of executive chef position at Mirbeau, Edward effortlessly transplanted his passion for regional, seasonal, and artisanal ingredients to the Finger Lakes.

Elements important to Edward's cooking philosophy include balance and focus. Rich textures are counterbalanced with vinaigrettes, soft textures with "crunch," and spice with sweet. He strives for harmony in each presentation, taking care to see that no single flavor dominates. His inspired and unconventional combinations, such as Asparagus Soup with shaved summer truffles and pan-seared scallop and Roasted Venison Chop with sautéed bulgur wheat, roasted squash, and berry gastrique, demonstrate the breadth and depth of his balancing act. Local garlic-crusted Beef Tenderloin is served with "Whatever the Farmer Brings."

The sense of community gained from working with local growers is shared by everyone on his crew. Excitement flows through the kitchen with the delivery of baby fennel from Tierra Farm or when a flat of micro-greens arrives from Sunset Hill Farm. The greens become almost a work of art, offering intricate detail, delicate textures, and mild exclamations of flavor to so many of his dishes. The mix of vibrant, spicy arugula, tender red oak, and feathery mizuna is kept in the walk-in cooler and snipped fresh as needed.

The restaurant's ethos is to capture Monet's aesthetic sensibilities, not only with the idyllic setting and mood-enhancing French music, but with food worthy of the artist's table. Menu themes include "Monet's Rising" at breakfast, "A Visit to the Greenhouse" at lunch, and "The Painter's Palette" at dinner, all communicating what Edward calls "an impressionistic approach to the culinary arts." He compares the rim of a plate to a frame around an artist's work, only, instead of oils, his creations are developed from a spectrum of flavors. The kitchen is his studio.

To heighten the Mirbeau experience, Edward collaborates with food and beverage manager Randy Miller on a food-friendly wine portfolio for thoughtful regional picks that include Treleaven Chardonnay, Heron Hill "Ingle Vineyard" Riesling, Standing Stone Gewürztraminer, and Fox Run Meritage.

Exquisitely prepared and beautifully presented food is an art form that, like a Monet masterpiece, lingers in the imagination and the memory. The consummate artistry of chef Edward Moro has resulted in his dining room being named one of "The Best New Restaurants in America" by *Esquire* magazine. Under his guidance, Mirbeau stands at the highest echelon of wine country dining.

The Restaurant at Elderberry Pond

See Elderberry Pond Farm (page 175) . . . .

Rosalie's Cucina

841 West Genesee Street
Skaneateles, NY 13152
(315) 685-2200

Hours: Sunday–Thursday,
5:00 p.m.–9:00 p.m.;
Friday and Saturday,
5:00 p.m.–10:00 p.m.

www.rosaliescucina.com

Everyone comes to Rosalie's. Native bluebloods, wine country tourists, even a president of the United States—Bill Clinton, along with Hillary and Chelsea, ate dinner here in 1999. Except for a couple of months during the heart of winter, this is the hottest table in Skaneateles, a self-consciously old-fashioned village that seems an unlikely location for an exuberant, high-energy outpost of Italian culture.

The restaurant was the brainstorm of Auburn native Phil Romano, who earned a national reputation with multi-unit theme eateries such as Fuddrucker's, Eatzi's, and Romano's Macaroni Grill. Rosalie's reminds me of the latter with its engaging style of traditional Italian fare, only slightly more upscale.

Parking is provided at the rear of the restaurant, where you'll have an opportunity to stroll through the chef's herb garden, planted under an old railroad trestle, and pass by the stacks of hardwood he uses in his Tuscan oven. The sprawling pink stucco building is surrounded by a cluster of maple trees, rustic patio, and bocce ball court, and as aromas from the long-cooked sauces and Italian melodies waft in the air, the mood is cast before you even set foot inside.

It's difficult to say with absolute certainty what's best about Rosalie's— the bustling trattoria setting, the well-trained servers, the sensational food, or the whole idea of this restaurant as a gift from Romano to his sister, Rosalie, who directed the operation for only a year before she passed away in 1996. The answer is all of it.

In a small bakery at one corner of the restaurant, the staff begins arriving at six in the morning to start the day's "bone bread" from scratch, producing 150 loaves each weekday and more than 250 loaves on Friday, Saturday, and Sunday. "The bread might be more famous than the restaurant," says owner Gary Robinson.

It isn't typical French bread with a hard-as-nails crust and light, airy middle. This soft bread, shaped like a bone, has a rich, moist consistency, and it arrives at the table along with fragrant olive oil and a "spice plate" with crushed garlic, red pepper flakes, oregano, and shaved Locatelli Romano cheese, mixed to your specifications right in front of your nose.

But don't fill up on bread. First courses include thin-crust Pizza Margherita with tomatoes, mozzarella, basil, and oregano, grilled, then finished in the wood-burning oven, and Antipasto Affettati, with sliced prosciutto, sopressata, capocollo, and almond-olive tapenado. Spinach for Insalata di Spinaci is sautéed for just a matter of seconds with olive oil, roasted garlic, and Asiago cheese.

Chef John Gow executes each generous entrée with honesty and self-assurance. Arrosto di Maiale is slow-roasted pork with oregano, garlic, cannellini beans, and greens; Scampi alla Rosalie includes shrimp, artichokes, oven-cured tomatoes, and garlic butter, served over angel hair pasta. Owner-inspired Penne Regine alla Robinsono is a sauté of broccoli, bell peppers, hot peppers, chicken, olives, and feta cheese. Regular visits to the local farmer's market add sparkle to his ingredient-driven menu, most notably in the daily specials.

Dessert is considered part of the meal at Rosalie's, and the kitchen impresses with housemade tiramisu, cannoli, biscotti, chocolate cake, and, if you are up to it, the most amazing banana pudding you could ever imagine. A phyllo shell is piled high with a rich banana cream, layered with bananas and crumbled almond cookies, topped with fresh whipped cream, and served with a whole almond cookie for good measure.

For wine enthusiasts wanting to match Finger Lakes regional wine to Tuscan cuisine, Rosalie's does not disappoint. Although reasonably priced Italian vino dominates the offerings, regional stalwarts, including Heron Hill Riesling, Hazlitt Gewürztraminer, Hermann J. Wiemer Dry Riesling, and Treleaven Meritage, hold up to the rustic fare.

With a policy of no reservations, the wait for a table at Rosalie's has become the stuff of legend. But Gary admits that when regulars call, even during the busy summer months, they get special treatment. "It's a perk they deserve," he explains. In fact, 2,000 of the local gentry have endorsed their enthusiasm for the restaurant with personal signatures scrawled across the dining room walls.

This is the kind of food you never tire of, and that partly explains the popularity of this place. But Rosalie's impresses because it executes the basics. In fact, the basics are so well done here, you realize how often they're poorly done in other restaurants. I can't think of a more enjoyable dining experience in the Finger Lakes, even on a theatrical level. Singing hosts Rafael Guido and Paulo Salterello send every customer off with a song.

Accommodations

CANANDAIGUA LAKE

Canandaigua Inn
770 South Main Street
Canandaigua, NY 14424
(585) 394-7800
(800) 228-2801

www.visitinnonthelake.com

Hotel and Conference Center with 134 guest rooms
(16 lakefront rooms) on the north shore of
Canandaigua Lake.

Grapevine Inn Bed & Breakfast
182 North Main Street
Naples, NY 14512
(585) 374-9298

www.grapevineinnbb.com

Surrounded by vineyards, this English Victorian Tudor
home was built in 1923 by William Widmer, son of
John Widmer, founder of Widmer Winery.

Sutherland House
3179 Route 21 South (Bristol Street Extension)
Canandaigua, NY 14424
(585) 396-0375
(800) 396-0375

www.sutherlandhouse.com

Henry C. Sutherland was the youngest of five brothers
who built their homes on Bristol Street. This regal
1885 Second Empire Victorian offers five guest room
accommodations.

Thendara Inn
4356 East Lake Road
Canandaigua, NY 14424
(585) 394-4868

www.thendarainn.com

Four guest rooms in the former lakeside estate of
State Senator John Raines. Formal dining room or
casual dining at the Boathouse (see Canandaigua
Restaurants, page 16).

CAYUGA LAKE

Aurora Inn
391 Main Street
Aurora, NY 13026
(315) 364-8888
(866) 364-8808

www.aurora-inn.com

Federal-style country inn with ten luxurious guest
rooms, some with balconies furnished with rockers,
benches, or swings. Located near Wells College in the
tiny village of Aurora. Lakeside dining on a porch and
veranda overlooking Cayuga Lake (see Cayuga Lake
Restaurants, page 159).

Gothic Eves
112 East Main Street
Trumansburg, NY 14886
(607) 387-6033

www.gothiceves.com

Bed and breakfast lodging is offered in an 1855 Gothic
Revival home in the village of Trumansburg. Its location
puts it between Cayuga and Seneca Lake Wine Trails.

La Tourelle Country Inn
1150 Danby Road
Ithaca, NY 14850
(607) 273-2734
(800) 765-1492

www.latourelleinn.com

A thirty-five-room European-style hotel located on sev-
enty acres of rolling hills near Ithaca College, on South
Hill. Downtown Ithaca is only three miles away.
Adjacent to John Thomas Steakhouse.

Taughannock Farms Inn
2030 Gorge Road
Trumansburg, NY 14886
(607) 387-7711
(888) 387-7711

www.t-farms.com

Twenty-two guest rooms are located on the grounds of
an 1873 estate overlooking Taughannock State Park
and connected by hiking trails to Taughannock Falls,
the highest waterfall in the northeastern United States.
The restaurant is open April to November.

William Henry Miller Inn
303 North Aurora Street
Ithaca, NY 14850
(607) 256-4553

www.millerinn.com

Rich in architectural detail, this beautiful bed and breakfast inn began as a private home built in 1880 by Cornell University's first student of architecture, William Henry Miller. Located in downtown Ithaca just off the Ithaca Commons, at the foot of Cornell's East Hill, it is in easy walking distance of many of Ithaca's fine restaurants, theaters, and shops.

KEUKA LAKE

Esperanza Mansion
3456 Route 54A
Bluff Point, NY 14478
(315) 536-4400
(866) 927 4400

www.esperanzamansion.com

Historic Greek Revival estate with a spectacular view of the lake, developed into nine mansion guestrooms, twenty-one additional accommodations, a banquet facility, and a restaurant (see Keuka Lake Restaurants, page 42).

Keuka Overlook B & B
5777 Old Bath Road
Dundee, NY 14837
(607) 292-6877

www.keukaoverlook.com

In this Victorian farmhouse, open weekends only, year-round, there is a choice of four guest rooms, each with a private bath and each with a lake view. The wrap-around porch provides a good location for sipping wine produced at the adjacent winery (see Keuka Lake Wineries, page 29).

Radisson Hotel Corning
125 Denison Parkway East
Corning, NY 14830
(607) 962-5000
(800) 333-3333

www.radisson.com/corningny

This hotel and conference center on historic Market Street in downtown Corning is in easy walking distance of The Corning Museum of Glass and Rockwell Museum of Western Art. You'll also find glassmaking studios, antiques and specialty shops, and restaurants. Keuka, Seneca, and Cayuga Lakes are just a short drive away.

Trimmer House
145 East Main Street
Penn Yan, NY 14527
(315) 536-8304
(800) 968-8735

www.trimmerhouse.com

You'll find four guestrooms, all with private baths, and one suite in this Queen Anne–style home built in 1891 by a wealthy Champagne merchant. Breakfasts include pancakes and waffles made with buckwheat from nearby Birkett Mills.

SENECA LAKE

Belhurst
4069 Route 14 South
Geneva, NY 14456
(315) 781-0201

www.belhurst.com

Three distinct hotels are among the offerings at Belhurst: chambers in century-old Belhurst Castle; guestrooms in White Springs Manor, a Georgian Revival mansion; and new luxury accommodations in the Vinifera Inn. Dining options include the formal Edgar's restaurant and the informal Stonecutters. Also here is the tasting room for Belhurst Winery (see Seneca Lake Wineries, page 52).

Geneva on the Lake
1001 Lochland Road/Route 14 South
Geneva, NY 14456
(315) 789-7190

www.genevaonthelake.com

Built in 1914 as a private home and modeled after Villa Lancellotti in Frascati, Italy, this historic landmark is now a European-style resort with twenty-nine romantic suites and studios on ten acres set amid spectacular lakeside gardens. Candlelight dining in the grand Lancellotti Dining Room completes the experience (see Seneca Lake Restaurants, page 104).

Idlwilde Inn
1 Lakeview Avenue
Watkins Glen, NY 14891
(607) 535-3081

www.bbhost.com/idlwildeinn

An eighteen-room 1892 Victorian mansion on 2.6 acres of land in a parklike setting with great lawn and formal gardens. Several of the guest rooms, the sunrooms, and a huge, breezy wraparound porch overlook Seneca Lake.

The Inn at Glenora Wine Cellars
5435 Route 14
Dundee, NY 14837
(607) 243-9500

www.glenora.com/inn

Here is total wine country experience. Thirty guestrooms are furnished with elegant Stickley furniture, some have fireplaces and Jacuzzis, and a view of the lake may be enjoyed from guestroom balconies or patios. The inn is adjacent to the winery, Glenora Wine Cellars, and the winery restaurant, Veraisons (see Seneca Lake Wineries, page 65).

The Inn at Seneca Springs
4881 Route 414
Hector, NY 14841
(607) 546-4066

www.senecasprings.com

Accommodations are available in either an 1860s post and beam farmhouse or a rustic stone and cedar lodge, both overlooking Seneca Lake in the heart of wine country.

Ramada Inn Geneva Lakefront
41 Lakefront Drive
Geneva, NY 14456
(315) 789-0400

www.ramadageneva.com

This 148-room hotel is located on the north shore of Seneca Lake. Lakefront dining is on the property, at Pier House Restaurant.

SKANEATELES LAKE

Hobbit Hollow Farm
3061 West Lake Road
Skaneateles, NY 13152
(315) 685-2791

www.hobbithollow.com

Four rooms with air-conditioning and private baths are available for guests in this 100-year-old Colonial Revival structure set on a 320-acre horse farm overlooking the lake.

Lady of the Lake
2 West Lake Street
Skaneateles, NY 13152
(315) 685-7997
(888) 685-7997

www.ladyofthelake.net

Stella, Mary, and DeEtta are guest rooms named after the ladies who owned the home in years past. This turn-of-the-century Queen Anne bed and breakfast is just a block away from shops and restaurants in the village.

Mirbeau Inn and Spa
851 West Genesee Street
Skaneateles, NY 13152
(315) 685-5006
(877) MIR-BEAU

www.mirbeau.com

This small luxury hotel complex reminiscent of a French country estate is set around Monet-inspired gardens. Six buildings house eighteen chateau-style guest rooms, a full-service spa, and an award-winning dining room (see Skaneateles Lake Restaurants, page 184.)

Sherwood Inn
26 West Genesee Street
Skaneateles, NY 13152
(315) 685-3405
(800) SHERWOOD

www.thesherwoodinn.com

A Skaneateles landmark since it was built as a stagecoach stop in 1807, with twenty-four antique-appointed guestrooms in a setting overlooking the lake. Separate menus for lunch and dinner served in dining room and tavern.

Annual Events/Attractions

Cayuga Waterfront Trail

www.cayugawaterfronttrail.com

A six-mile scenic route that links the city of Ithaca with Black Diamond Park. Walk, run, bike, blade, or stroll along the waterfront, stopping along the way at various points of interest such as the Ithaca Farmer's Market, Cass Park Playground, and the Tompkins County Visitors' Center.

Corning Museum of Glass
1 Museum Way
Corning, NY 14830
(607) 937-5371

www.cmog.org

Here, at the glass capital of America, you can stroll through the sculpture gallery and learn about thirty-five centuries of glassmaking from around the world. The 30,000-piece collection includes goblets and jars, vases and paperweights, chandeliers and beadwork, tables and chairs, statues and mosaics, and a Louis Comfort Tiffany stained-glass window.

Finger Lakes Race Track
5857 Route 96
Farmington, NY 14425
(585) 924-3232

www.fingerlakesracetrack.com

Thoroughbred racing, April to December.

Finger Lakes Trail

www.fingerlakestrail.org

This 562-mile-long footpath, popular with hikers, backpackers, and runners, wanders through large wilderness areas and infrequently traveled roads throughout the Finger Lakes.

Finger Lakes Wine Center
151 Charlotte Street
Canandaigua, NY 14424
(585) 394-9016

www.fingerlakeswinecenter.com

Sonnenberg, a fifty-acre estate with a Queen Anne–style mansion, nine formal gardens, an larboretum, and a conservatory, has become a wine center for thirty Finger Lakes wineries.

Finger Lakes Wine Festival
Watkins Glen

www.flwinefest.com

Glenn H. Curtiss Museum
8419 Route 54
Hammondsport, NY 14840
(607) 569-2160

www.linkny.com/curtissmuseum

This museum showcases a collection of historical aircraft and antique motorcycles, highlighting the achievements of Glenn Curtiss, motorcyclist, aviator, engineer, and entrepreneur.

Granger Homestead and Carriage Museum
295 North Main Street
Canandaigua, NY 14424
(585) 394-1472

www.grangerhomestead.org

Built by Gideon Granger, Postmaster General under Thomas Jefferson, the Granger Homestead was home to four generations of the Granger family. Fifty horse-drawn vehicles are on exhibit, showing the history of nineteenth-century transportation in western New York.

Great New York State Fair
Syracuse

www.nysfair.org

Harriet Tubman Home
180 South Street
Auburn, NY 13021
(315) 252-2081

www.harriettubmanhome.org/home.htm

This home preserves the legacy of the woman who rescued over 300 slaves through the Underground Railroad.

Herbert F. Johnson Museum of Art
Central and University Avenues
Ithaca, NY 14853
(607) 255-6464

www.museum.cornell.edu

One of the finest collections of art in New York State and one of the most important university museums in the country. A small masterpiece, designed by I. M. Pei, with stunning views of Cayuga Lake, the Cornell campus, and Ithaca.

MacKenzie-Childs
3260 Route 90
Aurora, NY 13026
(888) 665-1999

www.mackenzie-childs.com

A winding red brick road leads to the home of whimsical, handmade ceramics, enamelware, glassware, furniture, and home accessories. Tour the manufacturing process to observe artisans hand-forming, hand-painting, and hand-trimming each extraordinary piece.

Museum of the Earth
1259 Trumansburg Road (Route 96)
Ithaca, NY 14850
(607) 273-6623

www.priweb.org/museumoftheearth

The Palentological Research Institute permanent collection includes the 12,000-year-old Hyde Park mastodon.

National Women's Hall of Fame
76 Fall Street
Seneca Falls, NY 13148
(315) 568-8060

www.greatwomen.org

A permanent exhibit in the birthplace of women's rights. It was here, in 1848, that Elizabeth Cady Stanton, Lucretia Mott, and 300 other individuals held the first Women's Rights Convention.

Newfield Covered Bridge
Main Street
Newfield, NY 14867

www.nycoveredbridges.org

Built in 1853 to cross the west branch of Cayuga Creek, the historic bridge is the Finger Lakes' only covered bridge and one of the oldest covered bridges still open to vehicular traffic. Follow the signs on Route 13, either northbound or southbound, as you approach Newfield. The bridge is in the center of the village and well marked.

Rockwell Museum of Western Art
111 Cedar Street
Corning, NY 14830
(607) 937-5386

www.stny.com/rockwellmuseum

The largest collection of American Western and Native American art in the eastern United States is on display at this museum.

Roseland Waterpark
250 Eastern Boulevard
Canandaigua, NY 14424
(585) 396-2000

www.roselandwaterpark.com

Kids have a field day in this fifty-eight-acre forest filled with water rides and the Finger Lakes' largest wave pool.

Sagan Planet Walk
601 First Street
Ithaca, NY 14850
(607) 272-0600

www.sciencenter.org/SaganPW

Built to honor Ithaca resident and Cornell professor Carl Sagan, the Sagan Planet Walk is an outdoor, permanent model of the solar system that stretches from the sun on the Ithaca Commons to Pluto at the Sciencenter three-quarters of a mile away. It consists of ten monoliths, one for each of the nine planets and one for the sun, spaced on a scale of one to five billion.

Sapsucker Woods Bird Sanctuary
159 Sapsucker Woods Road
Ithaca, NY 14850
(800) 843-2473

www.birds.cornell.edu

Home to the world-famous Cornell Lab of Ornithology. Four miles of trails wind through woodland and over swamps and ponds, habitat for waterfowl and other wildlife, and a bird-feeding garden.

Seneca Museum
89 Fall Street
Seneca Falls, NY 13148
(315) 568-1510

www.senecamuseum.com

Seneca County and Finger Lakes history of waterways and water power, which gave rise to industries and the spread of reform movements, is on display at this museum.

Seward House
33 South Street
Auburn, NY 13021
(315) 252-1283

www.sewardhouse.org

This is the home of William Seward, former State Senator, Governor, and Secretary of State under Presidents Abraham Lincoln and Andrew Johnson. It features a mixture of Federal- and Tuscan-style architecture surrounded by two acres of gardens.

Waterloo Outlet Mall
655 Route 318
Waterloo, NY 13165
(315) 539-1100

www.premiumoutlets.com

Bargain hunters will love the "thrill of the hunt" in over ninety famous-brand factory outlet stores.

The Wizard of Clay
7851 Route 20A
Bloomfield, NY 14469
(585) 229-2980

www.wizardofclay.com

This pottery complex is housed in seven geodesic domes designed and built by master potter Jim Kozlowski.

Hot Air Balloon Rides

Wind Rider Balloon Company
44 Deer Run Road
Newfield, NY 14867
(607) 564-1009

Lake Cruises

Canandaigua Lady
Canandaigua

www.steamboatlandingonline.com

Captain Bill's Seneca Lake Cruises
Watkins Glen

www.senecaharborstation.com/cruise

Cayuga Lake Cruises
Ithaca

www.cayugalakecruises.com

Keuka Maid Dinner Boat Cruises
Hammondsport

www.keukamaid.com

Mid-Lakes Navigation
Skaneateles

www.midlakesnav.com

Picnic Sites/Recreation Areas

CANANDAIGUA LAKE

Onanda Park
4965 West Lake Road
Canandaigua
(585) 394-1120

Located eight miles south of the city, the park includes a two-mile hiking path, tennis and basketball courts, and playgrounds. Rustic cabins, pavilions, and lodges available for rent in summer.

CAYUGA LAKE

Long Point State Park
Lake Road (4 miles south of Aurora, off Route 90)
Aurora

The park provides a picnic area, beach, boat launch facilities, and fishing access. Open year-round.

Stewart Park
Routes 13 and 34
Ithaca

Located at the southernmost tip of Cayuga Lake, the park includes hiking trails, playing fields, a children's playground, picnic area, concession stand, tennis courts, and a restored carousel. The park buildings here date back to the time when Pearl White, Lionel Barrymore, and Irene Castle starred in films made at Wharton Studios.

Taughannock Falls State Park
2221 Taughannock Road
Trumansburg
(607) 387-6739

Located off Route 89 eight miles north of Ithaca, this beautiful state park's best-known feature is its namesake, Taughannock Falls, which tumbles 215 feet over a rock cliff. A scenic hiking trail rims the top of the falls, while a more challenging hike descends downward to the pool. Picnic areas, cabins, and camping sites overlook Cayuga Lake, with marina, boat launch, and beach nearby. Open year-round.

KEUKA LAKE

Keuka Lake State Park
3370 Pepper Road
Bluff Point, NY 14478
(315) 536-3666

Besides great views of vineyard-covered slopes, the park includes a swimming beach, picnic shelter, boat launch ramp, docking space, hiking trails, and 150 tent and trailer sites.

SENECA LAKE

Sampson State Park
6096 Route 96A
Romulus, NY 14541
(315) 585-6392

Rolling woodlands and ravines are part of the attraction here, but a central feature is the 123-berth marina for seasonal boaters. Visitors will also find picnic areas, tennis, basketball, and volleyball courts, swimming beach, 245 electric campsites, and 64 nonelectric sites.

Watkins Glen State Park
Main entrance is in the village of Watkins Glen
(Near the south end of Seneca Lake, off Route 14)
Watkins Glen

A spectacular 1,000-acre park with an erosion-sculptured gorge, craggy rock formations, nineteen waterfalls, and 300-foot shale and sandstone cliffs. A foot trail with over 800 stone steps follows the gorge, passing over and under waterfalls. Rim trails overlook the gorge. The park has 305 campsites and an Olympic-sized swimming pool. Open year-round.

SKANEATELES LAKES

Fillmore Glen State Park
1686 Route 38
Moravia, NY 13118
(315) 497-0130

Located one mile south of Moravia and south of Owasco Lake, this wooded park features hiking trails that offer spectacular views, unique geological formations, five waterfalls, and a botanically rich glen. There are picnic tables, sixty campsites, a stream-fed swimming pool, and fishing is available in the Owasco Lake inlet. Hiking, cross-country skiing, and snowmobiling are permitted in winter.

Picnic Supplies

Arbor Hill Grapery Store and Wine Shop
6461 Route 64
Bristol Springs, NY 14512
(800) 554-7553

www.thegrapery.com

In addition to a wide range of wines, Arbor Hill produces its own jellies, preserves, vinegars, mustards, salad dressings, barbecue sauces, and dessert toppings. Enjoy a free wine-tasting while you stock up on picnic supplies.

GreenStar Cooperative Market
701 West Buffalo Street
Ithaca, NY 14850
(607) 273-9392

www.greenstar.coop

This consumer-owned, democratically run co-op market offers hundreds of organic and natural products. The bakery and deli provide a wide range of take-out supplies for a delicious healthy picnic.

Ithaca Bakery
400 North Meadow Street (Route 13 North)
Ithaca, NY 14850
(607) 273-7110

www.ithacabakery.com

Mothership of the Brous & Mehaffey empire has the heart of a hippie, the soul of a townie, and the style of a gourmet. Five satellite stores provide bagels, stacked sandwiches, salads, cheeses, and you-name-it.

Ithaca Farmer's Market

545 Third Street at Steamboat Landing
Ithaca, NY 14850
(607) 387-6952

www.ithacamarket.com

A focal point for community life and an Ithaca institution since 1973, local food vendors at the vibrant, open-air market offer fresh produce, jellies, honey, baked goods, and ready-to-eat vegetarian and ethnic specialty foods. Weekends from April to December.

Ludgate Farms

1552 Hanshaw Road
Ithaca, NY 14050
(607) 257-1765

www.ludgatefarms.com

Family owned and operated farm market and specialty food store, filled with fresh organic produce, local dairy and cheeses, organic and natural groceries, and bulk specialty foods. Open 9:00 a.m. to 9:00 p.m. daily, year-round.

Wegman's

www.wegmans.com

This full-service supermarket chain has several stores in our region where you can assemble the makings of a gourmet picnic. Wegman's has an excellent selection of cold cuts, cheeses, imported olives, and freshly baked breads, along with an array of seasonal fruits and vegetables from local farms, bags of ice, and the *New York Times*. Use the store locator link on the company website to find a Finger Lakes Wegman's.

Windmill Farm & Craft Market

3900 Route 14A
Penn Yan, NY 14527
(315) 536-3032

www.thewindmill.com

Nestled among pine trees five miles south of Penn Yan, three main buildings on a twenty-six-acre site house 250 vendors, including many Amish and Mennonite farmers and artisans. Picnic tables are provided on the grounds. Open Saturdays, late April through mid-December.

Skiing

Bristol Mountain Winter Resort

Canandaigua

www.bristolmountain.com

Greek Peak Mountain Resort

Cortland

www.greekpeak.net

Song Mountain Resort

Tully

www.songmountain.com

Spas

Mirbeau Inn and Spa

851 West Genesee Street
Skaneateles, NY 13152
(315) 685-5006

www.mirbeau.com

Treatments feature a selection of wraps, massages, facials, and mineral baths, all provided in rooms with fireplaces for luxurious, indulgent comfort.

Visitor's Information

Canandaigua Wine Trail

www.canandaiguawinetrailonline.com

Cayuga Wine Trail

www.cayugawinetrail.com

Finger Lakes Artists and Crafters Network

www.fingerlakesartists.com

Finger Lakes Bed & Breakfast Association

www.flbba.org

Finger Lakes County Visitors Connection

www.visitfingerlakes.com

Finger Lakes Culinary Bounty

www.fingerlakesculinarybounty.org

Finger Lakes Cycling Club

www.flcycling.org

Finger Lakes Regional Tourism

www.fingerlakes.org

Finger Lakes Runner's Club

www.fingerlakesrunners.org

Finger Lakes Trail Conference

www.fingerlakestrail.org

Finger Lakes Wine Country Tourism Marketing Association

www.fingerlakeswinecountry.com

Finger Lakes Wine Guild

www.fingerlakeswineguild.com

Keuka Lake Wine Trail

www.keukawinetrail.com

New York Wine & Grape Foundation

www.uncorknewyork.com

Routes 5 and 20 Driving Tour

www.routes5and20.com

Seneca Lake Wine Trail

www.senecawine.com

Finger Lakes Limousine & Coach
(315) 539-2235

www.fingerlakeslimo.com

Finger Lakes Vision Tours
(607) 532-9370

www.fingerlakesvisiontours.com

Finger Lakes Winery Tours
(585) 329-0858

www.fingerlakeswinerytours.com

Grapevine Country Tours
(315) 585-6769

www.grapevinecountrytours.com

New World Tour Company
(607) 387-6292

www.newworldtour.com

Quality Winery Tours
(877) 424-7004

www.qualitytran.com

Wine Tours

Canandaigua Bus Tours
(585) 396-2799

www.canandaiguabustours.com